BETWEEN THE TIDES

Shipwrecks of the Irish Coast

Roy Stokes

AMBERLEY

First published 2015

Amberley Publishing
The Hill, Stroud
Gloucestershire, GL5 4EP

www.amberley-books.com

British Library Cataloguing in Publication Data.
A catalogue record for this book is available from the British Library.

ISBN 978 1 4456 5333 4 (print)
ISBN 978 1 4456 5334 1 (ebook)

Map design by Thomas Bohm, User Design.
Typesetting and Origination by Amberley Publishing.
Printed in the UK.

Contents

Introduction

It was curious, just how many of my diving buddies loved a drag of a fag immediately after a dive. Almost inexplicably, even though divers might be better acquainted with the benefits of a good set of lungs, and with the damage that smoking can do to them, many continued to puff away, and some still do.

The unique planning that was involved in trying to keep a packet of fags and matches dry during a long sea journey, in a continually swamping inflatable boat, was often stretched to ingenious and secret lengths. With the dive accomplished, the celebratory cigarettes were revealed. The pleasure from igniting the fag with cold and dripping wet hands, and finally getting it going, felt great, but was purely temporary. It soon broke up after a couple of puffs and was reduced to a sodden mess.

The inflated pontoons of the rubber boat were carefully avoided, but those closest to the petrol supply were a little uneasy with the practice.

Alone, this little anecdote may only appeal to another diver, an older one perhaps, but as the reader progresses through the book, I hope he will gain some insight into the thrill we have experienced through the years, searching for and diving on old shipwrecks.

Underwater archaeological discoveries included, an explanation for the diver's addiction to this aspect of the sport might lie in the occasional reward for his personal endeavour, overcoming a range of obstacles to make that dive of discovery. It may just be the camaraderie and the trust shared with fellow adventurers in a dangerous element, or simply an itch to solve mysteries, a trait present in most of us. For a few, it's all about 'the story'.

This volume contains three detailed accounts of specific shipwreck events and of the contemporary salvage and diving associated with them. After they were relocated in modern times, they were explored by the author and others, and their experiences are included with a history of the shipwreck. The shipwrecks span a period of over 200 years from the eighteenth century up to the First World War.

Shipwreck is seldom a singular event but often involved a myriad of subplots and dramas. The ship and its owners, the lust for profit, the skimping of crew, and the seaworthiness of a ship. Exploration, the aftermath of survival in remote regions of the world, and the interaction with local inhabitants are the stuff of storybooks, great novels and factual accounts.

The salvage of shipwrecks and their cargoes is an epic tale of adventure and a belief that there is huge wealth to be wrestled from shipwreck and the sea, more easily than from a bank.

The causes of shipwreck might seem to amount to more than one can estimate, but despite all the technical and social progress to date, these have hardly changed at all. Ships still wreck for the same reasons.

The first chapter, Shipwrecks, is a brief description, a snapshot of the interest that has been generated in shipwreck and salvage and the fascination that has grown for the subject from the earliest times to the present.

Chapter Three, The Wreck They Keep Secret, is the story of a large East Indiaman built in Liverpool in the eighteenth century, ostensibly for the Habsburg empire, but secretly being run by a syndicate of international businessmen and adventurers. She was lost off Dublin within 24 hours of setting sail from Liverpool for China. Carrying a fortune in silver, an attempt to salvage her began almost immediately, but failed. Two notable Scottish bell divers of the period died during the attempt from an unknown cause. Along with a small team of divers, the author has been attempting to relocate the remains of the ship for a number of years.

The wreck of the *Queen Victoria*, although responsible for a considerable loss of life when she sank in the mouth of Dublin harbour, might not have been remembered as a significant event. As shipwrecks and their loss of life go, the event paled in comparison to the 400 passengers and crew that were lost on the emigrant ship *Tayleur* the previous year, when she wrecked on Lambay Island, off north County Dublin. Significantly, the *Queen Victoria* was rediscovered by the author and the Marlin sub aqua club in 1983, and the find prompted changes to the legislation protecting historic shipwrecks in Irish waters. The wreck was the first of its kind to be issued with a protection order, made under the National Monuments Amendments Bill.

Chapter Four, Into the Yawning Abyss, is the story of Ireland's worst emigrant shipwreck disaster. A relatively new, popular, and well-built American clipper ship, the *Pomona*, was lost off Blackwater, County Wexford, in 1859, with the largest loss of emigrants on the Irish coast. The figure stands at 424, mainly Irish emigrants sailing from Liverpool to America. Twenty-four were saved, and these proved to be crew. The story will explain the discovery of the wreck in 2013, and why not one passenger survived.

The fifth chapter, The Drowning Command, is a compilation of events during the First World War in the Irish Channel, known here as 'U-boat Alley'. They involve the sinking of a number of ships by some notable German submarine commanders during 1917. German minelayers might have changed the course of the war if extreme measures had not been taken against them, measures that are still shrouded in some secrecy.

The final chapter, The Well-Head of All Pyrates, is an account of shipping, shipwrecks and salvage in and around Broadhaven, County Mayo, collected from the earliest records available to the present time. Some particular examples are expanded here and elsewhere in order to highlight local practices, and to explore the vexed and historic question of 'wrecking'.

Where is 'between the tides'?

The casual visitor to a harbour or seashore will observe the level of the water rising and falling and knows that this is the natural phenomenon called 'the tide'. Produced by the gravitational effects of the Sun and Moon, this difference between the lowest and highest level of the tidal water is more pronounced in different parts of the world – being as little as a couple of centimetres in parts of the Mediterranean, and as great as 15 metres in the Bristol Channel and the Severn Estuary. By and large, these differences are more pronounced in the northern hemisphere.

When this differential, say an average of 4 metres, impacts on an area spanning thousands of square miles, it becomes apparent that, when such an enormous mass of water begins to move during a rising or falling tide, it is bound to create an incredibly powerful dynamic. When the sea flows through narrowing geographical features, such as loughs and channels, or against and over a steeply rising seabed or obstructions, the rate of flow can increase dramatically.

Around the British Isles, there are four tidal movements in a 24-hour period. The sea will rise for 6 hours to its full height and fall during the next 6 hours. This rise and fall of the tide will occur twice in a full day, at a time which will alter progressively daily. These tidal movements are currents of water, which vary in different parts of the world. They can go from barely noticeable in some parts of the world to places like the Severn Bore in the UK, which can produce currents of up to 14 knots.

In the north-west of Europe, the differences in tidal current can be quite dramatic. The position of rivers, estuaries and geographical features can dramatically influence the movement of tidal water and create localised anomalies. These can occur around headlands, within channels, over rising or narrowing seabed, estuaries, even over and around shipwrecks and many other seabed features. In effect, any fixed feature in the path of moving water may change its direction and rate of flow, just as around a rock in the river.

Large features may have such an effect on the tide that it will not begin to stop rising or falling in accordance with the tidal prediction, and will instead maintain its own 'local times' in the area of these natural phenomenon.

In order for scuba divers to avoid and guard against these tidal streams, it is imperative that they become fully aware of local conditions before entering the water. On the plus side, nature has made a neat provision for those working on the sea, and the diver.

When the tide has reached its zenith – has ended its flood, and has filled its sea – it will then cease to flow. After giving a short respite of still or slack water, it will begin to give back the sea it has filled and begin its ebb. It is this stop or 'turn', this short respite between the tides, when divers can safely enter the water to investigate that other world. It is the sweet spot, a brief interlude, which can vary dramatically in places, and from one tidal period to another.

This period between the tides can vary quite significantly in its length and time of occurrence. In areas on the east coast of Ireland, the time can be as short as just a couple of minutes at the top of a spring tide, and almost 2 hours during the bottom of a low neap tide. If one has experienced just how much energy can be expended during a dive against flowing water, diving in that sweet spot becomes very sweet indeed. And as it happens, and probably not too surprisingly, this is also a great time for angling on shipwrecks.

These slack times can vary, sometimes significantly, from the tidal predictions, especially in areas of anomalous marine topography – such as in the North Channel, where the tide from the Atlantic, north of Ireland, meets that of the Atlantic from the south, which pushes up through the Irish Sea. The channel narrows and the contour of the seabed alters significantly here, resulting in long periods of slack water, and what are called 'standing waves' in places.

The strength of the tide can also alter at times, with what are called neap and spring tides. These are periods when the amount of tidal water varies, from low to high volumes. During neaps, amounts of water in motion can be far less than during springs, thus altering the strength of the current.

Being caught out on the seabed, in an area where tides can be difficult, has proved fatal for far too many divers. Thankfully, observing such disciplines has now become more considered and thoughtful.

Synchronising this sweet spot between the tides with a work schedule, the availability of other divers, suitable weather conditions and a half-ordinary home life, in order that one might indulge a passion for diving shipwrecks, has been the bane of my life – utterly frustrating and an insatiable time monster, but forgivingly addictive.

Shipwrecks

History and causes

From the time it is first laid down, and after artisans have fashioned hundreds of tons of materials into a floating vessel, until the moment she ceases to be a ship, a considerable number of people will have interacted with something that has become more than just a vessel that can float. Fortunes will have been won and lost and battles fought. Many will have depended on her for their lives and some will have been lost in her. This harmony of timber and man will only cease when she is lost, or after her final voyage to the breaker's yard.

The surveyors will record her specifications, where she was built and the details of her owners into the *Lloyd's Register of Ships*, and after the dog-shores are finally knocked away, a ship is launched. Through her time afloat, she will be constantly resurveyed from stem to stern, and maintained as required, and any alterations to her original details updated in the registers by Lloyd's of London. In the vast majority of cases, nothing more is ever heard or remembered of her.

During her time afloat, she will have sailed thousands of miles. At any given time, her position in the world will have been recorded by a few short staccato-like words in the maritime journal *Lloyd's List*. The constant record of her comings and goings, continually reported from around the world, are meant more for the benefit of her owners, and the merchants who have transported goods in her, than those who will have waited patiently for news of the loved ones who sailed in her.

The whereabouts of ships throughout the world were collected from shipping agents, ships' captains, extracts from letters, and entered under the Marine List in the twice-weekly – though the frequency of publication altered slightly through the years – maritime news sheet *Lloyd's List*, begun as a journal by Edward Lloyd in 1734. Most newspapers of the day also had shipping columns, which were not comprehensive and often relied on *Lloyd's List*. Some researchers claim that the origins of Lloyd's marine news sheet reach back to 1692.

The production often consisted of just one page, printed on the front and reverse sides, and the effectiveness of its economy of words is a remarkable tribute to the English language. From coffee house beginnings, Lloyd's extensive network of agents and communications spread to countries all around the world, and became of strategic importance to the British government during all of the global conflicts. What might seem surprising is that *Lloyd's List*, now a magazine, is still in production.

In the earlier production model, within the section Marine List, and under the heading of Ports – such as 'Port, Dublin: arrived from' – a list of entries would appear. Such an entry would read: '*Cerese*, galley, Richards, London', which meant that the galley *Cerese*, with Captain Richards in command, had arrived at Dublin. And a similar type of entry for outgoing traffic under the heading 'sailed for'.

If a ship is 'spoken of', or news of her loss has been reported, it would appear as follows: 'The *Aid*, Captain Cranitch, from Leghorn and Bristol for Dublin, is wrecked at Wicklow Head'.

The impending arrival of ships was not only of interest to their owners, merchants, and those waiting on loved ones. The ladies of the night also had an interest in sailors arriving on shore after long voyages, which supposedly gave *Lloyd's List* that other name: The Whores' Gazette.

One can immediately see that during the average lifetime of a ship, say between thirty and forty years, apart from those who had directly interacted with her, the rest of the world might well be oblivious to her existence.

Once having wrecked however, news of the disaster often reached the general media, and then a wider public. Not all shipwrecks were considered notable, and news of those that were not faded as quickly as the earlier reports of the ship's comings and goings. When lives or a valuable cargo were lost, depending on the significance, newspapers were more than willing to run a feature on the incident, or it might just get a couple of words in a ships news column.

Prior to the latter half of the nineteenth century, it was unusual for journalists to travel to the scene of a shipwreck, relying almost entirely on reports from pillars of the community such as policemen, customs and excise officials, men of God, letters from 'esquires', ships' captains, and so on. Exceptions were often made in cases of a significant loss of life or property when the incident was relatively accessible by road or local coasters.

If the event proved significant, the story was copied on, and would appear in multiple newspapers. It was not uncommon to read a story produced in Dublin one week and see it reproduced verbatim in New York just a few weeks later. And then in Brisbane, as soon as shipping and post would allow. Time to print was shortened considerably when the telegraph was introduced in the mid-nineteenth century.

Certain shipwrecks have almost become industries now, such as *Titanic*, *Mary Rose* and *Vasa*. Historic notoriety of an otherwise dubious nature can befall a ship once having wrecked or, in the case of *Marie Celeste*, abandoned.

The fascination of shipwreck

Why do shipwrecks fascinate? If, instead, we ask ourselves 'did shipwrecks always fascinate?' the road to an answer might shorten.

Notwithstanding exceptions, when the earliest forms of water transport sank, they were small enough to represent only a minor loss of goods or personal possessions. Retrieving the raft or boat was often not too difficult as they were built entirely of timber or reeds and could have remained buoyant. The loss, and maybe the recovery, of such vessels would not then have been of great significance, and may even have been commonplace, not attracting notable attention.

Only when ships increased in size, and became weapons, makers of fortunes, floating ideologies and the bringers of religion to new lands, did the fascination begin.

With larger ships, a shipwreck represented a larger commercial loss. It could also mean a significant naval disadvantage. If a ship was lost in shallow water, free divers were able to retrieve some of the valuable cargo. The wrecked ship itself still did not fascinate, but what Marten Triewald in 1734 dubbed the 'art of living underwater' did. If a man could descend to a shipwreck, and work there, he might become wealthy.

With the developing science of diving, a wrecked ship, and the possibility of raising it, also became a fascination.

Early divers were extremely canny about the methods and equipment they employed to recover valuables from sunken ships. Even during the earliest days there was significant competition. Just as with tales of shipwreck and survival, the public's curiosity grew and was constantly entertained by the mystery of how they did it as reports of recovered treasure grew.

Sunken treasure such as precious metals and gem stones has a lure and reward that needs little explanation. Men have invested fortunes in search of further riches. Nowadays, it tends to be someone else's fortune that gets spent.

The constant probing of history and the progress of civilisation has meant that the time capsules of shipwrecks continue to provide opportunities for social scientists to study the development of navigation, ships, trade and, by extrapolation, people. Discovery by divers of early and complicated navigational aids from shipwreck sites, such as astrolabes and sunstones, has astounded scientists and historians with both their complexity and simplicity.

Centuries-old shipwrecks, the ocean-going craft that extended man's ability to discover and conquer – their remains are now of great interest to scholars.

Undoubtedly lost from one of the many ships that have wrecked there, one of the most amazing finds I have witnessed was an eighteenth-century octant, discovered on the Kish Bank off the coast of Dublin. Appearing to be delicate, this intricately constructed scientific instrument of ebony, ivory, brass and glass seemed none the worse for its immersion in sand and seawater for almost 250 years, and was in almost perfect working condition.

The owners of these timber ships and those who travelled in them grew proud of their craft, and for centuries ship art was either commissioned or fashioned by them. The ship, the violence of shipwreck and the agonising fate of its victims, became a popular subject for artists – a new voyeurism began. Early biblical representations, such as 'St Paul's Shipwreck', depicting frail humans and their craft being dashed on the rocks by their maker's tempest, being just one example. Not short of dramatic instances of shipwrecks and large numbers of victims, when the early Victorians took the subject to their hearts, as only they could, interest in the subject grew. Matched with their remarkably descriptive language, the public couldn't get enough of it.

Ancient stories of ships, adventurous quests and shipwrecks, mythological or real, have filled shelves in libraries all over the world. The Victorian accounts of shipwreck survival sparked an even wider public appeal. The stories moved betwixt book, pamphlet, and the press. Shipwreck and all its aspects eventually became a source of fascination among a wider population, scholars, historians, salvors, and the general public.

The United Nations has estimated that there are more than 3 million shipwrecks dotted around the world. Begun in 1984 on an Amstrad 64, my own electronic database of Ireland's shipwrecks, available online at irishwrecks.com, now contains more than 14,500 entries. As it is now conjectured that this amount could be less than half of the actual amount, it would seem that the UN estimate, as in the nature of many other estimates, should be altered upwards, maybe doubled.

From the time I first began to research the incidences of shipwreck, when there were relatively few microfilm machines in Irish libraries and no electronic databases, until the development and expediential growth of available data on the internet, we have accumulated a vast storehouse of digitised shipwreck history. To own or have need to reference any of the printed volumes of shipwreck inventories, such as those compiled and recorded by Edward J. Burke in *Shipwrecks of the Irish Coast*, Bridget and Richard Larn's *Shipwreck Index of the British Isles* and Karl Brady's *Shipwreck Inventory of Ireland*, which is still a work in progress, is almost unnecessary now. Although these publications remain remarkable sources of reference, such printed works are quickly being outpaced by online access to the vast new storehouses of data.

I say 'almost' as, though most of the data have been captured from these written works, just as in times past, certain material and detail can be either lost or dropped in the transcription. Drawing down a hefty volume in order to consult and read references still has its own reassuring attraction.

Of special interest now is the huge number of high quality seabed surveys being undertaken by mineral exploration, aquaculture and governmental agencies, such as the partnership of the Geological Survey Office of Ireland and The Marine Institute, known as Infomar. Leading the field, they are well on the way to achieving their goal of surveying and charting Ireland's entire seabed. It is a truly pioneering and commendable task.

Their work has meant that the remains of a sunken vessel can be easily detected and a 4D survey completed from a desktop. Precise positions are recorded for any further on-site inspection by divers or by a camera mounted on a remotely operated underwater vehicle (ROUV).

Ships and boats have been sinking since they were first built. The oldest known 'under the water' shipwreck is the Dakos shipwreck (wrecked 2700 BC) off the Greek island of the same name. There are, however, additional classifications and new discoveries being constantly added, so this claim might be gazumped by the time this work reaches the reader. If we were to include earlier routes and means of transport, such as by river, lake, and craft peculiar to inland seas and estuaries, the record might age dramatically.

The recently discovered 4,500-year-old log boats, found by Captain Trevor Northage in Lough Corrib in the west of Ireland in 2014, and an earlier carved oak dugout discovered on the shores of Lough Neagh in Northern Ireland and dated to 5490–5246 BC, are interesting indicators.

The preservation of construction materials from these ancient wrecks remains an ongoing problem of their discovery and recovery, as does their aging and identification. If the water level around the world was once higher, are there even more shipwrecks to be found on land?

The most common method of denoting the presence of a shipwreck has been the use of a symbol, a horizontal line crossed by three equally spaced verticals, that was adopted by the Admiralty in 1920 and remains in everyday use on navigation charts. Earlier variations were in use on charts that were not drawn by the British Admiralty. The derivation of today's symbol is unclear, but may have been meant to represent a depiction of a sunken sailing ship with three masts showing above the water, or the basic construction outline of a ship: keel and ribs.

The adoption of a wreck symbol was not confined to the Admiralty. From very early times, charts of the sea were drawn up by all sorts of cartographers and sold to mariners over the counter, as they still are today. Earlier methods of denoting shipwrecks were small drawings of the event, or the use of the word 'Wreck' on maps was common.

Although there were a number of private companies still producing paper navigation charts until recent years, such as Imray and

Kingfisher, these are now compiled, by and large, by state institutions around the world, such as the US-based National Oceanic and Atmospheric Administration (NOAA) and the UKHO.

Use of the paper chart has been supplemented, and overtaken in many instances, by a variety of digitised charts which are now available on a micro memory chip or online.

Naval or commercial mariners were not the only people to use maps of the sea however – landowners also found a very special reason to map their foreshore. Thanks to their pecuniary astuteness in recording the details of their property and its legal boundaries, they often recorded shipwrecks. A landowner's property or property rights might extend a considerable distance from dry land, to a point where the tidal water will recede no further, and it is here, and beyond in some cases, that ownership and control of all on it might cease.

Early mapmakers began the process of making an actual sketch, and even painted known shipwrecks on the land-deed title maps of wealthy landowners. Long before that, the sinking and wrecking of ships were being recorded by artists and historians.

Fishermen, yet another group of people interested in the sea and the creatures and habitats within it, have also recorded bathometric anomalies, such as depths, rock, sandbars and shipwrecks, for generations. Since man began to fish, it has always been in their interest to know what the seabed was like as different species of fish-life and their numbers are attracted to its variable features. When sail trawling began, it was of paramount importance to be able to avoid obstructions in order to preserve valuable nets and to continue fishing.

At first, fishermen recorded these obstructions by referencing their positions to the alignment of different features on the land – mountains, steeples, the entrance to a river etc. – and called them transit marks. When motorised trawling and navigation by radio waves (Decca) progressed after the Second World War, they were able to plot all of their 'snags' or 'fastenings' on simple graph paper.

Positions were determined by cross referencing numerical 'lanes', with a colour code across the top, against another scale along the side of the graph paper.

Remarkably accurate, the copy of the fisherman's trawl chart (snag or fasteners chart) for the area around the Arklow Banks and

Cahore, off the east coast of Ireland and seen in the illustrations accompanying this book, shows lines which are the routes of a particular trawl and a plethora of dots and circles, which are obstructions that include shipwrecks.

In respect of shipwrecks, and Ireland's place in this league of misfortune, the record is notable. The number of shipwrecks that are in lakes, rivers and in the sea around Ireland is probably comparatively disproportionate to its land mass, even when measured against the overall length of its large number of bays and inlets.

Uniquely situated, Ireland is the most westerly landmass off the north-west of mainland Europe; it is the last, or the first, sight of land that mariners venturing deep-sea or returning from trans-global voyages will observe. For mariners navigating this huge expansion of ocean, this meant that it had a special significance in maritime history, and for their safety.

Ireland's position in the geography of north-west Europe became strategic hundreds of years ago, and will remain so until there is no longer an ocean, or until we cease to use it. When the whole of Ireland was occupied by Britain, her naval supremacy over seaborne traffic from northern Europe was extended from Dover to the extremities of the south-west coast of Ireland. The north of Ireland was of somewhat similar strategic importance, especially during the World Wars, when Britain maintained two exit and entry points to the Atlantic for her naval and commercial fleets.

To the north, control was exercised from the deep-water ports of Lough Swilly, Lough Foyle and Larne, and, to the south, from the ports of Rosslare, Cobh and Berehaven. Any disagreement with its north European neighbours meant that Britain, through her dominance of this northern access to the Atlantic, could effectively sever or drastically reduce the other's global commerce and the influence that it derived from the use of these areas.

When viewed against other areas around the coast of Ireland, one might be tempted to consider its west coast as a 'flat spot' in terms of the amount of available shipwreck data and record of maritime traffic. An inventory of shipwrecks shows a marked decrease in the record between the entrance of the River Shannon and north-west Donegal. However, due to an insufficient record of older events, those available are only able to give the smallest glimpse of the huge amount of traffic that did take place along these shores during an earlier time. This traffic included the fishing fleets from Holland, Scotland and England, Spain and Portugal, and the almost incalculable amount of maritime interaction that took place between the clans of western Ireland and Spain and Portugal.

Neither was it an area ignored by the British navy. Britain deployed naval and revenue vessels at various stations along this coast from the sixteenth century, ostensibly to combat smugglers, but, more importantly, to prevent France and Spain developing the notion that, although it was a sparsely habited and difficult area of Ireland to control, it was not being left unguarded. The zeal with which this policy was applied in 1588 was to prove a bitter lesson for the Spanish when their storm-battered Armada ships were swept onto the coast of Ireland.

Ultimately, by virtue of Ireland's unique strategic geography, its invasion or occupation became an attractive proposition for Britain's enemies, of which there was no historical shortage. Ireland became a strategic and sometimes willing pawn in a number of regional and global conflicts, and many ships were sent to the bottom of the sea as a result.

More recently, the role which Ireland played during the Second World War, one always thought to have been strictly neutral, has proven to have been secretly more sympathetic towards the cause of the Allies.

Naval ships

Sunk in battle, warships, whether they be those in the air or the sea, are not the shipwreck material of this review. Nonetheless, the wrecking of naval vessels is deeply interwoven in the narrative of shipwreck. By virtue of the fact that naval discipline required such detailed record keeping, we have been fortunate to have inherited some of the most graphic and detailed accounts of naval shipwreck.

The Swedish warship *Vasa*, built in 1628, was to be a gleaming example of premium naval shipbuilding. Unfortunately, the arrogance that comes with vanity capsized and sank her before she sailed a thousand yards. The national reputation was somewhat redeemed later by the tenacity of archaeologists when the wreck was rediscovered in the 1950s, removed from the mud, and reconstructed for public display.

Not naval in a modern understanding, the remarkable stories of the East Indiamen, such as the *Grosvenor* (wrecked 1782) and *Halswell* (wrecked 1786), also come to mind. As do those of the naval vessels that participated in great periods of exploration, including voyages to the polar regions and Anson's 1740–44 voyage, which was less an attempt to sail around the world and more of an adventure for treasure.

In his attempt to round the Horn and reach China by way of the Pacific, Anson was also intending to capture the richest prize of all the oceans, the annual Spanish treasure galleon *Nuestra Señora de Covadonga* that travelled from Acapulco to Manila. George Anson set out in convoy from Spithead in September 1740 with 152 ships. His own ship, the *Centurion*, was the only ship to reach Canton. The remainder were either lost or returned to England. Contained in the story of the voyage, there are a number of individual and regrettable stories of shipwreck.

Of the 1,900 men that left Spithead, almost 1,400 died in the misadventure. Anson did capture the treasure galleon, which did indeed carry a vast fortune, and upon his return to England was celebrated and compared to Drake. The Crown counted not the cost, but the booty.

Instruments of politicians and government policy, naval vessels have nevertheless been at the cutting edge of civilisation's technical advances in their construction, voyages and their recovery after having been wrecked. Their sailors and commanders have been at the vanguard of exploration down through the centuries, with several resulting in notable shipwreck events.

One example is HMS *Association*, which lost her entire crew of 800 after she grounded on the Scilly Isles in 1707. More examples are the submarine *Thetis*, wrecked in Liverpool Bay in 1938 with 99 lives lost during commissioning, and the nuclear submarine *Kursk*, which lost all 118 of her crew when she was lost in 2000 due to catastrophic mechanical and human failure. Each of these, and many more, in one way or another, became a focus of remarkable feats of salvage.

Providing more exciting clarity, and heightening the fascination in shipwreck, a later modern world has managed to pull all of these exciting strands together and present them in films and documentaries. There are now millions who view shipwreck features in cinemas, on television and, more recently, on the internet. The birth of new media sources and the marriage of film with history has popularised the subject and continues to do so.

A surge of interest in shipwrecks emerged in the middle of the twentieth century at the same time as the not unconnected development in scuba diving equipment. Untethered, divers were free to roam around the seabed with portable breathing equipment, and then with cameras.

Having ancestors lost in ships for whatever reason, readers and viewers are now able to relate to these events from their desktop. Accessing history and tracing ancestry has become much easier, and big business. Technology and the media have adopted 'shipwreck', and continue to enhance its fascination.

The causes of shipwreck

On the face of it, from the time of reed craft and dug-out canoes to the most sophisticated water craft known to man – the nuclear submarine – it might seem that ships have been wrecked for an ever-increasing number of reasons. Given that ships' propulsion, materials and methods of construction and safety at sea have undergone such fundamental evolution, one might expect that the dynamics which have caused the loss of ships would also have changed.

Ships have been lost at sea for a wide variety of reasons on a micro level. However, excluding the deliberate sinking of a ship during conflict, or by a violent attack by others, the crucial factors leading to the loss of a ship have remained the same, and can be largely categorised under one of three headings: the state of the weather, the condition of the vessel or the condition of the crew.

Putting exceptional weather conditions aside for a moment, one might observe that all shipping casualties are caused by the top of the pyramid, man, as it is he who constructs, maintains, manages and mans the vessel in which he puts to sea. Some have believed that the two have always been irreconcilable, and that shipwreck represents a disagreement between man and his maker.

He doesn't, however, have any influence over the weather, and until very recently his capabilities of forecasting it relied on trend and day-to-day observations. Notwithstanding, it is important to understand the influence each of these other downstream categories can have on the successful operation of vessels, and, when they are below par, how they can impact disastrously on a ship and its crew.

When the mercantile marine division of the Board of Trade was established in 1859, the process of tabulating the various losses and damage to ships had already begun. They itemised four categories causing the loss of ships: arising from stress of weather; inattention, carelessness and neglect; various causes; causes unknown.

In 1864 they produced a nine-year report which showed that 1859 was the worst year for the loss of ships, and that the highest loss of life occurred in the Irish Sea. The stress of weather was the reason given for the greatest number of losses. The tragedy of the American sailing ship *Pomona*, wrecked off Wexford in 1859, was the most significant loss, and the story of that event is included in this book.

Weather

The early transmission of impending weather conditions – forecasting – began side by side with the advances made in communications, with the telegraph arriving in the 1840s. However, the science of predicting the weather only began to make real advancements when the Irishman Francis Beaufort applied himself to it in the 1850s. This is not to belittle the remarkable studies and recordings of weather and maritime phenomena by others and, specifically, the little known about eighteenth-century dock-master at Liverpool, William Hutchinson, who plays a role in the story featured in the chapter 'The Wreck They Keep Secret'.

It was not until much later, however, that weather prediction reached any degree of accuracy or reliability.

Today, we can predict weather with a good level of accuracy for almost a week ahead, and much further than that with varying degrees of success. More importantly, we can receive weather forecast updates on demand through a range of media and electronic receivers.

Previously, sailors had to rely on trends and their ancient knowledge of metrological observations passed down through generations.

Coastwise voyages, lasting only a few days, had the protection of coastal shelter from sudden changes in weather conditions, and their level of risk differed considerably from that of deep-water voyages. With land far behind them, these much longer voyages, once begun, could not be abandoned at the first sight of storm clouds.

A ship might set out on a voyage from Bristol, bound for Africa and from there to America, with an expectation of returning to England in one piece and with a profitable cargo a year later. Apart from their position in the world, previous experience, and the time of year, they had no idea what extremes of weather might be visited on them.

If a ship is said to have been lost due to foul weather, the statement would appear to be self-explanatory. If caught in a storm of extreme weather, for instance, a ship can suffer such violent buffeting that the integrity of its construction suffers to the point that the ingress of water compromises its ability to float, and she sinks.

This would seem to be a clear case of cause and effect, but weather may only be a contributing factor. For example, a ship blown nearer to a coastline with hidden shoals and reefs that are totally unfamiliar to its crew. This alone, being driven by weather, should not and did not always mean the destruction of a ship. A total loss usually only occurred when other factors came into play. Such trials with stormy weather can also test the condition of a ship's equipment and the metal of its crew.

Returning to weather that is truly exceptional, it is obvious that very little could be done to save a ship of timber and canvas when it found itself in conditions so extreme that they were often described as a total storm, or a fierce hurricane, and so on. And even today, such conditions can prove challenging for large powerful ships. The only factor that may help to save a ship in such weather conditions is its ability to remain afloat. If a ship is well built and maintained, and remains tight, her ability to remain buoyant might save the ship and those in her.

Proving fatal to ships of many kinds, extreme weather events have been recorded since very early times. Most notably, earlier versions of the volcanic eruptions at Krakatoa in 415 and 535, and the well recorded one in 1833, where more than 36,000 people were killed. Numerous ships were sunk by the resulting tsunami and the red-hot ash that fell from the sky for miles around.

The terrible weather conditions that lasted throughout 1639 were heralded in the beginning of the year with 'Great Storm of rain, hail, snow and great thundering and lightening, striking people with panic and fear'. The great storm was ushered out in December with an incalculable loss to shipping, extensive damage to private and civic buildings in Britain, and Archbishop Laud calling it, 'The greatest wind that ever I had heard.' The fact that one cannot see the wind, but can clearly see the effects of it, can be a fascinating feature, but one that has perturbed many in years past.

Estimated today to have measured a magnitude of 9, the 'Great Lisbon Earthquake' occurred on All Saints' Day, 1 November 1755, and its effects were felt all over Europe. Utter devastation was visited on Lisbon, and the resulting tsunami travelled all along the eastern seaboard of the Atlantic, flooding the market place in Kinsale and damaging the Spanish Arch in Galway. When the sea receded in Lisbon, it revealed a sea floor littered with lost cargo and shipwrecks.

It was a sad feature of this disastrous event, in which it is estimated that upward of 100,000 people perished, that at first belief was suspended. The population of Europe was slow to grasp the enormity of this catastrophe as news of it, which included descriptions of Lisbon and where it was situated, did not reach a sizeable portion of the population until almost a month had passed.

Reported in such graphic terms as 'Lisbon is no more', maritime commerce was obviously affected significantly. True to its penchant for brevity, however, the event, or any interruption of trade with the region, was not mentioned in *Lloyd's List* up to the end of that year.

Ireland had its own 'Night of the Big Wind' on 6 January 1839. Said to have been the worst storm in 300 years, it was responsible for a large loss of life and calamitous devastation onshore. Extensive damage to buildings and the loss of hundreds of boats and ships were recorded around the coasts of Britain and Ireland. As Peter Carr writes in *The Big Wind*, 'Herrings were found 6 miles inland, and in County Galway the risen tide left the dunes and beaches squirming with herring, cod and congers.'

The vagaries of the weather were a mariner's lot, but significant weather events continue with equal, if not more disastrous, results today.

Condition of a ship

At different times in our history, the short-cuts taken by shipbuilders and owners during the construction and maintenance of their ships have attracted considerable amounts of criticism. One example of a modern kind is the use of single-hull tankers, which have been responsible for incredible cases of pollution after collisions, and another being giant bulk carriers which have fractured unexplainably during heavy seas. Modern materials have proved stronger and more durable but can suffer similarly to any other material from bad design and neglect, causing structural failure and disaster.

Incidents of neglect involving older timber sailing ships attracted particular attention, when greedy owners and agents ignored the dangerous shortcomings of their vessels during the period of Ireland's Great Famine, and the large migration of Europeans during the nineteenth century. The transport of people in ships reached considerable proportions during this period, and promoted skimping for profit during the construction and maintenance of emigrant vessels, as well as insufficient provisions for suitable onboard living conditions.

Both before and after landlords began to be charged with certain obligations to their impoverished tenants, there were moves to eject the tenants from their lands. In an unashamed opportunistic rush for profit, the greedy ship owners skimped on the quality of the crew and the maintenance of their ships. Squeezing as many emigrants as possible into terribly cramped and unhealthy conditions, and then crossing great oceans in vessels that were so deplorably inadequate, they became known as coffin ships.

Included in such criticism was the use of unsuitable and unprepared lumber for the construction of a ship. This was less a crime of construction and more a result of the over-extended service of the ill-conceived ship by its avaricious owners, when it should have been condemned far earlier.

Overloading was rife, leading to the loss of many ships, and only came to an end with the introduction of the Plimsoll Line. This was a mark put on a ship that indicated a maximum height the water could rise to on its hull, thus regulating the amount of cargo or people that could be loaded into a ship. Although the principal of using such a load line was invented in the 1870s, by Samuel Plimsoll, it took many years for its use to be universally accepted and implemented.

The criminal use of 'rotten' ships for profit is well recorded, and even remembered in song. The following verse, one of three, in a tribute to the stand taken by Mr Plimsoll, captures the mood and the difficulties he undoubtedly encountered while attempting to outlaw the practice:

> There was a time when greed and crime did cruelly prevail
> And rotten ships were sent to founder in the gale
> When worthless cargoes well-insured would to the bottom go.
> And sailors' lives would were sacrificed that men might wealthy grow.
> ('A Cheer for Plimsoll' by Fred Albert, 1876)

Not all ship owners were so callous or short sighted. There were many well-respected owners and companies and, in particular, some families who had been in the business for generations and carried on their business honourably. For many others, sufficient profit did not always suffice.

Passengers and crew alike suffered and died from chronically poor shipboard conditions. Badly treated crew deserted when they could. Timbers sprung, and rotten rigging failed at the first glimpse of bad weather. But if a ship could pump out water faster than it came in, though, it could remain afloat.

A ship would almost certainly sink if it could not beat the ingress of water and foundered. Wrecking from this single cause, however, may not have been the most common. Such a fatal outcome often required an additional element.

There are numerous aspects of shipbuilding – design, materials used and aftercare – which, when neglected, have contributed to the loss of many ships. The following two are worth mentioning as their effects were at first unknown but, even when discovered, they were ignored by so many, leading to disastrous results.

From the moment a tree is felled, its natural fibre can decline – it will just decompose if its integrity is not preserved. When it is used in the construction of a ship and launched into water, it has a life expectancy than can be dramatically altered either way by the quality of the care it receives.

The hull of a wooden vessel will rot prematurely if it is not cleaned and treated regularly. This is not so prevalent in colder waters, but once a ship travels to warmer climes the dreaded teredo worm will eat the bottom of a ship until it becomes like a sieve and causes the ship to sink or break open. When the phenomenon was discovered, one of the remedies was to cover the bottom of a ship with copper sheets in order prevent the worm getting to the timber. The chemical reaction of the copper in the seawater was also thought to play an important part in repelling the organism. The copper had the double effect of not only reducing the effect of the worm on the timber but also preventing the growth of weed and other organisms that could quickly accumulate on a ship's hull.

The value of the copper remedy was discovered in 1705, but was not introduced until about fifty years later. Coppering of a ship and its subsequent maintenance was an expensive consideration, and it was not a compulsory requirement. A consequence of this was shortcuts; planks were replaced and worm holes were filled in.

When ship's fastenings moved from timber to metal, the reaction of the different metals to one another, in a ship immersed in sea water, led to their sinking. When the chemical reaction between the different metal fixings in the ship's hull first became evident, it was not understood. Over time, and before the life of the timber had ended, iron fixings in a ship could corrode in the sea. However, the quality of some iron fixings, such as those used in Viking boats, was such that they seldom showed any signs of corrosion. Experiments with brass, bronze and copper showed that these metals had a longer and more reliable life, and, though more expensive, they gradually came into common use.

During intervening years, when iron fixings were showing dangerous signs of corrosion, either naturally or from the use of non-iron fixings in the same hull or in the copper sheeting, these were individually replaced by bronze or brass ones. It was soon discovered that an electrically induced chemical reaction between the two metals in seawater was taking place, which gave rise to an even faster deterioration in the remaining iron fixings.

With the prospect of a major engagement with France and Spain over America looming, the British navy began a programme of coppering all of its ships. This was soon followed by a programme of retro-fastening all of its ships with single metal fastenings.

A considerably lower level of urgency was evident in commercial shipping, with only the more progressive and wealthier coppering their vessels. Ships just fell apart at sea or were left to wreck and ruin.

A fundamental change to shipping and practices began during the latter half of the nineteenth century. Iron was now been used to construct the hulls of ships, and steam engines were being used to replace sail. New routes were being opened, and sailing times were dramatically reduced. Ship owners unable to extricate themselves from timber and sail were finished. The remaining timber ships could not compete or attract the expensive reinvestment in their upkeep and just disappeared.

Condition of the crew

This third element, condition of the crew, has a number of facets. It might mean that the crew had suffered from an over-extended voyage, or had become malnourished due to a lack of suitable food, or any food at all. They may also have become incapable from a prolonged period of bad weather, suffered from fatigue, or been injured in a conflict.

'Condition' also include illness which, having overcome senior members of the crew, captain and officers, might lead to reduced effectiveness in managing the ship. In this instance, we might also include those who succumbed to the effects of alcohol – drunkenness.

Lastly, a ship lost due to the condition of the crew could also mean that the captain and crew were incompetent, or lacked the suitable experience and maritime skills necessary for the voyage on which they had set out.

There are some recorded incidences where the drastic and risky step of subduing a sick captain – one who has temporarily lost the normal function of his mind – was taken in order to steer the ship safely to port. Such a measure was considered mutiny without very strong evidence to the contrary, and was punishable by hanging. Some of these succeeded, and some failed with fatal consequences for the mutineers.

None are so gruesome as that which occurred on the brig *Mary Russell* returning to Cork from Barbados in June 1828. Aboard was the demented Captain William Stewart, six dead crew members and the passenger, Captain James Gould Raynes. All seven lay dead on the cabin floor. They had been killed by the captain and their heads battered in with a crow bar, an axe, and a harpoon. There were six others on board, comprising crewmen, one passenger, and two stablemen.

Flying a flag of distress, Captain Stewart was still in command of the *Mary Russell* when she fell in with the American ship *Mary Stubbs* 300 miles off the coast of Cork. Captain Callendar of *Mary Stubbs*, and two of his crew, boarded the *Mary Russell*, and discovered the macabre massacre. They also discovered seven other crew members in various degrees of injury and terror.

While the two ships proceeded to Cork, Captain Stewart threw himself overboard and had to be rescued from the sea three times.

Captain Stewart was arrested when the ships berthed in Cork harbour and charged with the murder of Captain Raynes. During the trial, Stewart declared that he had suspected mutiny. This was apparently brought on by Captain Raynes speaking in Irish to the crew. The survivors denied that there had been any notion of mutiny, and counterclaimed that the captain had lost his mind.

The jury found Captain Stewart not guilty, but insane, and he was committed to an asylum until he died in 1873. No one was tried for mutiny.

Once again, the ship will remain afloat if it does not totally fill with water, and will rarely sink because a captain or its crew are temporarily incapacitated or incompetent. The ship may find itself in a place not intended, choose a course too close to shore or one which narrowly avoids a remote reef, but unless there is a second, or even third, element present, shipwreck is often avoidable, and was not common in these lesser circumstances. If a ship could stay afloat, there was always the prospect of assistance from another passing vessel.

Examples of shipwreck and their causes

Built of iron, the White Star clipper ship *Tayleur* was heralded as a fine and particularly strong new ship. Bound for Australia on her maiden voyage, she set out from Liverpool into the Irish Sea in January 1854. The weather was described as being thick at times, and the ship was buffeted by strong winds that were predominantly westerly at first. It was not described as a storm when the ship was thrown off course in the direction of Ireland.

Doubting the accuracy of her compasses, position and heading, confusion grew as to the ship's true course and position. The *Tayleur*'s course had initially been WSW, but her actual heading brought her dangerously more westward, towards the coast of Ireland. The dangers inherent in continuing on this unsuspected heading were compounded when the wind strengthened and turned more south-easterly.

Eventually, looming out of the darkness ahead, the captain became alarmed when he caught sight of the high cliffs on the shoreline of north County Dublin. Unable to get off the lee shore, he let both his anchors go, one after the other. Both chains broke and failed to halt the progress of the 2,000-ton ship, now travelling in the direction of Lambay Island, or prevent it becoming a total wreck. Reports on the number of victims varied and it is put at approximately 400 souls who were either lost or drowned.

Testimony confirmed that the ship was a strongly built vessel and not leaky. But if the evidence reported subsequently is to be believed, the ship was wrecked by every other possible means except otherwise manageable weather!

The number of crew was insufficient, they were inexperienced, and some could not speak English, meaning orders were difficult to relay efficiently. The ship had not undergone the normal trials expected. The rigging was new, not broken-in, and the sails split during the strong winds. The compasses were inaccurate due to not being swung properly after the ship had been fully laden – the entire ship was constructed of iron, and there was an 8-ton iron steamer stowed on the deck of the ship, supposedly after the compasses had been corrected.

Compounded by strong and contrary winds, one might expect that a ship with such deficits was clearly in some danger. She struck on the rocky shore, filled with water and sank quite quickly. One aspect of the controversy surrounding the accuracy of the new compasses was striking – doubt. The captain and crew, at an early stage in the voyage, would seem to have begun to mistrust the accuracy of the new compasses and consulted each in turn, expressing scepticism in the accuracy of both.

A useful lesson taught to me when I began boating and diving was to have faith in your compass. If, after testing, it consistently works with some measure of accuracy, always believe it. If it doesn't appear to work well, throw it way. Scurrying around the seabed in a dark environment is no place for a diver to lose faith in his compass – the same goes for on the sea.

A faulty compass was often cited by survivors as a reason for damage to their ship or its loss. This may very well have been a valid criticism in many cases, when the compass had not been properly swung after taking on a significant cargo of iron. But unless recovered undamaged, and tested again in similar conditions, this was impossible to verify.

The Russian nuclear submarine *Kursk* (wrecked 2000) was lost, in as much as naval secrecy allows, as a result of two elements. It was holed, and then sank, as a direct result of its declining condition, and the incompetence of its crew.

Another defeated by two elements was the liner *Costa Concordia* (wrecked 2012). Although not suffering from being under maintained, she was holed while sailing too close to shore and failed to remain afloat. Once more, this was a direct result of mismanagement by its crew.

Confluence of the elements

A stout ship, with sails that are in good condition and well-trimmed, crewed by a sober and competent crew, has excellent chances of surviving the most deplorable weather conditions and completing her voyage – even after it has been completely abandoned by its crew, a well found ship can remain afloat, and be saved later. If either of these elements is under par, the ship is in danger. If two of these factors are deficient, the ship and its crew will be very lucky to avoid coming to harm.

A ship with a leak that cannot be stemmed, and which has no means to pump the water out, will fill totally and then sink. If the ingress of water can be stemmed, allowing the ship to maintain some buoyancy, then there is hope of reaching safety. But if, in addition, the ship is dismasted, or the rigging damaged to the extent that steering a safe course is not possible, then the chances of being wrecked are dangerously multiplied. If the ship is leaking badly, the rigging is unmanageable and the crew incapacitated, the situation would seem to be almost hopeless.

The well-respected bankers and ship owners Joseph Wilson and his son Thomas sailed one of their ships from Port of Spain, Trinidad, in 1859. The ship was named after Wilson's club, which was named after an earlier and more controversial ship of the same name, the *Ouzel Galley* (wrecked around 1700). Packed with 400 hogsheads of sugar from his plantations, this younger *Ouzel* was bashed by severe storms off Bermuda, injuring members of the crew and killing one Robert Owen from Dublin. The ship was badly damaged, losing her bulwarks, mizzen-mast, and jib boom, and her sails and rigging were torn to shreds.

The remaining crew survived, after a gallant rescue by the passing American ship *Ann E Hooper*. The *Ouzel Galley* was later reported to have been wrecked, lost and abandoned. Nevertheless, the ship did not in fact sink under the water. We know this as she was encountered and identified by another passing ship, several days after being abandoned.

The *Ouzel Galley* had taken so much water over her decks that the hatches were damaged, and her ability to keep out of the sea was compromised. The ship filled, but as she was packed so tight with barrels she remained afloat. Heavily insured, her ultimate fate went unreported.

This was a well found and well insured ship, under the command of the respected Captain Thomas Halpin, brother of the famed Robert, captain of the *Great Eastern*. She was the victim of hurricane weather, badly damaged rigging and injured crew, leading to her filling with water.

Here we have a ship which suffered onslaught from all three elements but didn't sink, and all the crew, bar one, were saved. We remain unsure of her ultimate fate. Not an isolated case – the odds against survival were overturned by chance, a passing ship in the middle of an ocean.

King Philip of Spain sent forth his huge armada of ships to conquer Britain in 1588. His captains covered all the odds. The invasion was timed for the fair weather of late summer and early autumn to make the best of the English Channel. They were well prepared for battle and for landing and conquering Britain. What they were badly prepared for was losing the battle at sea, and being routed 'northabout', in a desperate retreat to Spain.

Many of the ragtag collection of fleeing ships had been damaged during the conflict. They ran short of food and water with crew becoming sick and helpless. Ships that had been suitable as an invasion fleet were soon found to be unsuitable for the North Atlantic. That other element, the weather, for which they believed they had prepared, turned dramatically against them. The North Atlantic produced an unseasonable storm, 'the storm of the century', from the not unusual direction of west and north-west. Of unpredictable ferocity, it dashed many of the Spanish ships to pieces on the west coast of Ireland.

Although the weather had been contrary, and many of the Armada vessels were badly damaged, and their crews were sick, the ships were not lost until they were holed on the coast of Ireland.

Ireland lost her sail-training vessel *Asgard II*, a modern production utilising classic sailing ship design, in the Bay of Biscay, in 2008. A timber brigantine, built at the renowned yard of Tyrell's in Arklow, the ship was in excellent condition. And although a sail training vessel with part-time inexperienced crew at times, she was permanently manned by a competent full-time crew.

The cause of the sinking was the ingress of water from damaged planking, the cause of this damage being unknown. After the sudden and surprising discovery, the water rose rapidly, and the captain gave the order to abandon ship. The captain was reported to have said that he did know how the water entered the ship. The weather conditions during the night were unremarkable.

When examined later, divers reported that there was some damage to the planking below the waterline. This gave rise to a belief that the vessel may have struck a submerged object – possibly a steel container. To lose containers overboard in heavy seas is not an unknown occurrence. It might also have been caused when the ship struck the seabed.

The vessel was in excellent condition, her crew competent, and the weather fair – none of the three elements were present. If the cause of sinking the *Asgard* was as reported, then it was pure chance that such a collision might occur, and that sea would have entered the ship so quickly and the crew would be unable pump it out and keep afloat.

If there is any criticism to be made in the above example, it might be levelled at the early warning systems that are installed in modern vessels. Unless a catastrophic event, these will indicate any increase of water in the bilges, giving time for measures to be taken to save the vessel. Those on the *Asgard*, on the other hand, may not have been sufficient, fully operational, or, less likely, not fitted.

Other causes of shipwreck

It has already been pointed out that a study of naval engagements and resulting losses are not included in this review as they are a deliberate act by man intended to sink ships, and this needs no further explanation. However, I would like to digress briefly in order to demonstrate the extent to which such terrible acts occurred in the Irish Channel during the First World War, and how this aspect of the war has passed into history largely unnoticed.

The channel between Ireland and England, relatively narrow in places, was for many years thought not to have unduly suffered in comparison to other places in Europe during the World Wars. Some might consider that it was less affected during the Second World War, but this was certainly not the case during the First World War, and, unlike the west coast of Ireland, could never have been described as a flat spot. Quite the opposite was in fact the case, with hundreds of ships having been attacked and sunk there by German submarines.

Lending support in maintaining such an illusion, the Admiralty went so far at one point as to describe the Irish Channel as a quiet lake, even when German submarines appeared to be roaming there almost at will. The Channel contained some of the most important maritime and industrial centres of Great Britain and Ireland, and the seabed between the two countries is now littered with the evidence of German submariners' handiwork.

During the four years that immediately preceded the commencement of the First World War, there were eighty-nine shipping casualties recorded in the area now known as U-boat Alley. For the next four years of the First World War, there are 718 entries. These include all losses and attacks by U-boats.

U-boat Alley represents the sea off the coastline from Antrim to Wexford and areas such as the North Channel, the Irish Sea and the St George's Channel.

Even taking into account the additional classifications and those entries that did not result in a loss, the magnitude of the increased figure speaks for itself. Not so obvious are the reasons for the low casualty figures in the years preceding the conflict, which is explained by the near disappearance of sailing ships. It also reflects the proliferation of iron and steel in motorised vessels, the considerable improvement in maritime regulation and practices, and the safety at sea that resulted.

The terrible increase of the casualty figures over the next four years, during the First World War, demonstrates the destruction man is capable of when he is bestowed with new weapons.

Some additional reasons for the loss of ships are collision and fire. Seemingly separate causes, they nevertheless, in the first instance, fall into the categories 'condition of the ship' and 'condition of the crew' for our purposes.

Today, collision is normally caused by the mismanagement of the ship. The modern ship, with so many navigational aids, means that the old bugbears of fog, poor lights, or a sudden gust of contrary wind can no longer be excused. During the era of sail only, a ship may at times have found it hard to steer safely in certain weather conditions, or became obliged to reduce sail and speed in order to lessen the possibility of a collision, or the damage from one. There were also times when a captain, even with all sail reduced, could do next to nothing to reduce his rate of progress through the water.

Just as with fire, collision by ramming was also a weapon of aggression. And if one recalls the Cod Wars between Great Britain and Iceland during the latter half of the twentieth century, we might conclude that it is another feature of shipwreck which hasn't gone away.

Collision between sailing vessels was not uncommon, and despite all of the advances in technology today it remains a recurring feature of accidents at sea. Barely moving, the MV *Kilkenny* was lost in Dublin Bay in 1991 with loss of life and the complete destruction of the vessel. Not all collisions are pure chance.

Fire aboard a sailing ship remained a constant fear of captains and crew. Although sailing ships had fires on board for cooking, there was exceptional care taken with any flame or hot embers. Fire could start on a ship through negligence. It could also start by pure chance – lightning. It could begin with spontaneous combustion, due to badly managed bulk cargoes of grain or bituminous materials, or, our old friend, during conflict.

Just as with ramming, fire was also used as a weapon against ships. If not hurled from battlements, then fire ships could be packed with inflammables or explosives, lit, and guided among enemy ships. Philip's Armada was scattered in the English Channel when the English sailed a number of fire ships among them. Terrified, many of the Spanish ships cut their anchor hawsers and fled, losing valuable anchors they would later discover they had a dire need for when they found themselves off the west coast of Ireland in fierce storms.

Amid familiar charges of faulty lifeboats, and negligence by the crew, 128 people were lost from the liner *Lakonia* in 1963 when she caught fire off the island of Madeira. She sank later while under tow. The fire began in the hairdressing salon.

The Norwegian cruise ship *Nordys* did not sink but suffered serious damage from fire off Aalesund in 2011. Fires of this nature are rarely caused by chance.

Demons and curses

A figurehead or image was placed on the bow or sail of a ship as far back as the Vikings, Phoenicians and the ancient Chinese. Later, placing a figurehead on the prow of ship was meant to indicate the status of the owner, or the name of the vessel, or both. Not unlike the names that appear on boats today, these can often represent a characteristic, allegiance or escapade of their owners – they are making a statement about themselves.

In their earlier use, figureheads were also meant to represent an appeasement or a plea to the gods for safe and rewarding voyages. Some images were obviously intended to frighten the opponents of their owners.

It was believed during earlier times that a race of gods and demons, when angry, were responsible for wrecking ships. The Egyptian demon Aldinach might appear as a woman on the prow of a ship shortly before casting it away. It was also believed that the same fate might befall ships if any of the wind gods, such as Vesper or Boreas, were angered by mortals.

On rare occasions, a ship may be thought to have been doomed to wreck by being cursed, whether it be the curse of the White Star, or a red haired lady crossing the path of seafarers, who are notoriously superstitious. Suspecting anything out of the ordinary, sailors could become extremely agitated with a crewman who might begin to behave unusually, whistle, speak ill of the cat, or wear the wrong colour. Secreting bottles of blessed water and small religious icons throughout a ship was common.

In 1884 the British naval vessel HMS *Wasp* was believed to be heading for the islands off the north coast of Ireland to collect overdue taxes. With the impending arrival of the naval vessel, the King of Tory Island performed a ceremony with the island's cursing stones that was said to have caused the wrecking of the vessel under the island's lighthouse. The wreck of *Wasp* does lie at the bottom of the cliffs under the lighthouse, and the victims of the incident are buried on the island. The stones are still in the possession of the King of Tory.

The use of Tory's cursing stones tends to be treated as a great yarn, but stories concerning the use of such stones are not peculiar to the remote island of Tory.

Accounts of stones with similarly strange powers survive in Erris, County Mayo. The Godstone was meant to calm waters, while small mounds of stones called *Caislean Pleminhin* were said to have had the powers of demons and could be used to call up the wind in order to wreck ships. The stones were piled up and an opening in the mound was created in the direction the storm of wind was required to blow in order to wreck the ship.

An account of the practise is recorded in Caesar Otway's *Sketches in Erris and Tyrawly*, published in 1841:

> The erection and use of *Caslaan Pleminhin*, these are small castles, somewhat like those children build of cards, raised up of nine stones in a conical form, and with a door towards the ART from which the wind is required to blow. Some magical rites attend the building of these castles, whose efficacy the most incredulous of the country fellows do not attempt to deny; but they have an objection to try the operation of the act, as they consider the meddling in such practises might place their souls in the power of the demon; but they are said to have been extensively used in the former 'wrecking times' when ships were considered fair booty, and the hanging out of false lights was not considered unwarrantable.
>
> Indeed, how could the poor have a scruple on the subject, when the practise was countenanced and taken advantages by persons who ought to know better. When a ship was seen off the coast the *Caslaan Pleminhin* were erected to effect the wreck; the calm which generally succeeds a storm was looked to as part of the required effect, affording the opportunity of approaching and plundering the unfortunate vessel and her crew.

Seemingly equally unlikely is the possibility that ships might be sunk by sea creatures or demons from the deep, which is not actually unlikely at all. There are a number of well documented cases where whales have attacked timber or fibreglass vessels and sunk them. *Moby Dick* was a novel and movie, but based on the true story of the sinking of the whale ship *Essex* in 1820. Still surviving, there are a considerable number of accounts by fishermen encountering giant octopi which threatened their lives and the safety of their vessels. The octopus reported by Indians in December 1902 was certainly not one you would like to encounter while sunbathing on your lilo. It was caught in Neah Bay, USA, and measured 55 feet across, and weighed 2,500 lbs. Each of its tentacles had 350 suckers.

A number of encounters with giant octopi or squid were also reported by submarine commanders during both World Wars, and maybe not so giant by Greenpeace researchers in 2014.

> Then once by and angels to be seen,
> In roaring he shall rise and on the surface die.
> (*The Kraken* by Alfred Tennyson, 1830)

The giant octopus Kraken is classed both as mythological and legendary. Nonetheless, there is no apparent reason why, if the northern hemisphere is so bountiful, and can produce such big fish, that either now, or when other large creatures lived on earth, that huge marine creatures such as Kraken might not also have lived there. Other huge creatures still do.

Stranding or fraud?

Not to be confused with being shipwrecked – that is, a ship that is wrecked and totally lost – the stranding of a vessel can be quite a different event. Often mistakenly reported as wrecked, a ship that is accidentally or deliberately grounded on a sandbar or shoreline is normally only in the early stages of a marine accident, which can go either way. Many such occurrences were mistakenly reported as shipwrecks, but after a high tide, or having been subsequently lightened, the vessels sometimes got off and were saved. However some, badly bilged, just filled up and sank soon afterwards. If Noah was around today, he would tell you that the Ark was not wrecked, it just stranded when the waters receded.

How often ships were lost as a direct result of fraudulent action by their masters, crew and accomplices, by its nature a secretive event, is difficult to estimate. The consequences of the evolution from sail to steam, already outlined, impacted considerably on this phenomenon. The numbers of such acts began to increase during the middle of the nineteenth century, and some qualified concern was expressed in 1858 in vol. 42 of *Merchant's Magazine*, when they reflected on the shipwreck returns released by the Board of Trade that year, and stated:

It is not long ago that the master of a ship was tried and convicted in the Old Bailey for scuttling his own vessel off the Downs. Who can tell how many more vessels have been wilfully destroyed, in addition to those that have been lost through gross and culpable neglect? For it must be remembered that, in consequence of the almost universal custom of insurance, the shipowner has often no pecuniary interest in the safety of his vessel, and may even benefit from her loss. It cannot be wondered at, therefore, if here and there an unprincipled man should lend himself to the commission of a fraud for his own advantage.

Loss caused by wreckers

Falling into the same category as 'by man', as in ships lost as a result of a deliberate intention (but not a naval engagement), 'wrecking' became another historically contentious practice. The term is generally understood to have meant the deliberate act of presenting a false light or signal to a ship that is offshore and either in distress or seeking an entrance to a nearby harbour. The ruse was intended to confuse the ship's crew as to their relative safety, or to indicate a false course for safe passage, in order that the ship might become wrecked. The act, possibly only a perception in many cases, is raised consistently in accounts of shipwreck and smuggling, and some examples are contained in this book. These factual accounts may help to throw some light on whether such a practice existed at all, or, indeed, if it might only have occurred on some infrequent occasions.

If one can imagine the captain of a ship on a dark night in the eighteenth or early nineteenth century, struggling to remain distant from a lee shore, lest he be blown helplessly onto the coast, he is otherwise making all possible progress towards his destination. Associated with stormy weather, as the stories are often inclined to be, the sudden appearance of a light on a cliff-top is of no significance or help to him unless he can identify it. The presumption that a captain would order his ship to be steered for, or on a course relative to, an unknown light in these circumstances is not credible.

There were precious few lights maintained by municipal authorities at this time, and unless a captain believed he was near such a light, he would not use an otherwise strange and small illumination to navigate by.

There is, however, another possibility. When a ship found itself unable to claw off a lee shore, being driven closer to eternity, is it probable that those witnessing the drama from shore would recognise the ship's dilemma and attempt to guide it into a cove or onto a sandy part of the coast as a possible means of escape? How many times did the captain of a ship have to make this last throw of the dice and run his ship ashore in a place indicated by lights held by land people, amid the boiling surf on the shore?

The use of a light by the landsmen to signal a smuggling ship lying off, which was meant to indicate they were ready to receive its contraband, is quite a different matter. Although mobile phones have almost eliminated the practice, this type of signalling is still in use today.

Whether these stories were fact or just folklore, a similar ruse was constructed during the First World War when the Admiralty moved the position of prominent light buoys and lightships in order to confuse enemy submarines. German submarine commanders used these lights to navigate by, and by calculating bearings to them were able to lay their mines in the most strategic positions.

Causing the submarine to come to grief on a nearby sandbar, or laying its mines in a useless position, was the aim of the ruse. It would seem that the ruse had limited success, if any.

It is undoubtedly true that the local inhabitants of many countries felt they had some kind of right to wreck. Falling on a wreck and carrying off its valuables was common practice, but its acceptance was tolerated less the closer you got to large towns and cities, where there was some semblance of law. The more valuable the ship and its cargo, the more the law sought to stamp out the practice. When the United States of America was established, under Article IX of the Treaty of Amity and Commerce they sought the following agreement with the King of Prussia in 1786: 'The ancient and barbarous right to wrecks of the sea shall be entirely abolished, with respect to the subjects or citizens of the two contracting parties.'

My own belief is that the word wrecker fell into confused use, and often deliberately so, in order to describe the practice of coastal inhabitants, who descended with lights on to the scene of a helpless ship – but one that had already become wrecked onshore through no fault of theirs. As you might imagine, smugglers and those who salvaged goods from ships that came to grief on their coast were sometimes the same people, as were those who rescued survivors from the surf. In many instances, these were all tarred with the same brush, and lumped together under the law-breaking description of 'wrecker', purely for the convenience of reprisal by the authorities.

Salvaging shipwrecks

The men who get a living by trying to raise wrecks are farseeing, sparing of words, patient where patience is demanded, quick as a rapier thrust where quickness is essential, capable of toiling until they drop if it be necessary. They ponder over every possible contingency, but the weather is something beyond their control. They pray for fine weather, and fight against foul weather to the best of their ability; but when the wind takes charge, man and his endeavours are as nothing. (*The Wonders of Salvage*, David Masters)

It seemed the most natural thing in the world when, after learning to swim, I then began to venture under the water. Little games were made up to test one's ability for breath-holding, and then the recovery of items from the bottom of the pool. Coins would be thrown in to see who would be first to recover them, and then thrown increasingly further away.

Sometimes considered a romantic and a financially rewarding practice, the saving or raising of sunken ships, the act of recovering valuable cargo or shipboard materials, is as old as ships themselves. The recovery of food, medicinal remedies, and lost valuables from the water stretches back considerably further. Trying to see what is under the water, as fascinating and compelling as it is today, is probably as old as man.

There is increasing evidence that the ancient Greeks and Macedonians were capable of creating machines that would allow them to stay under the water for varying lengths of time. But it is still not satisfactorily explained why such a curiosity should provide so much romantic fascination, and why so many cannot resist entering an otherwise dangerous environment.

It was not until the seventeenth century that losses of precious metals and valuable merchandise by shipwreck, of one kind or another, reached intolerable proportions. Men soon began to realise that there were growing opportunities to become wealthy from salvage. The more adventurous realised that in order to have any chance of retrieving these treasures from the deep they would need to remain underwater for longer than just a breath-hold.

Slow at times, the next few centuries witnessed the development of diving apparatus. With a vessel placed over one's head, a man could descend to the seabed and breath there for a short time. This moved on to even larger vessels, and then to the diving bell. The earliest diving bells may have been fashioned from potting clay or Roman cement, but are commonly recorded as being coopered with timber. The bugbear was the limit to the breathing time provided by the volume of air in the bell. In order to overcome this, it was necessary to lower additional barrels of air, and to decant their contents into the bell by way of leather tubing.

In search of science and fortune, philosophers progressed matters and began the pumping of air into a diving bell, either from above or from within the bell itself. This further developed into pumping air into a diving helmet and suit. The suit then developed into massive indestructible proportions, which allowed the diver to reach tremendous depths – though he remained tethered to a service vessel on the surface.

Compressing a large volume of air into a portable diving cylinder, coupled with the invention of a method that would regulate the delivery of that air, revolutionised the science and allowed the diver to dive and swim freely, restricted only by the laws of gas and physiology.

Spurred on by the loss of so many ships during both World Wars, and the ingenuity of the salvors who continue to search for their valuable cargoes, the advances in technology continues to play a parallel and pivotal role in searches to ever-increasing depths.

Countless books and articles have been written about salvage operations following the First and Second World Wars, and the hunt for millions of tons of valuable metals, precious and industrial, that have been lost to the bottom of the sea during conflict. This attracted some of the most unlikely candidates to the profession of marine salvage, and men like Ernest Cox became leaders in the field. He was a clever engineer, but it was more through his sheer tenacity and determination that he succeeded at Scapa Flow.

A man who had never raised a ship in his life, a scrap merchant, Cox, performed one of the biggest operations in the history of salvage. His is an epic tale of salvage work on the remains of Germany's High Seas Fleet, which surrendered at Scapa Flow at the end of the First World War.

In a final act of defiance, depriving the Allies of a convenient opportunity to recommission the powerful German ships into their own navies, German officers scuttled their fleet of huge warships in the British naval base at Scapa Flow, Scotland. The scrapper, Mr Cox, purchased twenty-eight of the wrecks from the British Admiralty and salvaged the lot. A few were left for divers, who still enjoy diving on the historic remains of a once powerful battle fleet.

On an almost industrial basis, the Frenchman Alain Terme and the Italian company Sorima, followed by Risdon Beazley, all made significant amounts of money salvaging war wrecks around the world.

The previous examples may appear to have been motivated exclusively by financial gain, but just like many adventurers and explorers spurred on by the wondrous possibilities presented by Jules Verne, they were there by choice. Already relatively well off, they too were seduced by maritime adventure. As David Masters put it in *When Ships Go Down*, it was well-known that '... the salvage game is indeed a gamble. For every shilling won, a pound is lost.'

Scouring the oceans for lost ships and cargos continues to keep pace with the development of its technologies. New craft – underwater submersible vehicles – which have obviated the need for complicated diving and recompression procedures can now reach almost any depth, and recover tiny artefacts and the largest valuables. The exploration and recovery of shipwrecks, wartime and ancient, continues to attract archaeologists, those interested in an easy buck and other adventurers. It has however, become a different game.

The more recent advances in underwater imaging and seabed scanning, and in the use of remotely operated underwater vehicles, have meant that is almost unnecessary for divers to leave the comfort of a screen monitor to visit or work on shipwrecks. These new technologies allow salvors to continue their adventures to ever-increasing depths, enabling them to recover tons of silver and gold, and to explore areas of the deep where no man has gone before.

As the consumer's appetite for accounts of historic salvage and archaeology increases, and the lure of recovering large amounts of wealth from shipwrecks becomes less risky and easier, one can't help wondering if the legislation in these areas will, at some point, completely exclude the involvement of amateurs? After all, it is a finite and valuable resource, and we know from experience what becomes of those.

Maritime salvage remains big business today, but it can be risky, both physically and commercially. Tales of recovering sunken treasure remain among some of the most fascinating stories of the sea for both children and adults. Why do these tales of treasure-seeking from shipwrecks, and not the stories of the desperate efforts of miners to retrieve it in some of the remotest regions of the earth, have such unequal fascination for readers? Maybe it's just the way you tell 'em.

Where in the story of shipwreck are we now?

Extraordinary feats of salvage are not confined to monetary gains alone. Following on from earlier discoveries and recoveries of ancient ships and cargoes in the Mediterranean, great feats of archaeological salvage have continued. The Tudor warship *Mary Rose*, the seventeenth-century Swedish warship *Vasa*, and the Viking boats at Roskilde remain fine examples of what can be done by marine archaeologists, and of the technological advances that can flow from such projects.

Notwithstanding the commercial gain from tourism, lessons learned from these huge projects with costs that often become open-ended have proved invaluable.

The recovery of two galleys, enormous even by Roman standards, on Lake Nemi, Lazio, Italy, is another fine example of archaeological salvage, except in this case the water element was removed! Built for the first-century emperor Caligula, they lay at the bottom of the lake until the first attempts at salvage began in 1827. After some early diving on the wrecks, they finally broke the surface when the drastic but successful measure of draining the lake was completed in 1932. Destroyed by the fleeing German army during the Second World War, they were reconstructed and are permanently housed on site.

Today, the appetite for raising wooden ships from their marine environment has been dampened considerably. Pressure on government finances increasingly weighs against any attempt at justifying such expensive projects, and studies in situ have now become more the norm.

Exceptions have been made in the past, and hopefully will be made again, where an input from the private sector can be facilitated and even welcomed. Sought by some is a balance between what is desirable, from an owner or investor's point of view, and the preservation or improvement of archaeological standards, along with some return for the state.

Hopefully, new avenues that will prove beneficial to all concerned will emerge, and will help to promote such operations. The squabble between the Irish government and the owners over the First World War liner *Lusitania*, and the sometimes controversial but ongoing operations of the company Odyssey Marine are interesting and useful examples one might learn from. Countries like the USA and the UK would appear to have reached a resolution that provides a gain for most concerned, and where valuable maritime projects continue to flourish.

Shipwrecks will continue to occur but less frequently. The number of wrecks in space will grow, and will eventually replace an old fascination with a new one.

As I write, it has been reported that artefacts and cannon from Armada shipwrecks have been recovered by members of the Underwater Archaeological Unit of the Department of Arts, Heritage and the Gaeltacht at Streedagh Strand, County Sligo. Their recovery

was prompted by the discovery of the remains of the wrecks, exposed
during winter storms. The action is to be congratulated.

Victims of shipwreck

> The wreck, the shores, the dying and the drown'd!
> The generous natives, moved with social pain,
> The feeble strangers in the arms sustain;
> With pitying signs their hapless lot deplore,
> And lead them trembling from the fatal shore.
> (*The Shipwreck* by William Falconer, 1762)

Stories of shipwreck victims are many. Volumes have been written
on the violent event, from *Robinson Crusoe* to the historic losses in
the North and South Poles and from war victims stranded on Pacific
atolls to the great story of the *Essex* (*Moby Dick*) and its aftermath
of forced cannibalism. Acts of cannibalism during the aftermath
of shipwreck and air crashes demonstrate the lurking trait for
self-survival buried deep in our psyche and remain of intense interest
to story tellers and readers.

Describing victims not of a shipwreck but a plane crash, the novel
Lord of The Flies is just one of a number of fine works on the subject.
It is a wonderful portrayal of how the characters of survivors can
alter, or seem to, when threatened or marooned from civilisation. The
so-called 'Miracle of the Andes', when flight 571 crashed in the Andes
mountain range in 1972 and the survivors lived for seventy-two days
before rescue by eating the flesh of victims, is another.

Not a category covered in this book, air wrecks, their causes and
the stories behind them, differ little from those of shipwrecks, with
the exception of age. In time, no doubt, the difference of a couple of
hundred years, here or there, will mean little, and they will have a
genre all of their own, as many already do.

Car wreck and train wreck, seemingly modern American terms,
really don't fall into the same wreck genre, and are ignored here.

Interestingly, and seldom considered in the same way, another
late entry to the wreck category is the loss of spaceships and their
crews. These, by and large, do not seem to have been impacted by
either weather or war (yet), but have occurred for some of the same

reasons outlined for shipwrecks. There are, however, other causes lurking in space – growing amounts of space debris and meteorite showers.

Man alone is seemingly responsible for any such tragedies to date, and they are an interesting subject for film-makers. They would seem to have a similar storytelling future to that of shipwrecks.

Like many other regrettable aspects of our society today, tales of shipwreck have at times been glamorised in order to sell. Nevertheless, these are extreme incidences of drama – a fight for survival. We are far removed now from the life and times of those who, simply through a need to survive, crossed oceans in relatively small commercial timber sailing vessels on journeys fraught with uncertainty and danger to life. The voyages of these ships, only slightly bigger than timber trawlers of the 1960s, across the Atlantic during the seventeenth, eighteenth and nineteenth centuries is a remarkable testimony to the skill and ability of those seafarers, and to how when 'needs must' one can overcome adversity.

Not so far removed, but equally difficult to fully comprehend, are the last moments of the thousands of sailors who were killed in warships when the mass of metal around them buckled from explosive heat, flooded, and plummeted their ship to the bottom. The men who sailed the North Atlantic convoys during the Second World War may have had their spirits buoyed by adventure and camaraderie, but they knew the terrible risks they were taking only too well.

Having studied many aspects of shipwreck from the eighteenth to the twentieth century, and observed the casualty rates dwindle through the introduction of codes of conduct and the technical advances of man's ingenuity, it is a shocking realisation that shipwreck has once again become synonymous with a re-escalation in the loss of life at sea.

The most regrettable aspect of this feature of shipwreck, loss of life, has re-emerged with a vengeance in the most unlikely circumstances and is killing thousands. Its victims are those in flight from conflict, disease and hunger in a variety of countries. Just like before, these are places that show little sign of evolving into places where their citizens can remain in safety and are able to progress with their lives. The discovery of mass graves of fleeing Asian migrants is the latest revelation in this epidemic of forced migration.

They come from the innermost regions of the African continent and the war-torn Middle East to the Mediterranean coastline. Here, separated from Europe, with a riviera of wealth and sunbathing on one side and conflict and death on the other, escape is only the width of a channel away in places. Gathered by the ruthless smugglers, they are packed into vessels that are totally unsuitable before making the crossing to southern Europe in search of rest, peace and hope.

In October 2013, it is estimated that somewhere between 500 and 600 migrants boarded a 60-foot fishing vessel in Tunisia to make this crossing. The vessel broke down off the Italian island Lampedusa. A fire was set to attract a rescue, and the boat capsized. It was reported that 155 were rescued and that divers witnessed dozens of corpses wedged in its lower deck.

Since that shipwreck shocked the world, the numbers have grown beyond all comprehension and it now takes more and more death to shock.

The reader will have recognised the uncomfortable similarities between the flight of nineteenth-century emigrants and victims of shipwreck, and their horrible treatment at the hands of greedy men, and those of today. One is only left to remark that some things don't change.

Thousands continue to die in this way, at the hands of people-smugglers – another age old and despicable practice. Procrastination by politicians has compounded their plight, and plays into the hands of the people smugglers. Dressed up as globalisation, free markets and progress, slavery has been resurrected. They flee a sub-human existence in places where some species of animals are better protected in search of a life fit for humans. This aspiration and attempt at self-betterment has now become a crime.

A solution to their plight has become mired in regional wars, self-interest, and insatiable appetites to control new markets and chase increased profit, and a lasting solution may never be attained.

A man familiar with sea travel, shipwreck and adventure may have put his finger on the essence of the contradiction between man's often regrettable and sometimes heroic behaviour when he is faced with the violence of shipwreck, sudden or otherwise. Robert Louis Stevenson wrote in *Strange Case of Dr Jekyll and Mr Hyde*:

With every day, and from both sides of my intelligence, the moral and the intellectual, I thus drew steadily nearer to the truth, by whose practical discovery I have been doomed to such a dreadful shipwreck; that man is not truly one, but truly two.

The fact that the development of watercraft and ocean-going ships has occurred alongside the development of mankind is undeniable. One can easily cite the milestones in the development of maritime commerce, exploration, and even conquest as examples. As with spacecraft today, the ship at one time represented the future. Its possibilities attracted the most ingenious, the bravest and the most adventurous among our kind. Might we then take a moment to ask ourselves – what path may history have taken if some of these exceptional minds had not been lost by shipwreck?

Dreadful Shipwreck at Howth

The wreck of the paddle steamer *Queen Victoria*, 1853

Captain William Harrison Walker left Ireland in April 1854 after he had established and completed an enquiry on behalf of the naval department of the Board of Trade (BOT) into the loss of the emigrant ship *Tayleur*. Given that Walker had been to Ireland the previous year in order to investigate another serious incidence of shipwreck for the BOT, we might expect that, by the time he left a second time, he would have been sick to the gills of the harrowing tales of shipwreck and the mounting loss of life on the coast of Ireland. If he was, he never showed it, and continued his duties as a senior inspector for the Board of Trade around the coast of England and Ireland as diligently as ever.

Unlike many captains of industry today, Captain Walker joined the Honourable East India Company (HEIC) when he was a boy and rose through the ranks to serve as an officer until the India Act was passed in 1839. Captain Walker became part owner in a number of East India ships, which he also commanded. He was a thoroughly well-respected and experienced mariner.

Taking a deep interest in the sciences of the marine, he proved a rewarding choice for the BOT when the Mercantile Marine Act was made law in 1850, leading to his hiring as inspector of ships and harbours.

Captain Walker was knighted for his services to the marine in 1871, and died at the age of sevety-two the following year.

After another winter tragedy on the Irish coast, Captain Walker's mission to Dublin in 1853 established this earlier enquiry into the loss of the popular packet boat *Queen Victoria*. This well-known paddle steamer struck the rocks under the Bailey lighthouse at the entrance to Dublin Bay and, after getting off, sank during an attempt to run for shore. The tragedy occurred on the morning of 15 February 1853, with the loss of fifty-nine passengers and crew and the total loss of the ship, though the casualty reports that were compiled on nineteenth-century maritime tragedies often varied with those that appeared in newspapers, as they did in this instance.

The City of Dublin Steam Packet Company

The Irish cross-channel service was the pride of the company's operations, and the owner was dedicated to the continual improvement of the company. He graduated at the Bar, but his heart was in shipping. From Drumcondra Castle in the suburbs of the north side of Dublin city, Charles Wye Williams entered the world of shipping in 1816 when he formed his first company, The Steam Packet Company. It failed after a short time as a result of disagreement among its partners.

Convinced of the future for the new power of steam, Williams threw everything into a second company which was established in 1823. It would achieve considerable success over the next century before finally failing as result of the commercial impact of the First World War. Williams first named this company after himself, but soon thought better of it and settled on 'The City of Dublin Steam Packet Company'.

The company was incorporated in 1833, and just a few years later, in 1838, it boasted having seventy-nine vessels in operation – from cross-channel passenger steamers to commercial trade vessels of numerous and various types; on the sea, in the canals and lakes, and on the River Shannon.

Williams was a man invested in the improvement of ships and machinery. One of the earliest to adopt steam, and to build vessels with iron, he allied with Laird's of Birkenhead for a historic career of shipbuilding excellence. Williams eventually moved his family to Liverpool and his company's connections with that city flourished until its demise at the close of the First World War.

Not satisfied with just building ships for profit alone, both yard and owner collaborated to introduce the innovative and life-saving feature of watertight bulk heads. One of an identical quartet when completed by Laird's in 1896, the twin screw RMS *Leinster* boasted an extensive system of bulkheads, twelve of which were watertight. Alas, though impossible to have foreseen, they did not save the *Leinster* or the *Connaught* from the catastrophic effects of being struck by torpedoes during the First World War twenty years later. The German submarine *U-48* sank the *Connaught* in 1917, and *UB-123* sank the *Leinster* more than a year later. The two ships were sunk in an almost identical manner. They were both struck by two torpedoes, one striking the starboard side and another on the port side. The RMS *Leinster* was sunk outside Dublin Bay on 10 October 1918, and the RMS *Connaught* was sunk in the English Channel in 1917.

Although the *Leinster* was packed with troops at the time she was torpedoed, her primary function was as a regular mail boat on her daily cross-channel run. The *Connaught,* however, had been requisitioned and was trooping when she was sunk in March 1917.

By that time, a mainstay of the company's operations was the contract to carry the mails between Ireland and England. As the *Connaught* had already been requisitioned and sunk in the English Channel by another submarine, the remaining sister ships in the quartet could not satisfactorily fulfil the company's contractual obligations. It ceased operating in 1922 and dissolved in 1937, ending a century of outstanding service in the Irish Channel.

Paddle steamers had become the core of the City of Dublin's fleet, and among the ships advertised in service by CDSPC in 1838 were the *Royal William, Dutchess of Kent, Duke of Cambridge* and the *Queen Victoria*. Naming these early steam-paddlers, Williams demonstrated how he meant to keep pride well massaged on both sides of the channel by naming some of his ships after Irish place names, and others, such as the aforementioned, after members of the Royal Family. The company maintained this practice throughout its existence.

Among others, the *Royal William* was heralded as being the first passenger steamship to cross the Atlantic when it completed the voyage from Liverpool to New York in nineteen days in 1838.

The *Queen* sails

Three years after Captain Walker's appointment, the esteemed Irish engineer and railway magnate William Dargan was working flat-out erecting the Great Hall in Dublin's Merrion Square. The advanced design of iron and glass would house the largest international event ever seen in Ireland – the Great Industrial Exhibition. Queen Victoria came to visit the exhibition, which was considered a great cultural success. However, due to lower than expected door receipts, Mr Dargan lost one of his shirts.

Passengers intending to board one of the City of Dublin Steam Packet Company's (CDSPC) most reliable packet boats, the *Queen Victoria*, on Monday 14 February 1853 might have been fortunate enough to have caught the earlier pantomime performance at the Royal in Liverpool. The more discerning may have preferred one of the series of French plays that were also running in Liverpool, or a concert with compositions by Henry Russell ('Life on the Ocean Wave') in the concert hall on Lord Nelson Street.

The concert hall also ran a series of 'Grand Prize Nights', during which your admission ticket was entered in a draw. If drawn on the night, the prize would entitle you to a free passage to Australia. The prize was a handsome one, valued at 30 guineas and transferable. The cheapest seats in the theatre were a 'bob' – one shilling.

Upon landing at the Custom House Quay on the opposite side of the channel, in Dublin, the passengers or the crew of the *Queen Victoria* might alternatively treat themselves to a night of Shakespeare. *As You Like It*, playing at the Royal, boasted entrance prices suiting deep pockets or the half-skint alike; from a half a crown in the dress circle to three pence in the upper gallery.

On Monday afternoon, boarding of the *Queen Victoria* at the Clarence Dock in Liverpool was completed at approximately 3.15 p.m. Having only five cabins, accommodating twelve passengers on the day, most of the remaining passengers – numbering 120 – and possibly some others travelled on the deck of the ship. It was left to each individual to secure any of the spaces that could provide a modicum of shelter or comfort from the elements.

Out of the biting wind and rain, situated aft of the centre-house and the funnel and directly over the boilers, was a favourite. Or if you could get a steward or a member of the crew to look out for you, you might be able to squeeze into one of the empty horse boxes situated below deck. Conditions during the 12-hour voyage bore no resemblance to a similar crossing today, and could prove quite harsh for some.

Considered the norm at the time, accommodation for animals on ships was often better than that provided for humans. Belonging to men of a high station, livestock represented capital and profit, and its preservation was considered considerably more important.

The managing director of the CDSPC, William Watson, later alluded to this social contrast when questioned during a parliamentary enquiry:

Q. If you have both cattle and passengers you give the cattle the preference?
A. We cannot have them both in the same places.
Q. But the cattle would be sheltered, and the deck passengers would not be sheltered?
A. Yes.

As a member of the community of financial wizards once pointed out, 'money will almost naturally migrate to where it is best looked after'.

Among the Steerage passengers huddled around the deck that afternoon was James McManus, as well as his wife with their three children. Not attracted by the lure of a winning ticket to Australia, James had not treated his family to a show at the concert hall, for it was to America he was wanting to travel. Unfortunately, as it turned out, he was unable to afford the passage for all of his family to America. Passage in a ship's cabin bound for America at the time was advertised by the Liverpool & Philadelphia Steamship Co. at 20 guineas, with some restricted number of places available for 6 guineas each.

Passage for dogs was advertised at £3. As guineas were associated with gentlemen and their property, it is obvious that dogs, associated with the lower order – trades people and the like – would have their passage valued in pounds. One wonders how the shipping agent might have billed the wealthy owners for their lap dogs?

Passage on a sailing ship was cheaper, but the actual costs were not apparent in the *Liverpool Mercury* that week. The McManus family had saved their meagre amounts of spare cash and had left Ireland in pursuit of a new life. Thousands were in similar straits, fleeing hunger and depredation at the time in search of a better life.

Alas, the family's accumulated wealth was insufficient, and they were now returning to a country and a life they had fled.

Guided out through the docks by Mersey pilots, the *Queen Victoria* left Merseyside and headed out into Liverpool Bay. It was cold. The wind, described as moderate, felt sharp from the north-east, but it was not strong. It was also described as 'North-east and favourable', 'remarkably fine', and 'smart'.

The captain went below a few hours later and left the running of the ship to the first mate, Thomas Davis. A man of good standing and long service, he had served as first mate on the *Queen Victoria* for the previous thirteen years. Captain Church's last instructions to Davis were to wake him at 'four bells' (two o'clock in the morning) or if the weather deteriorated.

The significance of this hour lay in the fact that the steamer was expected to arrive off Dublin about then, and Captain Church was expected to come on deck to make the final approach to Dublin Port.

One wonders if, while preparing to retire below that night, the captain might have given any thought to his son, who was serving as third mate aboard another company ship, the *Iron Duke*. She had also been berthed in Liverpool, and was expected to leave for Kingstown shortly after his own departure.

The company had suffered some earlier loss of ships, and the *Queen Victoria*, built in 1837, was no spring chicken. She was nevertheless maintained to a high standard and had provided excellent service on the Dublin to Liverpool route.

She was built in Belfast, by Messrs Charles Connell & Sons, a renowned builder of timber ships. Interestingly, it is declared almost everywhere that Charles Connell turned out the first passenger steamer in Ireland in 1838, the *Aurora*. But the *Belfast Newsletter* claims he launched the steamer *Queen Victoria* the previous year before proceeding to Killileagh (Killyleagh) Quay for final fitting out! And it was heralded by the press at the time as being the third steamer built in Ireland!

The appearance of the *Aurora* coming off the slip in the accompanying images was symptomatic of the growing commercial demands being made on shipbuilding at the time. Bulk and carrying capacity were essential, but the results were often not pretty.

The engineer McNeill, commenting in the *Athenaeum* after his frightening attempt at passage on the *Aurora* in 1839, observed that the ship was 'crank' and 'built like a sea chest or a log', and that a 'shallow log-like piece of avaricious ugliness is the worst of all forms for a sea going vessel'.

These demands for bulk space meant that the *Queen Victoria* wasn't designed to carry a lot of cabin passengers, having only five cabins, but did carry lots of deck passengers, cargo, and animals. She was initially ordered for the Down to Liverpool route, but was transferred onto the Kingstown and Dublin to Liverpool routes for competitive business reasons.

After leaving the Mersey, the first 10 hours of the *Queen Victoria*'s passage through the day and into the night were uneventful. There was really nothing of any significance to report until around one o'clock in the morning when Davis began to worry over the deteriorating weather.

A constant feature of the CDSPC's business life, lasting a century, was the continuous and often underhanded rivalry of its competitors. Competition for the lucrative contract to deliver the Royal Mail, cross-channel freight and passenger traffic was unbridled and aggressive. The CDSPC had successfully competed and survived on its ability to continually adapt and maintain reliable regularity.

So, when Davis first saw the snow begin to flutter over the paddle boxes, at about 12.30 p.m., he might be forgiven for thinking better of disturbing Captain Church.

The snow continued to thicken, but the lights at the Kish Bank and the Bailey lighthouse had remained visible. Davis let another 20 minutes pass before the lid on his anxiety popped. When he next looked at his watch, the lights, though still visible, were being obscured at times. Fear of rebuke behind him, he went below to warn Captain Church of the worsening weather.

Church, a man with decades of experience, was not in the least flustered. Keeping the *Queen Victoria* on time was paramount, and he told Davis to go back up top, keep a sharp look out, and, as the lights were still in view, not to reduce the speed of the ship. This was a good lick of 9 knots at the time. Neither did he give any instructions to commence 'swinging the lead' – performing soundings with a lead weight and line in order to detect any change in the seabed and its depth. Although such a precaution was considered standard practice in conditions of poor visibility, it was not always carried out. It was not carried out on this occasion, and it was a criticism made later by Captain Walker in the findings of his enquiry, which were submitted to the BOT.

It was not mentioned, and it is arguable, that even if soundings had been taken, little – if any – change in depth would have been detected until it became too late. The depths in the area of the Bailey, and the entrance to Dublin Bay, do not vary significantly until very close to the shore. Unless one is very familiar with all the nuances of the scours and sand drifts in Dublin Bay, significant change in depth might not become discernible or could even lead to confusion. Indeed, the place where the *Queen Victoria* finally settled, with its bow-sprit touching the shore, is a 'hole'. The hole is a 62-foot-deep, isolated and anomalous depression in the seabed, with surrounding depths being considerably less.

Continuous soundings might detect a slight rise in the general depth, and may give cause to reduce the speed of a vessel. Unless, however, the visibility had been greater than the 'less than a boat's length' that morning, the best that may have been hoped for was to lessen the impact. Which may of course have been enough to avoid the awful calamity that faced the passengers and crew.

Having left the captain again, Davis spent another hour straining to see the way ahead and trying to maintain a bearing on the lights that were now beginning to disappear altogether. The captain hadn't been on deck for nearly 6 hours, and Davis suspected that he might not have fully comprehended the true danger that was presented by the suddenness of the deteriorating weather. He returned below just before two o'clock, and again reported his misgivings to the captain. Once again the captain dismissed the mate's concern and told him to return topside and keep a sharp lookout for other vessels.

Davis returned on deck and sounded four bells before shouting to the crew to keep a sharp look out before heading straight to the bow of the ship in order to see just a little further. He was there no time when the veil of 'darkness you could almost see' parted and revealed a sheer wall of rock directly ahead.

Wrecked in sight of Dublin

The light in the Bailey lighthouse, later described as 'poor', had become obscured by the falling snow at the vital moment of impact and reported to have been blinding. The ship ran at full speed onto the rocks under high cliffs about 500 yards north of the Bailey lighthouse. The jagged rocks, on which the copper sheeting and the oak planking burst open, were aptly called, 'the Broken Hatchets'.

The issue of the Bailey light and its poor quality was alluded to by Captain Walker in his report. It was testified that the light was observed a little before 1.00 a.m. The loss of the ship occurred at approximately 2.30 a.m. If the *Queen Victoria* had been travelling at the 9 knots stated, this would have meant that the Bailey light was seen from more than 13 miles away. This would seem to indicate that the light was bright at the earlier time.

The sudden crash and lurch of the paddle steamer onto the rocks was so deafening that even the light-keepers in the nearby Bailey said they heard it. The violence of the sudden stop woke any of those on the *Queen Victoria* who weren't already busy preparing for their arrival at Dublin.

Captain Church had sailed the route hundreds of times. He knew it like the back of his hand and could sail it with his eyes closed. It was probably the case that good old Absalom was caught napping. After twenty-eight years of service he let his guard down, leaving command of the ship entirely to the first mate for an extended period during conditions when he should have been up top, sharing the responsibility of command in confusing circumstances. The wind was never strong or stormy, so the ship had not been unduly buffeted, and Absalom Church probably just assumed that a little snow could do no harm.

At what precise moment he arrived at Davis' side was not made clear. The captain shouted the order to back the ship off the rocks, but Davis expressed some doubt, maintaining that they should inspect the damage first, which they did. Finding only a small amount of water in the forepeak, the captain relayed the order to the engine room to reverse. The thrashing paddles began to scrape the ship off the rocks, but, before she did, some of the passengers and crew – eight in all – thought less of the captain and ship's chances and jumped ship on to the Hatchets. Jumping ship might have seemed cowardly, but no one remarked on it. As it happened, their decision may well have proved fortuitous.

At first the leak seemed tolerable, but no sooner had the captain ordered her to make for port than the water began to pour in through the badly damaged hull.

Having given terrifying shapes to the swirling wind, the thick snow began to part and revealed the sheer cliffs of Howth towering in front of the ship. Confused passengers and crew began to scramble about on the listing deck, seeking reassurance. Only barely able to catch an intermittent glimpse of the Bailey light, the captain decided to make a run for the inner part of the bay, on the Dublin city side of the lighthouse. There, at least, he knew there were shallow bays into which he could run the ship.

Luck might still have played a role when the wind unexpectedly began to vary to the north-west, giving some shelter and respite to a ship in desperate peril under the head. The *Queen Victoria* was now making way with a tide that had just turned and by then had begun to flow southward. Despite the clearing weather, it became more apparent that the ship was in a sinking state. The *Queen Victoria* ended her final run just south of the most prominent point of the jagged outcrop of the Bailey.

As far as tides and the movement of water in Dublin Bay are concerned, the old paddler was at first fortunate to find herself in such an unusual place. There is a very predictable anomaly in the effects of the tide which occurs in this exact position, and did so at the very moment the *Queen Victoria* began to sink under the Bailey. The sea, though ebbing elsewhere, had become slack here. It was, apart from any effect wind might have had on the surface water, not moving in any direction. With the bow to the north of the ship only 50 yards from the shore and the stern to the south, she began to fill rapidly.

This tidal respite can be quite short, but can at times last an hour or a little more. It was already underway for a half hour. The short time when slack water remained was probably instrumental in the successful launch of the lifeboat on the port side of the ship, saving a number of passengers and crew.

After the slack water period ended, and the tide began to flow again, launching any boat would have been almost impossible, especially on the port side of the vessel. With the tide in such a state, the current would have been slamming into the hull from the west, creating a terrible turbulence in the water.

More exposed to the ebbing flow of the tide, which will normally continue unabated only yards east of the promontory, an earlier attempt to launch a lifeboat on the starboard side had failed after it was lowered into the water and swamped, drowning its occupants.

The big hull gave a final lurch to her starboard and settled on the seabed below the swirling sea, where it remained upright. The only visible sign of the old packet boat was the top of her funnel, which protruded above the surface about 100 yards from the rocks.

The tide soon began its run to the east again, flowing past the base of the lighthouse and meeting the main southerly flow, which creates a swirl under the lighthouse. By the end of the day, and a couple of tides later, the mast, rigging and funnel had been swept down, and the water swallowed up any of the remaining victims. The *Queen Victoria* was gone.

Aftermath

Similar descriptions to those from the *Queen Victoria*'s sinking can be found in many other stories of shipwreck from the period – chaos. There were four lifeboats on the *Queen Victoria*, but these were stowed in their davits and inboard. In this position, they were useless unless the difficult operation to launch them could be accomplished successfully. Two managed to get away. The starboard side boat collapsed and was swamped, killing everyone aboard.

The second, on the larboard side, got into the water successfully but began to fill immediately. The bung for the plug hole was missing. Left unplugged, the hole was normally vacant in order to prevent the boats from filling with rainwater. Commended later by Captain Walker, a travelling sailor, Patrick Darcy, who stemmed the flow by keeping his finger in the hole, and a young passenger named William Kegg, a sailor between ships, were instrumental in getting this boat safely away with survivors.

During circumstances where life and limb is threatened, resulting actions are sometimes described as cowardice. Instead, these are the unfortunate loss of humanity to the overwhelming forces of self-survival and terror. On occasions, often for unexplainable reasons, terror is defeated and great acts of bravery occur.

On the one hand, the sinking of the *Queen Victoria* produced some regrettable occurrences, but on the other it brought to the fore that part of man's spirit where cool headedness and good judgement can overcome the natural reaction to save oneself alone, which is always to be admired and applauded.

Charles Ralph, a ship owner from Wicklow, and two young sailors, William Kegg and Patrick Darcy, managed the only boat that launched successfully. Patrick Darcy, twenty-three at the time, was from Sir John Rogerson's Quay in Dublin and went to sea at fifteen years of age. He had already assisted in launching a starboard boat before going to help on the port side. When Ralph and Kegg got into the boat, they found it to be leaky. Darcy got in last and searched around for the plug, which was normally attached in the area of the bung hole. Ralph began to bale the water with his hat, while Darcy put his finger in the hole. They rowed to the nearby shore and offloaded fourteen survivors. Unlike the actions of some of the crew and passengers earlier, they didn't jump off to save themselves, instead returning to the wreck to save others.

Before they reached the wreck, another paddler, the *Roscommon*, hove into view and began to lower her own boats. Ralph, Kegg and Darcy rowed to these instead in order to secure a cork for the plug hole, a successful endeavour, and then continued to make their way back to the wreck. They saved five more from the rigging before making their way back to the *Roscommon*. By that time the *Roscommon* boats, one which was, incredibly, forced to return to the ship to replace a missing plug from their own lifeboat, had begun to recover corpses and any survivors in the water, or still clinging to rigging.

The *Roscommon* was another ship owned by the CDSPC, but on charter to the Chester & Holyhead Railway Co. at the time. She had been alerted to the emergency after Davis had ignited some red flares earlier, warning anyone in sight of the ship's impending peril.

The scenes described screaming children parted from their mothers in heart-wrenching circumstances, husbands separated from wives, improper conduct of passengers and even crew – all similar to what one might read in nineteenth-century accounts of shipwreck.

'Every man for himself', a reaction to the deck skewing away beneath your feet, is an attitude we associate with the less disciplined in such circumstances. However, it was not peculiar to the nineteenth century and has unfortunately been found to be the case right up to the present day.

One of those saved by Ralph, Kegg and Darcy during their second rescue was the young naval cadet Robert Jennet, who was returning to his home at Nannywater, Laytown, County Meath. They plucked the fortunate young sailor from the water after he had been thrown from the rigging, when the force of the water inside the *Queen Victoria* erupted through her decks as she plummeted to the bottom.

Along with Kegg and Darcy, Ralph was also commended by the coroner, Davis, and Captain Walker of the BOT.

When the strength of the water, now flowing eastward over the wreck, conjoined with the general tide that was flowing south, the current was between 3 and 4 knots. With the temperature of the water being between 7 and 8 degrees at this time of the year, it was all over. Those who were going to be saved had already been rescued and the remainder had either perished in the sunken steamer or been swept away.

Later that day, the *Iron Duke* arrived at Kingstown and was immediately despatched to the scene of the wreck. The third mate on the *Iron Duke* was the son of Captain Church, who knew full well by then that the wreck at the Bailey lighthouse was his father's ship. His state of mind cannot have been in any doubt.

The casualty reports varied. Captain Walker returned that there were 112 people on board the *Queen Victoria*, passengers and crew, and that 59 were lost. Some reports had the death toll as high as 100.

As I have referred to them earlier in particular, the reader might well wonder what ultimately became of the unhappy emigrant McManus family. Sadly, they lost their two older children first. This was followed by a tremendous struggle, during which Mr McManus's wife and their youngest child were eventually torn from his grasp and never seen again.

Mr Ralph was able to save the 400 sovereigns he had on his person, and I wondered if Mr McManus was able to accomplish anything similar, and whether or not he eventually reached America.

The first mate, Thomas Davis, survived, but Captain Church was separated from him during the tragedy. He was last seen on the deck helping with the boats and trying desperately to calm the passengers. There was also some suggestion that he returned below as no one seemed to be aware of his whereabouts after that.

The captain was never seen again – unless a subsequent disputed newspaper article, reporting that he was later seen in his cabin with his glasses still on, was actually true. The report was said to have emanated from the salvage diver who had been employed to go down to the wreck. Its accuracy was subsequently disputed by the man in question, a celebrated diver named William Campbell, in his own written response.

Captain Church left two daughters, one son, and his wife, who was in Dublin and expecting their fourth child.

The enquiry

With the benefit of studying shipping losses for many years, one might well expect to have an increased awareness of the events which lead up to such tragedies, and what might be the reaction of crews and passengers during such terrible events. Notwithstanding the availability of so much data and accounts of shipwreck, I remain completely at a loss in any attempt to understand what goes through the minds of victims on such occasions. Someone like a child, a mother, or a farm labourer, maybe someone who has never even seen the sea – what flashes through their consciousness in the darkness as a ship breaks apart beneath their feet and they are faced with the prospect of been plunged helplessly into a raging sea?

If one examines the details of enquiries that have been carried out by the Board of Trade into shipping disasters, it will quickly be noticed that, despite many of the vessels and incidents being of a dissimilar nature, the witnesses are addressed with consistently similar questions, such as 'was the lead sounded?'

The process is derived from the Admiralty procedures in similar matters, an organisation with plentiful experience of the sea, men, ships and bureaucracy. So it is the agent of the BOT, often ex-Admiralty, who is seeking to establish a full account of events and to winkle out some of the relevant details that preceded the incident. Considering the variety of firmly held opinions that can be offered on such occasions, such as weather conditions consistent with those mentioned earlier, it was important to separate testimony given by those of an impressionable disposition from that of experts.

The questions posed by any subsequent enquiry into the loss of a ship will be concerned to establish if the ship was well found in all respects, whether the crew were competent and sober and what the state of the weather was at the time. The questions will have a huge range concerning the cargo, compasses, condition and course of the ship, observations made and the whereabouts and state of the crew at the time, among other things. Despite the wide range of answers tendered by the crew, officials, passengers, professionals and witnesses to the event, they can nevertheless be categorised into the three elements: man, ship, and weather.

In the case of the loss of the paddle steamer *Queen Victoria*, it is clear why the ship sank – she was fatally holed when she ran into the rocks at full speed. But who, or what, contributed to the collision with the rocks? Were there one or more indisputable factors or actions that caused the collision?

The BOT investigator, Captain Walker, arrived in Dublin on 20 February – within a week of the tragedy. An inquest on some of the deceased began at Kingstown the following day and he sat in on it as a welcome and interested observer. The inquest concluded on 23 February, and Walker promptly began his own enquiry on behalf of the Board of Trade the following day in Custom House, Dublin.

After interviewing the first mate, Davis, and some of the other survivors, an astute Captain Walker was able to separate impressions from fact, and produced the following findings:

To conclude, the result of my investigation is as follows:
1st. The *Victoria* was lost through the negligence of the master in not sounding, stopping the engines or taking proper precautions when the snow-shower came on.
2nd. The conduct of the mate was to blame. He supposed the master was below, and ought to have known that the danger was imminent, and should have stopped the speed of the vessel.
3rd. The steamer was well found in all respects, with the exception that the boats were not so placed as to be ready for immediate use.
4th. Had there been a fog-bell on the Bailey light, it is probable that the accident might have been prevented.
5th. That the lighthouse was not properly attended to.

The question of the fog-bell and the conditions of the lighthouse and its establishment are for your lordship's consideration. With regard to the boats, I deem it my duty to state my opinion, founded on the present and former cases of accident, and to suggest, that it would be very desirable, if in all cases the boats of steamers were so placed as to be immediately ready for use, and if the officers in charge were instructed to station portions of the crew to the boats and to hold them responsible for their use and efficiency when required.

The light-keepers were well on in years and, although the light was seen, it was said that its intensity was not what it should have been.

The boats were swung in, which was a common criticism. Considered impractical, the practice and the conflict with regulations continued for many years. Lifeboats are still swung in, but permanently so now as modern technical innovations have made it far easier to launch from that position. Reference to a bell was also interesting in that if one had already been purchased and installed at the lighthouse, as intended after an earlier incident, it may have prevented the tragedy. All reservations regarding the science of sound and detecting its origins during certain atmospheric conditions, and the proximity of geographical features, aside, one can only agree with Captain Walker's conclusion on this point.

As for the first mate Davis, it would seem he might have been given a raw deal. He twice warned the captain of the deteriorating weather. He warned the captain about the danger in reversing off the rocks. He helped save passengers and crew by igniting the flares and through his own gallantry. He didn't jump ship. In other words, he appears to have done his best. The first mate Davis did do his duty, but he failed to read the captain's mind and be more forceful when the captain did not respond to his pleas. Going against the will of a captain while at sea can have very serious repercussions.

'Sounding the lead', the perennial question regarding this must-do practice in all similar incidents, revealed that the lead was not employed. Captain Walker's procedural adherence to the question reminded me of the time when I was a driver for a government department. Following an accident in a vehicle, in which I was struck from behind, I was quietly advised to answer the totally irrelevant question on the company's standard accident report form 'Did you sound your horn?' in the affirmative! Despite my protestations that the particular question bore no relevance with the particulars of the incident and that I wished to answer with the truth, that I hadn't sounded the horn – or not answer at all – I was further advised that this would reflect the fact that I did not attempt any warning! Apparently, you always answer 'I sounded my horn'. Nobody is ever in a position to deny it after the event.

Captain Walker concluded that 'The ship was well found in all respects', and we are thus left with two of the three elements that caused the accident – the weather and man, i.e. the failure of his professional duties.

As to the tragedy, and the principal factor in the cause of the collision, the ship ran onto the rocks because those operating it couldn't see where they were going. The thick snow, which proved only fleeting, had reduced visibility to less than a ship's length. The mishandling of events before and after the collision compounded their predicament.

The neglect, or professional incompetence, was in this case unfortunate, and in better weather would not have caused the loss of the ship. Captain Church, and his crew for that matter, had become complacent. They had travelled back and forward on the route umpteen times. There was no constant position-taking or chart-plotting involved, there was little concern with weather and the lead, if it could be found, had probably been put to some other use.

The *Queen Victoria* was not a sailing vessel. It was a steamer, capable of crossing the channel in rough weather or calm. Put simply, you got the steam up, selected a heading and off you went. The ship could perform a predictable speed, and when land or lights were seen on the opposite coast, course and speed were adjusted for the final approach. They just got it wrong that night.

Salvage and divers on the *Queen Victoria*

The first person to discover the wreck of the *Queen Victoria* was the diver William Campbell. The celebrated diver was a professional helmet-diver but had trained in, and went down in, the older style diving bell. He descended to the wreck of the *Queen Victoria* two days after she sunk. The dive was reported to have been so terrifying that nothing could induce him to go down a second time.

The Commissioners of Public Works (Office of Public Works) employed a number of bell divers in their depots scattered around the country, but few marine divers. Whether or not Campbell was consistently employed directly by the Dublin Harbour Commissioners or the Commissioners for Public Works, or was hired privately by either at this time, is unclear.

Campbell may have trained and worked earlier as a diver in Scotland, where the activities of a bell diver by that name were reported on the west coast.

By 1846 he seemed to be in Ireland, where he is recorded as being a carpenter and diver at Sir John Rogerson's Quay, Dublin. He was later declared insolvent at that address.

A diver named William Campbell then appears to have lived in Kingstown (Dun Laoghaire) in 1852. If the *Waterford Mail*'s report dated 11 October 1852 is correct, it appears that by then he was working for the Dublin Harbour Commissioners based at Kingstown. It begins: 'Mr William Campbell of Kingstown, the diver employed by the Harbour Commissioners to remove the *John and Hannah* a brig sunk at Broomhill ...'

Campbell completed the dispersal of the *John and Hannah*, which had wrecked at Broomhill the previous year, by blowing it up and supplying a multitude of concussed fish for the locals in the process. He remained popular with local people for the duration of his stay.

When one is tracing people's lives and careers through the years, you just never know what will turn up.

The *Waterford Mail* also reported that Campbell had been keeping up with advances in science, in so much as these applied to his profession. It stated that he placed a large tank of gunpowder under the bow of the brig, which he exploded by means of a galvanised battery. The battery used was the kind known as the Reverend Dr Callan's.

Dr Callan was an Irish priest at Maynooth who had produced many firsts in the science of electricity, even before the likes of Sturgeon and Faraday. He died in 1864. The Nicholas Callan Memorial Prize is still presented each year to the best student in the field of experimental physics.

William Campbell was employed by the Office of Public Works the year after his attempts to raise the wreck of the *Queen Victoria* and in subsequent years.

The sinking of the *Queen Victoria* raised an interesting issue for the author. Believing I had only to look up the *Lloyd's Register for Ships* for that year in order to obtain all the relevant details regarding her construction, owners etc., I was surprised to discover that there were was little information about this vessel available. There was an unusually brief entry for her first year, 1837, but none for subsequent years.

This single entry shows the name of the vessel, the captain's name, tonnage and the port it belonged to. This raised the question – who was responsible for the insurance of the vessel?

It would appear that if a vessel was contracted to carry the Royal Mail, it became a Royal Mail steamer, and its loss was covered by the British government and, thus, did not concern the insurers, Lloyd's. There were a number of other steamers belonging to the

CDSPC, and surprisingly few of them were entered into the *Lloyd's Register of Ships*. The *Queen Victoria* is recorded as carrying the Royal Mail, in 1843, under the command of Captain Beazley. So we are left to wonder if the *Queen Victoria* was, in fact, the RMS *Queen Victoria*? And who instigated and paid for the salvage work on the wreck – the government or the ship owners?

Campbell was employed at the scene of the wreck from the very beginning, working out of a ship named the *Pride*, owned by Mr Teal (Teall) – a shipbuilder in Ringsend, Dublin. It is likely that he was still working for the Dublin Harbour Commissioners at the time, and working on the wreck on their instructions. He may also have maintained a business relationship with Mr Teal. They performed the first dives on the wreck. The ship's plate (silver) was recovered, as were some personal and valuable possessions, some of the cargo of fabric and the remaining bodies of the victims.

Campbell's associate, Henry Teall, came from a well-respected and competent family of timber merchants from England that had premises throughout England and Scotland. When Henry came to Ireland, he was warmly welcomed in Limerick, where he employed carpenters and built boats. He later moved to the old premises of the CDSPC, Dublin, situated at the lifting-bridge over Great Brunswick Street, on the Grand Canal basin, where he built and repaired many fine ships and yachts.

At Ringsend, Teal experienced ongoing labour problems with the local community, who seemed to have considered him an outsider. Some of these developed into more serious engagements. He persisted nevertheless, and gained a significant reputation in shipbuilding, as his family also continued to do. He built and repaired ships for many large bodies such as Kingstown Harbour Board, and the CDSPC. Interestingly, he continued with salvage work on the 262-ton schooner *Victoria* in Kingstown harbour in 1854.

Campbell was also instrumental in assisting Captain Dennis getting stout chains under the hull of the *Queen Victoria*. The chains were taken up, and then secured on to vessels moored over the wreck. The plan was simple. As the tide receded and the sea level dropped, the chains were tightened up. As the tide rose, the floating boats would slowly lift the wreck from the seabed, and it could then be moved to shallower water. That was the plan.

The wreck wouldn't budge however, and the floating boats were suddenly put in danger of being pulled under. Attempts to lift the ship were temporarily halted, and additional vessels were rafted to the existing ones in order to provide additional lift for a further attempt.

This next attempt also failed when the terrific strain snapped the chains. Despite subsequent attempts, the force of the tide passing under the Bailey lighthouse defeated them, and the *Queen Victoria* remained where she sank.

Diving the *Queen Victoria* 130 years later

I have only kept a diary for two brief periods in my life. Entries for the two occasions in question only lasted for brief periods while investigating two shipwrecks. The first occasion was the time my diving club, Marlin, of which I am still a member, discovered and completed an underwater survey on the wreck of the *Queen Victoria*. Almost simultaneously, the second occasion was during the search for the remains of Lord Cloncurry's mysterious and valuable wreck, the *Aid* (wrecked in 1804), which was supposedly lost in Killiney Bay, Dublin.

The remains of a ship, widely believed to have been the *Aid*, were discovered at Killoughter, County Wicklow, in 1985–87. The discovery was made by a team of sport divers led by Professor Dillon from University College Dublin (UCD). Lord Cloncurry was the owner of valuable cargo on board the ship, and was still on his 'grand tour' at the time. He was collecting and returning ancient and valuable artefacts to be installed in his large estate house that was being built at Lyons, County Kildare. One of his shipments was carried in the brig *Aid* and left Leghorn in 1803.

Looking back now, you could hardly call them diaries as they were not a daily record, but rather a diving log of relative events during a relatively short period of time. The log entry for 10 October 1983 reads:

Visit to Howth and the Bailey lighthouse with Jimmy [Diving buddy, Jimmy Elworthy]. Seen two large seals. Discovered steps leading down to Freshwater Bay [This bay is adjacent to the Broken Hatchets]. Still some doubt as to the actual position of the Bailey lighthouse in 1853. I am betting on the position of the

wreck as described in 1853 being the same, relative to the present
day position of the lighthouse.

In 1983, if you wanted to research a newspaper you had to identify
the date you were interested in and take yourself off to the National
Library or Dublin City Library in Pearse Street. There, you would
examine an index to the available newspapers and requisition the
relevant ones for the period. The newspapers were returned to you
for reading, either on microfilm or in hardcopy. The trick was, and
still is, to refine and narrow down the period of your research.

Your reading began, and would continue, until you were satisfied
that you had referenced all the available publications and all the
possible sources of reports on the incident – a lengthy process.

Although the process had already begun, newspapers were not
digitised then and a computer could not be used to search them.

So when Jimmy and I sat in the grass at the top of the Bailey, eating
our sandwiches and looking down at the water swirling around the
base of the lighthouse, you will understand that it was after a lot of
late-night work with the press.

Descriptions of the final resting place of the wreck were very good
in this case, and looking at the area from above the lighthouse we were
fairly sure we knew where the wreck lay. This was my first wreck, but
only one of more than 14,000 that I would subsequently record.

The log entry for 31 October 1983 reads:

Halloween. Two boats. Twelve o'clock, set out for Bailey on
slack tide. Located *Queen Victoria* 2–300 yards south of Bailey
lighthouse. Strong currents. Success! Present were; Jimmy Elworthy,
John Burns, Julian Byrne and myself.

We were elated of course. First time out looking for a wreck of our
own and bingo! What the entry doesn't reveal is the hand that Lady
Luck played.

Knowing nothing of the tidal anomaly at the Bailey, and when
slack water might occur there, we consulted the tide tables for
Howth harbour and set off in our rubber boat. When we reached
the Bailey, we began our search. Sizing up our distance and position
from the lighthouse, we threw out our anchor and began to tow it
around the place in the vain hope of catching in the wreck.

It was our first lesson in towing a grapple. We soon discovered that it must be heavily weighted, especially when it is attached to a long length of nylon rope being towed against a current. The grapple remained hopelessly suspended mid-water as we motored east and west and all around the Bailey. We were only going to catch a cold.

But we soon identified and overcame the problem. We attached a diver's weight-belt, 20 lbs, near the anchor and began to drag again. Believe it or not, it was only partly successful. If we didn't go against the current, and paused from time to time to let the grapple and weight sink, it would otherwise just 'swim' again.

Mystified by the tide, which was still running hard, we got fed up and decided to just drop the anchor in a spot we guessed would be best, dive and have a look around. The boat dragged the anchor at first and then it got caught in something. Wow! I can still remember the feeling of excitement in the boat.

The elation soon gave way to panic when the bow of the small rubber boat began to crease under the strain of the rope over the tube and gradually pull it under the water. If we cut the rope we'd lose the anchor and our new wreck. If we didn't, the boat would fill! We quickly attached more line to the anchor rope and let it off, and although the rim of the bow was still perilously only a couple of millimetres above the surface of the water, we began our wait.

We waited and waited, but there was no reprieve in the tide. If anything, it was getting stronger. The anchor was stuck in something, and someone had to get the club's anchor back. Julian Byrne, the leading diver, volunteered. Holding on to the anchor-rope, he slipped over the side and began his hand-over-hand descent on the rope. He was only briefly down before being back up – his mask had been pushed off his face by the force of the current. After suggestions, he put it back on and went down the rope with his head down and his back to the current.

It didn't take long before he broke the surface again, informing us that he had freed the anchor – 'it was stuck in a wreck'. Well, the cheers went up. Success! It was impossible to make any further dives safely, but we nevertheless returned to Howth harbour very happy bunnies.

We were well aware that we were due for a dressing-down for not sticking to accepted procedures for taking the club boat on a non-club dive. This was not hard to do as the situation had not previously arisen. A couple of celebratory pints in Howth later, we discussed the impending rebuke for the dodgy boat seizure, the importance of which faded by the hour. Caught between fame and rebuke, the club's committee opted for a slap on the wrist and a new dive schedule.

William Campbell finished up his salvage work on the *Queen Victoria* in 1853, and continued to work directly for the Office of Public Works on piers and harbours. While repairing harbour walls at Kilmore Quay in September 1854, Mr Campbell added further to his celebrity status.

While at work on 16 September he experienced an unusual occurrence, and recounted the following details to his employers and the press:

> ... When all of a sudden I heard a mighty rush of water against the back of a pier, and in a moment came sweeping round the pier head, full 3 feet high and abreast. It was within an hour and a half of Low water at the time. The inner dock was crowded with the small sailing craft of the place, and quite dry – the tide being no more than 4 hours on the ebb. In less than 5 minutes every boat was afloat and we had High water. In 5 minutes more the water ebbed again to the lowest spring tide. This was repeated seven times in the course of 2 hours and a half. St Patrick's Bridge was alternatively dry and covered to the extent of a mile, and the sea formed a cascade from the end of it, the influx appearing to come from the east ...

Described by some observers at the time as 'death waves', Mr Campbell had experienced a tsunami, brought on by an earthquake originating in the St George's Channel to the east of Wexford. The effects on land and at sea were experienced all along the coasts of Wexford and Waterford.

Not escaping his attention, Mr Campbell decided he was exceptionally lucky that he wasn't in his helmet under the sea, on the other side of the pier, when the waves struck.

Campbell continued in his capacity as a marine diver with the OPW until February 1856, when he was promoted as overseer of harbour works at Kingstown. He earned 9 shillings and 6 pence per day, with a house at Kingstown thrown in. The celebrated diver Mr

Campbell had arrived and remained as Superintendant of Works, continuing to live at Kingstown harbour until 1864.

Mr Campbell had indeed arrived, but he never seemed to fit in. From the time he was reprimanded over purchasing a set of replacement diving boots during his work at Kilmore Quay without prior approval to his sudden departure in 1864, the man just wouldn't conform.

As head of harbour works in Kingstown, he had considerable scope to spend on materials and labour as he saw fit – but, unfortunately, not as the commissioners thought fit.

William Campbell was granted seven days' leave of absence in December 1863, from which he never returned.

During the previous months, Campbell had been inundated with letters from the secretary to the commissioners regarding his blatant disregard of adherence to proper practice and requests for forecasts of expenditure. Seemingly ignoring these warnings, he had a tendency to procure materials from unauthorised suppliers and to run up excesses in labour costs. The letters kept coming.

His appointment to the position of Superintendant of Harbour Works at Kingstown came with an additional plum thrown in – the collection of the harbour dues. William Campbell had also gained the title of Collector of Harbour Dues. On 20 January 1864, the commissioners had to write to James Twamley Esq. at the Royal Saint George Yacht Club to inform him that Mr William Campbell had absconded, owing them £40. As he, Mr Twamley, had provided surety for Mr Campbell, the shortfall, excluding that which could be made up from money owed to Campbell by way of wages etc., was now due to the commissioners.

A similar letter was sent to Puliford Battley in Glenageary.

Mr Nicholas Berry, clerk of works at the lunatic asylum in Dundrum, got Campbell's job at 8s 9d per day. Said to have been the rate Mr Campbell had been on, it was actually 10d less than Campbell had received ten years previous. Mr Berry also got the job of collecting the harbour dues for £25 per annum. There was no mention of a surety in his case.

So, where did Mr Campbell get himself to? – *Sin sceal eile*.

Queen Victoria amends Irish legislation

The remains of one of Campbell's old places of work, the wreck of the *Queen Victoria*, was relocated by the MSAC during the autumn of 1983. Apart from annual diving holidays, the club became preoccupied with the wreck during subsequent years until we completed an elementary survey of the site and recovered a small number of artefacts. These now reside at the National Maritime Museum of Ireland in Dun Laoghaire.

Our method of locating the wreck on each dive was to use the lighthouse, a nearby set of painted steps and a flagpole, in two sets of transit bearings, in order to drag a grapple into the wreck. There's a knack in everything, and dragging a grapple behind a boat in the hope of snagging into a wreck 20 metres below might seem easy. From our first experience with the weight-belt, we discovered the need for additional weight and plenty of it. Dragging it to the surface afterwards is a pain in the neck, becoming a task requiring considerable refreshment of the kind which can only be achieved with the other elbow on the bar.

Although it made life considerably easier, keeping the position of the wreck quiet for the time being meant that we could not leave a buoy attached to it. So every time we wished to dive the wreck, we would have to align our shore transits and drag away until we hooked into it. We would then draw up on the rope until it was almost 'up and down'. Vertical was impossible as the current is so strong there that the bow of the heavily laden small boat was always in danger of going under.

After our initial dives in 1983, we recommenced early in 1984 and continued with more exploratory dives in order to work out when slack water occurred on the wreck.

We had realised early that our find might become an important historic milestone and we began a process which would eventually make a significant contribution to amendments being considered to the National Monuments Amendment Bill at that time.

We had decided during the previous November to make contact with the Maritime Museum. After a number of meetings with officials from the Office of Public Works, the Maritime Museum and the National Museum, the divers' governing body in Ireland – CFT (Comhairle Fo-Thuinn, Irish Underwater Council) – the shipwreck was designated as an Underwater National Monument in 1984 – the first in Ireland. The remains of the *Queen Victoria* had become the first protected shipwreck in Ireland.

Due to the growing popularisation of the sport, and technical advances being made in scuba diving and navigational equipment, the authorities were keen to prepare for the inevitability of further underwater discoveries of archaeological interest. Their concern was bolstered at the time by the discovery of the French invasion frigate *La Surveillante* (wrecked 1796) in Bantry, County Cork, in 1979, and three Spanish Armada shipwrecks that were discovered off Streedagh Strand, County Sligo, by a team of English divers in 1985.

Expecting the new legislation to have an unfavourable impact on the freedoms already enjoyed by sports divers, the move was nervously received by CFT and the diving community in Ireland. The discovery of the *Queen Victoria* was seen as a test case by all concerned.

During winter months, diving usually took a back seat as club boats were put to bed by then and the divers just kept water fit by snorkelling during the winter. This remains the practice, if only because of the restrictions on boat insurance for winter months, but the winter period of non-diving has now thankfully shortened considerably. For the *Queen Victoria* project, this down time was used to improve relations between the divers and various voluntary and official bodies.

Further meetings took place during the year and these resulted in new guidelines and suggestions for a new venture in Irish diving – an Underwater Archaeological Research Team (UART). This was later to be preceded with the word Irish, making it IUART.

With some training, it was envisaged that an amateur self-funded team, drawn from sports divers in the various diving clubs throughout the country, should be established. Under the auspices of the Maritime Institute, the organisation did not get off the ground until much later and, although it still exists, little progress was accomplished.

On the other hand, the lack of an official and professional team of underwater archaeologists had become apparent. This was rectified in the years that followed, and the work is now carried out by the professional staff of the Underwater Archaeological Unit attached to the department of Arts, Heritage and the Gaeltacht.

Although we recommenced diving on the *Queen Victoria* early in 1984, we still hadn't determined if there was more than one slack period. We had worked out that there was slack water 2 hours after High water in Dublin Port, but the determination of a reciprocal one around Low water continued to elude us. This proved to be of little wonder as there simply isn't one. Keeping with the anomalous nature of this particular geographical feature, there is not sufficient slack water at any other state of the tide to allow safe diving at this wreck site.

It was around this time that I invited some more experienced wreckers to visit the site. We were seeking advice as how best to go about a survey of the wreck site, how an airlift might be deployed and the steps we might take in order to recover some key artefacts. We were hoping that these might be displayed alongside the figurehead of the *Queen Victoria* at the Maritime Museum in Dun Laoghaire. The bust had adorned the bow of the *Queen Victoria* at the time she was lost and was picked up a few days after the sinking by fishermen near Howth.

There was little or no experience of underwater surveying among the diving or archaeological communities in southern Ireland at this time. But there were some divers with underwater skills of a different nature. Sitting in a bar in Sutton after the exploratory dive with the visiting wreckers, I can remember well the seriousness of the diver sitting opposite me when he suggested that he could 'give the wreck a bit of a shake'. These were divers with serious ability, and they had given a few wrecks 'a bit of a shake' before, but the idea didn't float on that occasion.

The notion of inviting some experienced old hands to have a look at the wreck in order to advise us on how best to proceed proved naive on my part. Shortly after, most of the copper and brass piping and flanges associated with the engines and boilers just disappeared from the wreck!

Trying to make the best use of time, tide and weather, impromptu mid-week dives soon began on the club's first wreck. As this was a departure from normal club practice, permission for such out-of-hours club diving was not easy to extract from the club elders and led to some resentment. Taking advantage of the hard-won permission, during August of that same year a small number of divers, including myself, took a day off work in order to dive the wreck. This gave birth to a term not immediately recognisable to the reader – 'mushroom dives'.

It should be explained that divers without the basic qualification of 'two star' were considered trainees and not encouraged to dive outside of normal scheduled and supervised club dives. It so happened that you could be a trainee for a very long time, as there was no compulsion to progress and take your two star test, which was the next rung up the ladder of diving qualifications. Taking another diver who had not achieved this level of certification on extra-curricular dives was forbidden.

A club diver, or possibly more than one, who couldn't make it on these extra-curricular dives thought they were getting a raw deal, and christened those who could 'the mushrooms'. Something in that must have resembled reverse logic – mushrooms are kept in the dark and fed the proverbial, so it really wasn't us that were the mushrooms. It was more that everyone ashore was, and we were just feeding them the smelly stuff. The catchphrase stuck, and I'm still accused of it.

The log entry for 18 August 1984 read:

Howth. Sutton Dinghy Club for Victoria. Pesent were Philip Ogelsby [RIP], John Long, Damien Finlay, Christy Kiernan, John Osborne and myself.
Dive cancelled due to rough weather.

The entry is hopelessly brief and gives no clue as to what was actually meant by the term 'rough weather' that day, or the dramatic events that led to the dive being cancelled. Fortunately, I remember them quite well.

We had launched from the Sutton Dinghy Club, situated on the south side of the head, on what was an okay morning. Launching a boat at Sutton was far more convenient than at Howth harbour. The slip was adequate and never crowded, and it reduced the length and prospect of a bumpy journey to the wreck site – it was great. Recovering the boat a couple of hours later, across a hundred metres plus of exposed mud, was a pig.

More than half way to the Bailey that morning, we passed the remains of the ancient landmark known as the Candlesticks. We had covered the few miles in a bit of a lumpy sea in good time and soon arrived under the lighthouse. Judging the distance to be about 100 yards off the shore, we began to drag the grapple. We hooked into the wreck, pulled in the slack as tight as we dared and began the wait for slack water. Not yet having mastered the full extent of the tidal anomalies at the lighthouse, we continued to experiment at Low water.

We had all left our homes early that morning and didn't hear any radio news broadcasts. Though if anyone had, it probably wouldn't have made any difference. We would not have made any connection between earlier radio announcements and what we were about to experience.

An event that had occurred a month earlier, on 19 July, had set a new record in the British Isles. The largest earthquake on record, 5.4 on the Richter scale, was recorded off north-west Wales. This was followed by a number of aftershocks, including quite a large one which was itself described as an earthquake. This occurred on 18 August and measured 4.3 on the Richter scale. It too was followed by a number of aftershocks.

We didn't know it then but yes, this was going to be our day!

Sitting there, firmly attached to our wreck, we waited to dive. Then, as often happened, the boat began to drift. The anchor had come out of the wreck and was dragging across the seabed. We paid out some extra rope and began trying to hook into the wreck all over again. Christy Kiernan, as I recall, was at the tiller of the inflatable watching his transits peeping into view and slowing, allowing the grapple to fall into the wreck.

'Go! Go! Go!' I shouted.

'Get the fuck out of here. Quick, haul up the grapple. Quick! Look!'

It reads panic, and that's exactly what it felt like.

Appearing to come from the south, it was the biggest wave I have ever seen – at least while sitting on the sea as it approached. At that moment, it was less than a thousand yards south of us. If we were going to get stuck in the wreck at that moment, with the end of the rope tied to a cleat on the transom, as it normally was, it would have secured us firmly to the wreck and prevented the boat from riding the oncoming wave. The disastrous combination would have almost certainly led to the boat being pulled under.

We hauled in sufficient rope just in time, which raised the grapple and prevented it from hooking into the wreck. We pointed the boat into the oncoming wave and motored gently ahead, slowly mounting the huge wall of water as it passed under us. The rubber boat bobbed into the sky atop the huge wave, followed by a stomach-wrenching descent into the following trough. This was repeated through two subsequent smaller waves.

In those days, there was no such thing as stainless steel, or even just steel bottle racks to secure your equipment to. Heavy gear was just stowed on the wooden floor of the inflatable. In the commotion, bottles and regulators were flung all around the boat, with some of the lighter stuff getting tossed over the side.

We were aghast. We had never seen such large waves and had no idea what had caused them. We discovered later that the aftershock had struck off Wales earlier and that we had survived its tsunami.

Needless to say, we returned to shore immediately after the sea settled, severely chastened. Just like Mr Campbell 130 years earlier, we could only imagine what might have been the result if any of us had been down on the wreck at the time.

I had pencilled the following entry into the diary shortly after: 'Very freak series of waves – see earth tremor in Wales approximately 2 hours earlier.'

The log entry for 22 October 1986 reads:

> After a successful preliminary survey by a combined team of divers from various clubs, the results were acknowledged when the report was received by the junior minister for state Avril Doyle. This is a first for the country, and augers well for the club. It reflects well on CFT for future applications being made under the new legislation. I hope that the sand will be removed from the wreck next year, but with the change in the committee, which will exclude myself, I am not sure when we are going to do it.

We had completed the underwater survey and submitted the results to the Maritime Institute and the Office of Public Works (OPW). Considering that this involved a number of other diving clubs from around the country, a tremendous feat in itself, our results were considered a success. We had applied basic archaeological principles and produced a drawing that showed an outline of the remains of the *Queen Victoria*. It took several weeks – or years, depending on your point of view. Today, high resolution sonar images can be captured in seconds.

Estimated from the construction length of the ship, and the scattered debris, we made the length of the site 60 metres, along which we laid down two base lines. The first was quickly torn off the seabed by the strong current, the second was more robust. This was fastened to metal spikes which had been driven into the seabed every couple of metres. Despite this, the tide deposited a daily curtain of seaweed along the rope, all of which had to be removed during every dive. If not, the increased resistance of the bulging amounts of seaweed on the line, against the flow of the tide, would eventually have broken the line or uprooted the spikes.

After noting their position on the site, we proceeded to recover a number of artefacts – a broken wash jug, a coat hanger, an oak cleat and a very heavy lead weight, which was used to keep a safety valve on a boiler in place, etc. The most interesting artefact was the remains of a snuff or match box. It is inscribed with a hunting scene, with 'Richard Dallaghan' on one side and 'Harkaway' on the other. Richard Dallaghan was identified as being on the *Queen Victoria*. The finds were presented to the Maritime Museum.

Once we had completed all our measurements of the artefacts, rough drawings were completed and presented to a friendly draughtsman, Martin Colbert. He completed the drawing, which was eventually presented to the OPW and to the relevant junior minister, Avril Doyle, at the Maritime Museum in 1986.

It was the early days of underwater photography in Ireland. But despite some terrible visibility on the wreck, Sean Rick from the Viking SAC was able to capture some images. Not comparable with today's GoPros and the like, but nevertheless a very large old encrusted lobster, who had set up home in the boiler's condenser, did present well.

There were extensive meetings between representatives from the Marlin SAC and officials from the Maritime Museum, the OPW, the Irish Underwater Council, IUART (Irish Underwater Archaeological Research Team) and probably many more than I care to remember. Discovering the speed and ways of bureaucracy was a steep learning curve. Not realising at the time that it was actually ground-breaking stuff, it nevertheless seemed excessively time-consuming and never got up a head of steam.

The log entry for 12 July 1987 reads:

Left Ringsend at 06.00 a.m. *Venture I* [Colvic] and 120HP dory. On board were Philip Oglesby [RIP] Jimmy Elworthy, Christy Kiernan, Cormac Louth, Pat Fulham, Pat Pender, Eddie.

Cage and drums.

Buoyed wreck fore and aft. Deposited cage and drums at Bailey landing stage. Made contact with lighthouse crew. All in all, a successful beginning.

Light winds SSW, Very high tide, 4-metres plus. There was still a current while diving in slack water. Cage floats well with drums attached. Gerry McGeeney visited us, but didn't dive.

With the survey complete, the next phase of the *Queen Victoria* project began. The club received notification of the granting of a licence. We had also learned that funding for the part-excavation of the site had been granted and would be administered through Kevin Crothers of the Maritime Museum. This was scheduled for the following year. This was another first for underwater archaeology in Ireland.

By then we were travelling from Ringsend. I had purchased a 26-foot Colvic half-decker in the interim and we were using it to dive from and to transport the heavier equipment to the wreck site. The boat, *Venture I*, was also used for diving and fishing charters in Dublin Bay.

The plan was to use an airlift to remove some of the sand that covered the lower part of the wreck, which might allow discovery and recovery of some smaller artefacts. After some study, we selected a road compressor along with some 4-inch pipes to do the lifting. The lifted material was to be emptied into a 3-foot cube cage, which would allow smaller gauge spoil to pass through and retain any larger items.

With a boat that was beginning to look frighteningly small, on 15 July the road compressor and all the associated pipes and diving gear was loaded onto the Colvic. We berthed and loaded all the gear at the *Queen Victoria*'s old berth on the north quays of the River Liffey. The cage had already been shipped out to the landing stage at the Bailey lighthouse the previous day. Continually waving for snaps, being taken from a dory, we eventually reached the Bailey and began to set up our gear. The cage was secured to a buoyed rope that had already been tied off on the wreck, as was *Venture I*, to two others. We set up the pipes and hoses and lowered them with divers down to the wreck.

The diving and use of the airlift continued until 19 July 19 1987.

The log entry for 19 July 1987 reads:

Wind 4-5 NE. High seas.
Proceeded to Bailey. Cage secured to buoy. Dived in the lee of
lighthouse. Recovered cage. Main buoy missing. Returned to
Ringsend with everything. Disappointing finish.

An exceedingly brief comment after such a build up, it probably
reflected my mood and the fact that the operation was something of
a disappointment. The airlift was only partly successful. It was heavy
equipment, and the set-up amounted to over-engineering and proved
just too much for a small band of sports divers. The compressor
delivered too much air and our equipment could not control it in
order to exploit it successfully. The 4-inch pipe to the surface was
not sufficiently secured and, disconcertingly, tended to get away
from us at times. The lift did work, but not consistently.

My lasting memory of the few years spent diving the *Queen
Victoria* was not the surveying or the recoveries, but of a lobster. I
had noble sentiments about fish life then, and still do, and refused
to take a lobster while diving with scuba – a practise against which
the Taoiseach of Ireland, Charles J. Haughey championed legislation.
With a taste for all fish, and the opportunities being abundant, this
was a considerable sacrifice. I eventually succumbed during a dive on
the *Vick*, to my regret.

While surfacing from a dive, the air refused to be drawn from
my regulator – it just ceased, though the gauge indicated there was
air in the tank! I was ascending a rope at the time so I was able to
have a quick look around when I noticed the lobster I had earlier
thought might fit in a pot. He had seized the hose to my mouthpiece
in his claw and had squeezed it so hard that he cut off my air supply.
Stupidly, I began attempts to prize the claw open with my knife when
his whole claw just came away. He never got to the pot.

A conclusion

We were, and still are, referred to by some as 'the mushroom divers'.
In no way different from other clubs then, when I first realised my
own diving club was shackled to conformity and almost incapable of

branching out into any adventurous new approach to wreck diving, I became determined to overcome it. And we did.

I was also determined that details of shipwrecks that were discovered by us would be made known to all clubs. For reasons of brass hunting, divers had a tendency to covet any information they possessed about shipwrecks. This I accomplished through the national diving magazine *SUBSEA*, where I submitted various stories of shipwrecks and diving as our progress unfolded. These stories included the relevant coordinates.

Wild yarns of shipwrecks, spun by wishful divers, had led to so much time-wasting regarding shipwreck research that I vowed to myself that I would pass on any and all factual data I held on shipwrecks. I hope I have remained true to this promise, and while at first I published details in *SUBSEA* I later published the fruits of a lifetime of shipwreck research on my own web site, irishwrecks. com. The work began many years ago on an Amstrad 64 and has been online since the year 2000 – access is still free!

Note

As previously discussed, the remains of a ship, which was widely believed to have been the *Aid*, were discovered at Killoughter, County Wicklow, in 1985–87.

After touching at Bristol, where she offloaded and took on additional cargo, she was subsequently wrecked at Wickow.

The *Aid*, badly damaged, was towed on shore near Killoughter, County Wicklow, in January 1804. What ultimately became of the majority of the cargo and the ship has remained a mystery. The rigging and spars, along with some wood barrel hoops, were auctioned in the King's Iron Store at Sir John Rogerson's Quay, in June 1804.

The underwater find attracted excited publicity, but none of Cloncurry's valuable cargo was located. The search for this shipwreck was a well organised and respectably funded project. However, after a study by our own team of the earlier detailed report, and the representations of artefacts that were recovered by UCD, it is now believed that the shipwreck they discovered could not have been the *Aid*. We began a new search of the area in 2015, with no additional information to report.

The Wreck They Keep Secret

The loss of the Imperial East Indiaman *Comte de Belgioioso*, 1783

If there was ever a class system in ships, a pecking order so to speak, you would find the East Indiaman at the top. Not because they were the most beautiful, swiftest or of superior construction, and not because they were the best fighting vessel afloat – it was simply because they were where the money was.

Such ships belonged to companies that had been granted exclusive licence by their heads of government to trade with specific countries. Probably the best remembered of these was the Honourable East India Company (HEIC) based in London. For 250 years this merchant trading company maintained its own fleet of armed merchant ships and an army of soldiers and marines, supported by its own organisations of medical and quasi-civil administration services. As well as being superior to the British Navy in many ways, it might also be seen as a mirror organisation of the British government.

Although supposedly independent, these companies extended their monarchs' influence in trade and politics and provided a platform from which colonisation might progress in any part of the world. The roll of investors reads like a 'who's who' of an elite class that dominated politics and mercantilism throughout Britain and Europe. These names are still to be found in the top echelons of the commercial and financial world today.

This is an account of a large ship that was built in Liverpool shipyard in 1782 for a foreign power. It had notched up less than 24 hours of sailing history before it sank with all hands on a stretch of notorious sandbanks called the Kishes. These mark the southern and eastern approaches to Dublin Bay. Although a significant vessel, she had the briefest history and her loss has become an enigma. Discovering the little we know about her has involved researchers in no fewer than five countries. The sum of that research has produced only the flimsiest of details regarding her ownership, construction, and purpose.

Brief as these details are, we are nevertheless able to construct a series of events which will shed some light onto the fascinating reasons behind the construction of this vessel, her ownership and who would benefit from the mysterious adventures that were planned for her in the Far East.

The genesis of the project emanated from the murky world of eighteenth-century bankers, business and insurance syndicates, and mercantile adventurers who traded into India and China. Licence to trade with these countries was in the gift of governments, and in the case of the Honourable East India Company (HEIC) it was an exclusive right granted by the British Crown.

In the case of Austria, it was an exclusive licence granted by the Habsburg empire and, in this instance, it was one granted to William Bolts.

Born in Amsterdam in 1739, William Bolts was multilingual and a prolific and adventurous traveller; a wheeler-dealer of significant persuasive powers. With such attributes, and his insatiable ambition, he also made powerful enemies.

Bolts spent some early years with the HEIC before he developed some troublesome history with the company. This eventually turned acrimonious and he was forcibly removed from it, as well as India itself, after being declared bankrupt. Other than pure commercial misadventure, it is believed that there were other reasons as to why Bolts fell out of favour, but these have remained uncertain. Scholars have speculated that it may have been as a result of his secretive trading in precious stones or his growing interest in the opium trade. Notwithstanding either, Bolts was a multilingual adventurer among many other westerners at the time who had little or no grasp of eastern languages. Primarily, he was a veritable powerhouse of ambition. His admonishment by the HEIC apparently left a sour taste with William, and a score that he spent a lifetime attempting to settle.

He spent the next few years roaming Europe in search of partners to join him on a new adventure to his old stomping ground, the Far

East. A man with a considerable knowledge of global commerce, and
an adventurous purpose in life, Bolts soon found a sympathetic ear
in the House of Habsburg.

He convinced the Austrian ambassador to London, Count
Belgioioso, as well as officials at the court in Vienna, of the value of
expanding their trading opportunities with India, Persia and China,
and soon received the required licence from the only female – and
last – Habsburg ruler Empress Maria Theresa. He later became an
Austrian citizen and obtained the rank of Colonel in 1775.

Acting through the existing Habsburg East India trading company,
the Ostend Company, which became the Triestier Compagnie, Bolts
traded to India with varying success until 1781. The imperative
of settling his debts, and refinancing adventures, prompted a new
partnership between the well-known banker Karl Proli of Antwerp
and two others, Borrekens and Nagels.

Although Maria Theresa had died in 1780, the licence remained
with Bolts. The new directors met in September 1781 and agreed
that they would send six ships to China and India, two for the
east coast of Africa and two for the North Whale Fishery. It wasn't
long, however, before serious differences surfaced between the Proli
Antwerp group and Bolts at Trieste. Emperor Joseph II intervened
and reconciled differences between Bolts, his partners and the
Habsburgs.

These then became directors in a new Societe Imperiale Asiatique
de Treiste (Imperial Asiatic Company of Trieste – IACT).

Bolts remained heavily in debt, and in order to settle these and
keep Proli on side, he entered into a new financial arrangement with
the banker. He agreed to relinquish the authority of his licence to
Proli, in return for cash, a small percentage of profits from voyages
and permission to run two Chinamen (ships trading to China) on
his own account. Trading with India and China continued, but
Bolts' interests in other adventures, and in developing settlements
elsewhere, also continued.

In September 1782, two ships were acquired by the directors of
IACT for the voyages to China. Acting for IACT in London, their
agents, merchants Anthony and Bartholomew Songa, informed
the English authorities of the purchase on behalf of his Imperial
Majesty. Anthony Songa was also the Imperial and Tuscan Consul
General at London when he purchased the ships from the merchant

Thomas Gildart of Gildart & Reid in London. Thomas would seem to have been directly connected to the well-known Gildart family of Liverpool.

One of these ships was the ex-East Indiaman *Duke of Grafton*, of 800 tons' burthen, which was totally refitted and renamed *Count de Zinzendorf*. The second ship was the 840-ton *Comte de Belgioioso*, still under construction in Liverpool at the time. At odds here is a statement made by William Bolts that, when he arrived in London, these ships had already been rejected by IACT. This apparently occurred when IACT instructed another of the company's agents, Andre Reid – who had captained the company's large East Indiaman *Kaunitz* to India – to cancel the purchase in London. Confusing, and maybe intentionally so.

Also confusing is how Bolts stated that the *Comte de Belgioioso* was pre-ordered by Songa through Andre Reid the previous winter of 1780/81. It is recorded as far back as August 1781 that, aside from a percentage of profits paid to the other directors, they renounced any rights or interest in the vessel *Comte de Belgioioso*, which was to call at Africa en route to the Far East.

The reason given for the rejection of the London ships was that larger and more suitable ships had been acquired in Europe. This change of heart seems to have eluded the attention of the English authorities and took Bolts completely by surprise. The syndicate continued with the project under a more outward and commercial perception that permissions to trade in the east, their flag of convenience, remained with the two ships acquired in England – effectively, running an additional two ships to the Far East under the same licence.

It would also appear that Bolts, through the good offices of the Imperial Consul in London, Anthony Songa, had made direct approaches to the hugely successful merchants Thomas Gildart and Andrew (Andre) Reid in London (Gildart & Reid). These included the presentation of a lucrative opportunity to run two Indiamen from England to India and China with a legitimate licence and the protection of the Habsburg imperial flag.

Understanding how he funded this massive undertaking, and who with, requires a little imagination. It was recorded in *Lloyd's Register of Ships* in 1783 that the *Belgioioso* was 'owned by London' – an elusive designation no doubt, but intended to mean that its owners were based in London. The second ship purchased by IACT, *Count de Zinzendrorf*, was registered by Lloyd's in 1783 and this was 'owned by Germany'. This clear distinction would seem to point to the obvious.

Whoever had legitimacy to acquire the ships, and invite participation in the adventure, Bolts seems to have persisted with his own plans regarding the *Comte de Belgioioso*. The offer was too tempting for the London merchants and plans to have a large ship built by partners in Liverpool, and to purchase another for this financial adventure, were put in place during 1780.

Whatever transpired during the negotiations at London, these two ships maintained the outward appearance of preparing for a voyage to China on behalf of IACT, while Bolts continued with his own plans for the voyage of the *Comte de Belgioioso*.

Bolts was also heavily in debt to the colourful Scot Quentin Crawford, who was a banker and an investor in the HEIC. Bolts borrowed further from Proli in order to settle his debt with the Scot and to pursue investment in his own ships, even though this meant that he was now further leveraged to the banker, a man he still didn't trust.

The intentions of Bolts, however, remained something of a mystery to the merchants in London and the bankers and officials at Antwerp and Trieste. Bolts seems to have had wide interests. Among them were places such as the islands off the Malabar Coast and Nicobar, the remote southern Atlantic island of Tristan da Cunha and factories that had been established in Delagoa Bay, on the east coast of Africa, by the Portuguese. He also appears to have had an even stronger interest in exploiting these and furthering new factories and his own career.

The shrewd merchants were not averse to making huge profits from dubious trading practices, so we might assume that they were unaware of any illegal subterfuge by Bolts. Unilaterally establishing new factories and interests might well have jeopardised their commercial future with their own Crown, or any other crowned heads, for that matter. Nevertheless, the lure of large profit and the opportunity of new streams of revenue had always proved irresistible to the insatiable investors, many times both before and since. Unfortunately, any other intentions that these merchants, bankers and adventurers might have harboured for the two English ships have remained elusive.

Notwithstanding all of the new arrangements, new monies, new ships and licences, greed and mistrust permeated the relationships between the principals and the directors. The mistrust was well founded as each desired to run their own ships for personal gain.

After a number of voyages, the loss of a number of ships and a financial collapse (another bubble burst) in 1783, the company went bankrupt in 1785 and the banker Karl Proli committed suicide. William Bolts ended up in a poor house in Paris, where he died in 1808.

The richest ship that ever sailed from Liverpool

From the time it was decided to secure two large East Indiamen in England for the Habsburg empire at Trieste, a veil or 'flag of convenience' was wrapped round this China adventure. It had begun when the secretive syndicate of merchants and bankers in London, Liverpool, Belgium and Austria conspired with other adventurers to secure a non-British licence to trade with China. These men, their type so aptly described as 'shadow men', and already significant players and investors in the HEIC, secured not one but two East Indiamen in Britain in order to sail and trade in the Far East in the name of the Imperial Asiatic Company of Trieste.

The slightly larger of the two was an Indiaman previously run by the HEIC to China on four previous occasions, the *Duke of Grafton*. As was the practice, she was then taken out of service and sold on and another ship laid down and built on her bottom. Permission to purchase the *Grafton* was secured by the point man Anthony Songa on behalf of the syndicate and the Imperial Asiatic of Trieste (IACT), and after a total refit in England, she was renamed *Comte de Zinzendorf* and registered as 880 tons.

The second Indiaman or Chinaman, the *Comte de Belgioioso*, was a new ship and seemingly under construction at Liverpool since 1780/81, when she too was purchased for IACT by the same agent, the Imperial Consul at London, Anthony Songa.

Songa was a wealthy shipping merchant in his own right and appealed many cases for ship owners in the Admiralty courts. The *Comte de Belgioioso* and *Comte de Zinzendorf* represented a partnership between merchants in Liverpool, London, Bruges,

Antwerp, Ostend and Trieste. It was a partnership in a mercantile adventure for fortune. The element of risk in regards to the cargo was reduced by syndicating the insurance of the vessel and its contents, and was sold at coffee houses in the cities of London, Portsmouth, Plymouth and Bruges, and probably many others besides.

The underwriting of the *Belgioioso* and its cargo would seem to have been a complicated affair and had all the appearances of being a scam. To what extent investors in the insurance were affected is not known, but after the loss of the *Belgioioso* the merchant F. Boghe of Antwerp became a very unhappy man.

Having petitioned for compensation on his insurance investment in the ship after its loss, he was refused. He was represented by Van Outryyne de Merckem, an investor himself, who went to the Chamber of Insurance before the Aldermen of the city of Bruges in order to secure a judgement. The case fell. Most interestingly, the insurers produced the original documents, which clearly stated that the ship was insured from London and not Liverpool!

One wonders what position the insurers might have taken if the ship had been lost in the Bay of Biscay, making no difference whether the ship had sailed from London or Liverpool? As if to make matters worse, it was also reported that the ship was only insured from Lisbon to the Indies.

Almost two and a half centuries have passed, and ownership of the remains of the vessel has filtered down through many acquisitions. Quite surprisingly, the present-day owner of the *Comte de Belgioioso* is the Axa Insurance Group.

The first East Indiaman built in Liverpool

The building of the twenty-eight-gun Royal Navy frigate HMS *Nemesis* was commenced by Jolly & Co. and completed by Rogers & Smallshaw in 1782. It is unclear if Rogers & Smallshaw were acting alone in the completion of the *Nemesis* as copper supplies for this ship were delivered by Forbes to Fishers' yard. The change of builders and the completion of the *Nemesis* would appear to have been the result of bankruptcy proceedings against the firm Jolly & Co. When a large ship was completed and sold, or abandoned, during its construction for reasons such as bankruptcy, partnerships in the enterprise were often dissolved, the assets sold, and new enterprises begun. This firm was represented by three ship's carpenters in 1778 – James Burton, Richard Leather and Edward Jolly, each prominent Liverpool shipwrights in their own right.

Edward Jolly was a ship's carpenter who worked or resided at 22 Edmond Street, South Shore, Liverpool.

Proceedings against the carpenters had ensued during 1779, when a 90-ton new brigantine being built by them was auctioned to settle creditors. The bankruptcy appears to have been finally adjudicated on by the commissioners in February 1780 at the Union Coffee House, Liverpool. Soon after the bankruptcy was discharged, the yard of Jolly & Co., South Shore, Liverpool – which may have been a wet dock – laid down a large ship for the East India Company, and this was completed in September 1782. The launch of the ship was announced in *Gore's Liverpool Advertiser*: 'The large ship built for the East India Co. will be launched next Monday from Messrs Jolly & Co.'s yard.'

The actual launch of the ship was not subsequently recorded in this publication.

However, although a similar pre-launch announcement was not made in the *Williamson's Liverpool Advertiser*, it did report the actual launch on 12 September 1782 as follows: 'On Monday last, a fine large ship built by Messrs Jolly & Co. for the East India Company was launched in the presence of a great number of spectators.'

Not immediately apparent are a number of important aspects in the above reports. It was subsequently claimed that this ship was the first East Indiaman built at Liverpool. Both reports deliberately mislead the general reader into believing that this ship was built for the East India Company when, in fact, it would fly the imperial flag of the Habsburg empire. Although not uncommon, there was no mention that it had been pierced for thirty guns. It was also suggested that the shipyard, a separate entity, was owned by Jolly & Co. and was where they built ships, though this would not seem to have been the case.

In examination of the above, one might concede the following. Firstly, the claim that the *Belgioioso* was the first purpose-built East Indiaman built at Liverpool has never been refuted. Secondly, there was no other East India Company in England, so your average reader would not assume anything other than that this ship was built for the East India Co., London. Thirdly, at a time when the country was battered by war in the Americas and elsewhere, it may not have been prudent to publish an account of building warships for a foreign empire. Might the same have applied for a private ship trading to the east?

Finally, when the *Belgioioso* was about to be launched, a major shipbuilder in Liverpool, John Fisher, advertised two ships for sale at his yard. Along with mention of various amounts and types of timber for shipbuilding, there was a vacant slip where a ship of 700 tons could be built. All at easy terms.

And when Jolly & Co. finished the frigate-type ship *General Elliot* the following July, a similar type of advertisement was placed by John Fisher.

These two advertisements, when taken alongside the following extracts from a letter from Liverpool published in the *London Gazette* in September – '... Indiaman built here in yard belonging to Mr Fisher – pierced for thirty guns ...' and '... the *Grampus*, fifty guns in same yard belonging to Mr Fisher ...' – may seem to clear up the matter of who built this Indiaman, and where it was constructed.

The *Belgioioso* had been laid down by the Liverpool shipwright and builder Edward Jolly & Co., which was bankrupted during the project. The bankruptcy took place in 1782, at about the same time the adventurer William Bolts was bankrupted for a second time. The large ship was completed by the yard's owner-shipbuilder, John Fisher.

Alternatively, and more simply, it might appear that Jolly & Company completed the ship in Fisher's yard. Just as with many other aspects surrounding this ship and its owners, nothing is as it seems.

The East Indiaman *Comte de Belgioioso* was launched in September 1782.

The method used to measure and describe a ship's size has varied considerably through the years and can thus be confusing. There is no better example than the different descriptions given to the *Belgioioso* – 800 English tons, 840 barrel capacity and, in *Lloyd's Register of Ships*, 750 tons. Suffice to say that the completion of a ship at Liverpool boasting measurements of this order was a significant event, and by any yardstick she was a large vessel for her time.

Quite remarkably, despite her significant size and status, little information about her construction and mission to China appeared in the local or national press. Neither did any adverts appear for the transportation of passengers or freight.

After more than 3,000 sheets of copper had been fastened to the hull of the new Indiaman, she slipped into the murky waters of Liverpool docks. She was then towed alongside the quayside of the Salthouse Dock, where she began her final fitting-out. Armed with twenty-four 9 lb and four 6 lb carriage guns, the fitting out of this much admired frigate-like ship was completed in December 1782.

To briefly digress, coppering was when sheets of copper of varying sizes, but sometimes as large as 4 feet by 14 inches, were secured to the hull of a ship to prevent it from being eaten by Torado worms. It appears that Fisher's shipyard was dry, and no damage was reported to the sheeting during launch. Any issue with insufficient fasteners in the copper sheeting on the *Belgioioso* was not reported.

The reader will notice by now that there was little reported about this large new ship, and there was a distinct lack of comment on any pre-voyage sea trials. Not unlike similar rush-to-completion projects that ended with an urgent need for quick returns, such as the *Tayleur*, the process of testing a ship and its crew for seaworthiness is overlooked at considerable peril. The practise of ironing out the wrinkles, so to speak, is one still strictly adhered to by shipbuilders and navies.

Silver and sing-songs

Almost immediately the new ship was packed with the valuable merchandise that had been imported into Britain from around the world and had lain in Liverpool warehouses for almost two years. The cargoes had not attracted the usual importation taxes as Anthony Songa had been busy assuring the English authorities that its owners were not British nationals and that the goods were either being exported to their own country or to an onward offshore residence.

This creative bookkeeping was a method used for securing a financial advantage and one exploited regularly but quietly. It remains very popular.

In the case of the *Belgioioso*, the cargoes were stored in bonded warehouses at Liverpool. They were declared exports and thus had, in effect, not entered or left Britain and therefore did not attract any of the punitive taxes.

Of Venetian and Austrian ancestry, Mr Paul Wagner was another Imperial Tuscan Consul, but residing at Liverpool. He was in regular communication with Anthony Songa in London and, on behalf of the investors at Trieste, oversaw the loading of the Indiaman's cargo and the embarkation of its passengers.

All the contrivances which surround the acquisition of these two ships, and the accumulation of their valuable cargoes, represented the not unusual practice of maximising profits. Remaining the financier's skill, the practice was not illegal then or now as its facade has been cleverly honed by experienced traders to meet the legal requirements of the relevant authorities.

Licences and tax exemptions were eventually granted by the government to the petitioner, the Imperial Consul Anthony Songa acting on behalf of Bolts and the merchant syndicate, but with certain provisos.

One was that under no circumstances were the two ships to be used for any military adventures.

A second condition meant that, other than for self-defence, any other use of the ships' armament, arms and munitions was expressly forbidden without authorisation from the highest level.

Letters of marque were not sought for either vessel in any jurisdiction. The ship was a merchant trader travelling under the imperial flag of the Habsburgs and, at this time, considered a neutral entity.

On the one hand, the make-up of this 'China voyager' and its cargo was in part just as one might expect. Purchase of the ship *Belgioioso* was completed by IACT in 1782.

On the other, though she was built by British craftsmen in a British dockyard, she was not a 'British ship' – that is, she did not fly a British flag. The ship flew an imperial flag that represented the Habsburg empire and would voyage to India and China via Lisbon and Leghorn under a trading licence granted by IACT. *Lloyd's Register of Ships*, however, recorded that her owners were registered at London!

Exactly where the ship was registered, and just who owned it, was the subject of some puzzlement at the time. Brought to the fore as a consequence of her loss, however, the following article in the *Freeman's* seems to have got the measure of the ruse: 'Whether the unfortunate *Belgioioso* was an Imperial East Indiaman or, what is more probable from the complexion of the times, she was English property, under the sanction of the emperor's flag ...'

The cargoes carried by East Indiamen continue to fascinate historians. Detailed inventories can reveal the state of commerce between exporters and importers of different nationalities during an important period of international development. Who was buying what, and who was selling what, indicated the state of economies and levels of industrialisation, etc.

East Indiamen of all nations continue to be a subject of special interest, and the *Belgioioso* was no different and, in this case, probably a little extra special.

A ship's manifest was created for the *Belgioioso*, as was a roll after her loss. We know a number of copies were made, but none have been discovered. Copies of both were sent from Liverpool to IACT's agent in London, Anthony Songa, who forwarded them to the office of the Austrian ambassador and from there to IACT. No record of either has been discovered, so the only available account of what was aboard and who sailed on her has been gleaned from the few documents that have been unearthed at national archives in London, Germany and Belgium, and from articles printed in contemporary sources such as newspapers.

The *Belgiosio* boasted three decks – upper, main, and lower. The main deck carried her twenty-eight guns and maybe some of the lighter cargo. The lower deck would have been packed with cargo, particularly the heavier items.

Due to the marked decrease in the amount of silver available for trade and export at this time, the movement of large amounts of silver bullion and specie from England was tightly regulated. Silver was an extremely valuable metal in the Far East where, in some parts and in some forms, it was said to have been valued almost as much as gold. This may seem something of an exaggeration, but the comparative value of gold against silver in China was below what it was in the western world at the time. And when pure silver was presented in the highly sought after form of shoe, horse shoe or boat ingots, it could attract a handsome premium.

After experimenting with paper money, the Chinese dumped it and returned to the preferred currency of silver. The quantities hoarded in the silver houses rocketed and proved to be an unsustainable drain on the resources of countries such as England and the Netherlands. Despite persistent opposition from the Chinese authorities, opium was forcibly introduced as a method of payment in lieu of silver and, after that, the whole thing just went up in smoke.

Silver was also a monetary metal and was traded by citizens and merchants every day – but not to China, where the East India companies were the only traders chartered to export silver for trade. A cargo of silver declared to be the property of the Habsburg empire was given permission to be loaded on the *Belgioioso* at Liverpool. Whether or not any additional amount of gold or silver was loaded on behalf of the London end of the syndicate is unknown and the value of the cargo quoted after the ship was lost varied significantly. Private trading-chests were not uncommon.

Stating that it was 'the richest ship to have ever left Liverpool', the newspaper reports valued the cargo at £150,000. It supposedly comprised silver bullion and specie amounting to $130,000, and was also reported as being valued at £40,000 – which was quite a lot more. 25 tons of the root ginseng was also part of the cargo and valued at £60,000.

The silver was probably stored in the aft end of the ship under the officers' quarters, where a close eye could be kept on it and where it might better resist temptation.

Considered to be as valuable as silver, a burgeoning trade in western root crops was developing with China and ginseng was an extremely popular remedial root. It was so popular that the Chinese couldn't grow enough of it. It was also believed by some to have a similar effect to that of Viagra and remains a popular alternative in some places today.

Six hundredweights of the ginseng was eventually saved from the wreck, valued at £705. This was stored in Black's bonded warehouse on Batchelor's Quay. Gifford and Westlake, the Dublin chemists who saved the root, got £33 (in excess of two years' wages for a craftsman) for their trouble.

An unknown amount of Chinese specie, probably copper coins, was also said to have been part of her cargo. Most likely stowed in the lowest part of the ship, there was a 300-ton consignment of lead valued at £5,200.

Rum, tar, porter, baled goods and hay were washed on to the shore at Dublin after the ship was wrecked. The extensive amounts of flotsam that had come ashore in places like Baldoyle, in north Dublin, were removed by carts under armed guard to the king's store in Dublin. These items may have formed part of her cargo or ship's stores.

Taking a figure in the lower range of estimates, the value of this cargo today is considered to be £25 million.

The *Belgioioso* is also believed to have carried a consignment of rare and exquisitely ornate clocks manufactured by the renowned London clockmaker James Cox, who also despatched several stone of seed pearls in the ship. These were less flatteringly described in the *Derby Mercury* as 'watches and jewellery goods ...'

Most readers will be acquainted with the wonderful rich cargoes that were coming from China in the eighteenth century – ceramics, silks, teas, etc. Little is reported on the cargoes that were outward bound to China. In reality, the Chinese thought the West had very little of any worth to offer them. Nevertheless, some British trade items gained popularity. For example: wool and cotton textiles, some iron and leather goods, such as tools, and a certain amount of ceramics.

Not unlike the wide range of other imports reaching Britain, the importation of lead was heavily taxed and exports were seen as a growing source of revenue. Lead had all kinds of applications in China such as linings for tea caddies, waterways and dressing for roofs.

Clocks or 'sing-songs', as they were known in China, were in a league of their own. The Chinese loved them and were fascinated with all types of mathematically intricate mechanical instruments that encompassed the relative sciences, particularly astronomy.

With his own cargoes heading east, Cox had already been busy developing his business interests in China at the time. The same was true of his son, John Henry, who was in a little more of a hurry with time and thought it better to move on into the opium trade.

The loading and stowing of the entire cargo on the *Belgioioso* was supervised by the dock-master. An ex-privateer, Captain Wignall was a particular man and took his job seriously, making sure all of the cargo was secured and stowed correctly for the long voyage ahead. His attention to detail would prove fortuitous when it came to identifying the ship that had been lost with all hands on the opposite side of the Irish Sea the following day.

The London-based syndicate of merchants refitted a ship and built a second. They sold interests in them to unwitting partners, skimping on construction and the crewing of one. They insured them by inviting investment from speculative investors and from those who were shipping cargo on them. They were then loaded with private tax-free merchandise bound for the Far East, where the value of the newly acquired goods would increase many times over.

When they reached the Far East, the imported goods would be sold and all kinds of valuable merchandise would again be packed into these ships for the return voyage to Europe, where profits would multiply even further through legal and not so legal commercial transactions. Financial instruments, as they are so cleverly referred to now.

The ship was finally joined by its commander, Charles de Coninck; its captain, Pierse (various spellings have been recorded); a surgeon, John Archbald; a merchant returning to his business in Calcutta, Thomas Hutton, and a number of ladies of noble birth. These are the only details of crew or passengers that have been discovered. As is often the case, the total number of people reported to have been on board is confusing. But given the contents of correspondence between London and Trieste at the time, it is presumed to have been in excess of the 147 quoted.

Unfortunately, none of the unwitting crew and passengers who boarded the magnificent looking *Belgioioso* in Liverpool were fully aware of the extent of her owners' greed. A contributing factor to the cause of the disaster may lie in the old saying that they 'spoiled the ship for a ha'pworth of tar'. The ultimate price for incomplete preparations of the ship was paid when she disappeared in the Irish Sea about 2 hours' sailing from Dublin.

Within 24 hours of her departure from Liverpool, disaster struck the big ship and all aboard her were lost. Two bodies were later reported to have been washed ashore with some rigging near Dublin, but where? As there had been several shipping disasters along the coast at the time and later, it is also unclear from which ship they originated.

A maiden disaster

A traveller's description of the bay of Dublin, written in 1800, states that the locality is a most dangerous one to shipping, and that 'The numerous wrecks which take place every winter, apparent from the masts, which are seen every here and there, peeping above the surface of the water, as it were, to warn others by their fate, are convincing proofs of the truth of this assertion.'

During a period described as near famine, and a brief respite in an otherwise extremely cold and stormy period of weather in February and March 1783, the *Comte de Belgioioso* hauled in its thick hawsers from the quayside and was towed from her birth at the Salthouse Dock in Liverpool. The long boats pulled the 850-ton vessel down the Mersey on 4 March before a light easterly breeze began to puff out the large square sails. The sails began to fill, the long boats let go, and she sailed westward before the wind on a falling mid-day tide. After having been spotted several hours later off Anglesea Head, she was apparently set on that customary course SSW.

Few had noticed, but the renowned and diligent ex-privateer captain, by then senior dock-master at Liverpool, did. Remembered for his remarkable record keeping of tidal and meteorological observations, William Hutchinson must have shuddered at the sight of the sudden plummeting of his gauges. The weather suddenly began to close in again, with high winds and snow from the south-east. The large Indiaman he had played a part in the design of had just sailed into the onset of an unexpected winter storm.

The beat down the Irish Sea is one that has brought so many vessels, big and small, to the brink of disaster and beyond. Looking out to sea from either side of the channel, it seems to be a vast expanse of water. However, though only 45 miles lie between Ireland and Wales, large sailing vessels trying to get out of the Irish Sea and into the open water of St George's Channel dreaded having to tack back and forward, east and west, down the channel in bad weather and poor visibility. Often making no progress for days, it was important to set a steady course early for a swift passage. This meant one that would not require significant alterations to rigging and direction and would see a ship into the south St George's Channel without delay.

Mentioned in the story of the loss of the *Queen Victoria* in 1853, the newly built White Star clipper ship *Tayleur* set sail in February for Australia in almost identical meteorological conditions to those present on the day and night of the *Belgioioso* disaster. Not only was the weather very similar to that on the night the *Belgioioso* was lost, but both were newly built ships and not fully prepared for the voyage ahead. No sea trials had taken place and the rigging had not been properly tested, tensioned or adjusted. Compounding the problems with the sails and rigging, the frozen hemp ropes must have played havoc with the handling of both vessels. In the case of the *Tayleur*, it was also reported that the ship's compasses had not been properly swung and compensated – a claim made by a number of ship's masters after losing their ships on or near the Kish Bank.

Another example, from 1856, is the large American clipper ship *Pomona* that sailed from Liverpool for New York and came to a similar fate further south, on the sand banks off the east coast of Wexford, while attempting to beat down the Irish Sea on a steady course. The weather deteriorated, observations of the navigation lights became confused and the ship struck a sandbank and sunk with the loss of 424 passengers and crew, mainly Irish emigrants.

We might be tempted to conclude, therefore, that the similarity in the course set by these ships from the time they left Liverpool is uncanny. The course was in fact quite a normal and desirable one for ships heading south on a deep-sea voyage. Despite being a well-travelled route through an 80-mile channel with a minimum land separation of 45 miles, these ships wrecked with some disastrous losses and regrettable regularity on the opposite side of the channel. The shallow shoaling sandbanks off the entrance to Dublin, known as the Kishes, had claimed many vessels and lives before the morning of 5 March 1783, and many more after that.

There was no Board of Trade enquiry – the entity didn't exist at the time. The Admiralty never made a report on the loss, as it was not an English ship, and there were no survivors to tell the tale. We are only left to wonder, and to speculate from the sparse documents and reports that are available, what might have taken place on board this large sailing ship in the pitch black darkness, during a blinding snow storm, off Dublin.

What events overtook the ship and crew of the large Chinaman during that night and morning we can only imagine. We are aware of certain facts, though, that help us form some kind of picture. The temperature had plummeted to below freezing. It was early morning and still dark. Strong biting winds carried heavy falls of snow from the south-east which veered east. Visibility was probably reduced to less than the ship's length. As she undoubtedly was unable to maintain a safe course, we might assume that her sails and rigging were damaged. The ship had been driven off course. Out of sight of any land or light, her estimated position at the time could only have been guessed at.

Despite the fact of the captain of the European leg's name, Pierse, possibly indicating that he was familiar with the Irish Sea, complete disarray and confusion almost certainly overwhelmed the ship and all aboard her.

During a reconnaissance of the wreck by bell divers later in June that year, her keel was said to have been off, but her hull and decks had remained intact in 10 fathoms water. Further reports indicated a deterioration of the hull's integrity – her deck was off and the hull was open.

We must therefore assume that the ship lost her way and met the same fate as so many other sailing ships beating down the Irish Channel attempting to reach the ocean – they miscalculated and wrecked on the dangerous shoals off the east coast of Ireland. As we can't be certain if the ship was mismanaged due to construction or the competence of the crew, nothing more can be assumed without some bias.

It is most likely that, when the sounds of crashing waves were first heard, the crew might have believed it was from the shore. When in danger of sinking, sight or sound of shore, no matter how dangerous the predicament, always offers hope. As the pounding grew louder and there was still no sight of land, Pierse might have guessed that the ship was approaching the dangerous sandbanks that straddle the east coast of Ireland. The extensive latitude of these banks means that it is hard to avoid them unless you know exactly where you are. Even then, Pierse might have remained optimistic. Although many ships had been lost on the Kishes, many more had just struck and passed safely over them, or remained stranded until a rescue.

When the 800-ton ship came down on the hard packed sand, every timber and mast in the big ship would have rattled and the crew would almost immediately have suspected the audible damage to have been fatal. The keel was badly damaged in the initial impact and later separated from the hull. She continued to blow over and bump across the shallow sandbar and was pushed on into deeper water on the landward side of the banks. Her fate had been sealed however; the damage to the hull had opened her up and she sank like a stone. Not one of those who stepped on to the big ship in Liverpool just a few hours earlier was ever seen again.

The fate and position of the *Belgioioso* are speculated on as a result of contemporary and subsequent reports by bell divers, reports from captains who were in the Irish Channel at the time, archival material of the revenue service and contemporary notes by the eighteenth-century philosopher James Dinwiddie. This is added to by a study of similar occurrences on the Kish Bank over a number of centuries.

Though this ship, the *Comte de Belgioioso*, was lost, another ship of the same name was purchased by IACT around this time in Bombay. Reports of her subsequent voyages led to some confusion between the two.

The celebrated Mr Spalding and his infernal diving machine

First reports of the loss of an Indiaman were sent from Dublin to Liverpool the next day, after cargo and wreckage from a large ship were washed ashore on the north side of Dublin Bay, Sutton and Baldoyle. Later in the day, a ship in the Irish Channel recovered a bail of ginseng from the sea and entered it in at Liverpool. The fastidious dock-master, Wignal, immediately recognised it as being part of the cargo that had been stowed aboard the *Belgioioso* under his supervision. Soon after, news of the wreck reached the offices of Gildart & Reid in London.

The 6–8 March 1783 edition of *Faulkner's Dublin Journal* reported:

> It is with much concern we acquaint our readers, that by the fishing boats that come in yesterday morning we learn that the topmasts of a large vessel appear on that noted shoal of our bay called the Kish; by every indication it appears to be the wreck of a new vessel lately built at Liverpool for the service of the East India Company. One man is said to be saved.

Despite the recovery of various items of cargo, topmasts and yards that had been picked up by passing ships, and which indicated to some mariners that they belonged to an East Indiaman, the first people to see the wreck were local fishermen from Dublin and Wicklow.

The fierce weather from the east had developed into a full storm from the south and subsided again by 6 March. The local fishermen from Dunleary, Bray and Wicklow returned to their fishing grounds on the Kish Bank in their yawls and discovered the mast of a large ship sticking out of the water off Bray Head.

This stretch of coast, particularly from the Bray to the Wicklow end, was well-known for smuggling activity, having obscure landing places named The Brandy Hole (there are two named thus, between Dun Laoghaire and Bray), and Jack's Hole. Slightly further south, the area of the Breeches, and the marshes around Newcastle, had a reputation for smuggling. There was no coastguard service then, but there was a band of men employed by the revenue commissioners in Dublin to ensure that all taxes and duties were paid and to prevent their circumvention.

The man responsible for this part of the Irish coast was from a military family and had three other siblings in the service in Cork and Clare. The man, Rumley, was the surveyor at Dunleary.

As revenue surveyors went, Rumley was diligent, efficient and a good record keeper. From the moment the wreck was discovered, and by command of his employers, he made sure that his men examined and rummaged all the boats coming ashore along the coast.

Unlike many other revenue officials at the time, Rumley didn't sit on his laurels when it came to catching smugglers and faced down a number in his day. He was also a congenial and well-liked figure. His family became popular in Dunleary, where they even had a street named in their honour – Rumley Avenue. Later, during a period of a different imperial shade, the street was renamed Mulgrave Street. In fact, the whole town changed shade to Kingstown. And, after a spat with the mainland, it changed once again to Dun Laoghaire, a Gaelic version of Dunleary.

More to the point, Rumley's letter-writing kept his employers in Custom House abreast of all the relevant developments on his patch, and sometimes beyond. Thanks to his diligence, we have been able to pull together some additional facts regarding this shipwreck.

Goods from the wreck continued to come ashore along the coast. They were put under guard and then transported to Dublin, where they were placed in the king's store. Rumley, too, was soon able to report some success to his commissioners when he informed them that 'quantities of goods supposed to have come from the wreck of a vessel that was lost on the Kish Bank on Tuesday night last were picked up by the fishing and other boats on this coast'.

By 14 March, the identity of the loss was confirmed in *Lloyd's List*:

> Liverpool Wednesday 12 – I am sorry to say that it now remains no further a matter of doubt, respecting the loss of the *Belgioioso*, bound from this port to Lisbon and hence to China, the accounts received here this day from Dublin mention that she was lost in a violent storm of wind and snow, upon the Kish Bank off Dublin Bay and that every soul on board perished; a number of craft are out of Dublin in order to pick up all they can, but the heavy part of her cargo it is imagined is in too deep water ever to be got up.

All of the cargo that was recovered, at sea or on shore by fishermen, was lodged in the commissioners' premises at the king's store in Dublin. The owners would soon come forward to claim their goods, but the commissioners required the space sooner and were anxious to settle the matter promptly. It was probably clear to them by then that the goods were being exported, and unless they were resold to a new owner in England or Ireland there were going to be no taxes or duties accruing. There would, however, be costs for storage and salvage, etc.

As was often the case with wrecked vessels, or any goods salvaged from the shore or at sea, these were auctioned soon after the event. The auction was commissioned either by the owners, the underwriters or, in the case of no survivors or the absence of a determinable owner, the Crown. Expenses and debts had to be settled, and the cost of collecting and reshipping damaged cargo often proved uneconomical.

In order to progress matters, the commissioners contacted Theopold Thompson and Travers Hartley, merchants in Dublin city. The two men were no ordinary merchants. Both were also members of the Ouzel Galley Society.

Any Dubliner worth his salt will be familiar with the colourful tale of the *Ouzel Galley*. Although it has some basis in fact, it has expanded to fanciful and unsupported proportions through the years.

A mystery ship that sailed from Dublin to trade in the Levant in 1695 and was seized by pirates, it remained missing until

1700, when it returned heavily laden with booty. In its absence, a protracted disagreement had arisen between the owners of the vessel and the underwriters, who refused to pay up, after it was believed that the ship was lost.

A number of merchants and underwriters eventually came together to adjudicate on the matter. So satisfactory was the outcome that it was decided to retain the services of this committee of arbitrators. Further complicating the earlier resolution, the ship eventually turned up back in Dublin, much the worse for wear. The ship may have appeared bedraggled, but its cargo was said to have been worth a fortune.

But to whom did the fortune belong: the insurers, the original owners or possibly even the crew? The committee was again commissioned to settle the matter. They did so to almost everyone's satisfaction, and thereafter called themselves the Ouzel Galley Society.

The society was made up of very prominent merchants from the city, their number representing the number of crew supposedly manning the *Ouzel Galley*. Official record of the ship has never been found, but it became the practise of the revenue commissioners to refer disputed or difficult cases involving ship cargoes, duties and taxes due to them to the society. Very conveniently so, one might suggest.

That year, you could buy a variety of lottery tickets in Dublin or deposit your money in the first office of the Bank of Ireland in Capel Street. If you crossed Essex Bridge into Dame Street, you could catch a glimpse of the offices of the newly formed Dublin Chamber of Commerce. It was expected that organisations like the Guild of Merchants, and the Ouzel Galley Society, would be subsumed into the Chamber of Commerce. Not so with the Ouzel Galley Society – at least not in total. It still exists alongside the Dublin Chamber of Commerce and is made up exclusively of its past presidents.

Thompson and Hartley suggested moving the salvaged merchandise to Black & Murray's bonded warehouse on Batchelor Quay and employing the chemists Gifford and Westlake to salvage and restore the damaged ginseng to full health. The commissioners agreed and the work commenced.

On the instructions of the underwriters in London, all the salvaged goods were subsequently auctioned and the salvage costs paid. The most valuable part of the cargo, the silver, remained at the bottom of the sea and still attracts the attention of salvors in the present day.

The ship's underwriters had been in touch with the Ouzel Galley members, and they had also been in touch with the Lloyd's agent in Dublin, Robert Black. His job was to secure as much detail as possible regarding the position of the wreck. Meanwhile, on behalf of their associate merchants in London, they also contacted Mr Charles Spalding of Edinburgh.

The divers are summoned from Edinburgh

Charles Spalding lived at Canongate, Edinburgh, and given the adventures for which he became famous, his full time profession was all the more unlikely – he was a confectioner. Charles and several members of his extended family were also early but accomplished bell divers.

Seeming a sweet-natured occupation, running a successful confectionary entailed a little more than just selling or producing cakes or sweets. The premises at Canongate were full of all kinds of exotic spices, liquors, wines and ports, all of which went into the production of confectionery, cooking ingredients, and remedies for ailments supplied to the apothecary profession. The confectionery was also well-known for its sticks of sugar barley.

More importantly, many of the ingredients arrived at Spalding's yard in barrels, and these needed to be maintained and constructed. It was a family business, and the coopering fell to his talented brother-in-law George Small. His nephew, Ebenezer Watson, was also employed in the family business. Charles had a brother, Thomas, a surgeon with the East India Company and a keen bell diver and inventor.

Being a keen bell diver did not mean that, if you fancied it, you could just go out and purchase a diving bell and start diving. This science was in its infancy, and diving bells could not be bought off the shelf. They had to be self-designed and constructed. There were no night classes or instructors to teach you how to use them. It required some skill and intelligence, a fair amount of guts and lots of cash. Constructing, transporting and manning diving bell expeditions to different parts of the British Isles was not an easy or inexpensive part-time occupation, as Mr Spalding and his family discovered to their cost.

Spalding was no ordinary 'rock-dodging-scrapper' scouring the coast in search of wreck and opportunity. Having cut his teeth with his large wooden diving bell on some earlier salvage operations, Charles had returned the previous winter, 1782, from Devonport, Portsmouth. The navy's huge warship the *Royal George* had embarrassingly keeled over earlier and Spalding had been called in to see what could be accomplished. The expectation was that most of her guns and other heavy gear could be fished up and the vessel could then be raised. Somewhat disappointingly, expectations were running a little ahead of what the science could accomplish.

They gave Spalding the use of an interesting brig, called the *Cabot*, which proved leaky but adequate. Assisting him on the project was Small, and a man named Winer. Even though Small dived during the project, he was also an excellent cooper, responsible for the construction of the oak-staved diving bells. Winer also proved to be an extremely accomplished diver and appears to have been Spalding's main man during the project despite, as Charles noted, being a man with attitude. The divers were successful in recovering much of the heavy rigging and several of the big guns, but slow to recover payment from the Admiralty for their efforts. Spalding retired to Edinburgh for the winter, somewhat peeved.

The acknowledged wisdom of diving science at this juncture was pretty basic. The technique employed by Spalding, and divers before him, was one discovered centuries before that. It is also one discovered by many a young boy or girl messing around with water. When the upturned glass is pushed below the surface of the water, the air inside the glass appears to remain unaffected, mysteriously keeping the inside of the glass dry even when totally submerged. The ideas the phenomenon suggests has always fascinated the curious young mind.

In effect, this was the exact same principle used in the Scotsman's diving bell in 1783. Spalding's great bell was almost 7 feet high and 5 feet in diameter at its open end. It was constructed by a cooper with oak staves into a bell shape, and these were all kept in place with iron hoops. Its capacity was 120 gallons. A prominent feature was its large open end, through which one or two divers entered. They sat on a plank within, which was fixed to opposite sides of the bell.

With the men inside, and a great weight attached to a pulley system within the bell, it was lowered to the wreck or seabed. The weight would rest on the seabed and the bell could then rise or fall by using the rope and pulleys. In an emergency, one or more weights could be let go, allowing the bell to rise quickly to the surface. The action was one of the very few emergency options that were available to the divers and could easily result in the bell becoming unbalanced and overset.

With the application of similar basic principles, a huge iron diving bell was constructed and used in the construction of quay walls in Dublin harbour. It was designed and commissioned by the engineer for Dublin Port & Docks, Bindon Blood Stoney. In a sad state of neglect now, and proving to be an embarrassing bad penny for the land sharks, it might still be seen sitting on Sir John Rogerson's Quay.

With the bell in position, the men inside were then free to work away, picking at whatever caught their attention. Any items needing to be moved or lifted were fixed with a rope from above and hauled out of position. And by means of a signal rope, those alerted topside could haul up any items of interest – a lot of ropes. Holes were made in timbers with augers or sacrificial ones embedded, ropes were then secured to the beams or planking and wrenched free of the wreck with a capstan or winch from above.

The same effect could also be achieved above the water by sinking hooks into the timbers or fishing with an assorted array of grapples. One implement called the 'creepers' became one of the diver's favourites. It surprised many that with only the most basic tools – tongs, augers, saws and axes etc. – just how much of a ship divers could dismantle in order to get at its valuable cargo. The operation would undoubtedly have been remarkable subject for a time-lapse camera study.

Divers did understand that when the bell descended in the water the air, which had been at normal atmospheric pressure inside, was then compressed into a higher pressure. The deeper they went, the higher the pressure in the bell. The fact that they were breathing compressed air within the bell, and that their physiology had adjusted to the effects of compression by the water, was not fully understood.

The divers' time underwater was totally reliant on the volume of the bell, but this could be extended after they signalled for a replenishing barrel to be lowered from the tender vessel above. This was a smaller weighted barrel, with an opening in its end, which was lowered to a position slightly below the bell and then guided over to the rim of the bell. A tube of leather fixed to the top of the barrel, with a stop cock fitted on its end, was hooked into the bell by the divers.

The diving bell contained air that was compressed to a higher pressure through the lowering, but was at a slightly lower pressure than the air in the replenishing barrel, which was positioned just below the bell. The stop cock on the end of the hose was opened and allowed the air in the barrel to decant up into the bell.

Although divers did not fully understand the dangers associated with breathing compressed air, they were aware that the air which they were exhaling was accumulating in the bell and was not suitable for breathing. So another small stop cock was inserted in the top of the diving bell, which allowed what they described as 'warm air' to escape. This was, in fact, air that was becoming more poisonous with its accumulation and time. Expunging the air, also described by early divers as foul and useless, by way of the stop cock in the roof of the bell was carried out periodically.

It was indeed fortunate for so many men experimenting with diving apparatus of one kind or another at this time that more of them were not killed. This was more due to the limits of their knowledge and equipment, and the fact that they did not seem to operate in excess of 10 fathoms, and more commonly between 6 and 7 fathoms (36–42 feet).

The smaller 60-gallon bells, effectively barrels with open ends and sometimes fitted with a viewing glass, operated in the same way. The diver, however, was less encumbered by these and could walk about the seabed more easily, or while working on the deck of a sunken ship. These bells could also be replenished from the surface in the same way as before.

It was reported that in some circumstances, using smaller barrels or helmets worn over the diver's head and reaching down to their shoulders, a diver could exit a larger bell to the same or slightly higher, but not lower, depth with a connecting tube. With one end of a tube in the bell, and the other end in the helmet, air would decant from the larger bell. This, I suspect, could be a very tricky operation if you consider one had to get down under the rim of the bell in order to get out of it! The method was difficult to master, if not highly suspect. Anyone remaining in the bell would need his wits about him.

Eighteenth-century diving was struggling to perfect suitable and less cumbersome apparatus. These early adventurers were attempting to plumb the depths in really strange contraptions, while others, even though they may have possessed a more enlightened understanding of the science and its application, were still stuck in the theoretical. Those who attempted to reach the seabed in no better than upturned barrels and buckets, with little care or understanding of the effects of underwater pressure on their bodies, were adventurous men. Those who were aware of the dangers, but persisted, were brave indeed.

Diving was new, and it was a favourite with newspaper readers. News of Spalding's activities was printed in all of them, but unfortunately, and such is the theme running through the stories in this book, most newspapers printed the same articles verbatim. Journalists rarely visited the scene of shipwrecks, and salvors certainly didn't invite them. Other than incidents that resulted in civil hearings such as an inquest, enquiry or court case, reports were solely at the discretion or ability of any surviving witnesses or, as in this case, the captain and crew of Spalding's salvage brig, the *Renown*.

A city of enlightenment, some of the best minds came from Edinburgh, as did some of the most successful merchants. The 'shadow men' contacted Spalding and offered him a generous salvage contract on the *Belgioioso* – so generous that he found it impossible to refuse. Information was relayed to London by Black in Dublin. This confirmed that part of the Indiaman's mizzen mast was still visible above the water, and that the general depth to the seabed was 10 fathoms (60 feet) – just within the proven maximum of Spalding's capabilities.

It is probably safe to assume that the fishermen who reported seeing the wreck continued with their efforts to relieve it of its valuables and to stay well out of Rumley's way. This was partly confirmed when subsequent salvors decried the number of 'grappling anchors' they discovered in the wreck. It was also understood that the chests of silver were fixed with buoys and ropes, and that it was the gunner's duty to make sure that they were made ready when such an event occurred. No one knew if this had been done or not, so reaching the wreck as soon as possible was imperative.

Details of the offer made by the merchants and underwriters were published on 10 June, as follows:

> Their agreement with him was truly liberal indeed. The cargo was valued at £150,000, of which there was £30,000 in silver and lead. He was to have one fourth of the silver and lead, and one half of the rest of the cargo, and although he should entirely miscarry, they were to defray all his expenses, from the day of his leaving Edinburgh to the day of his return.

The value of the cargo was considerable and the depth to the wreck was within his capabilities. The hard weather of March would soon give way to the more clement spring and summer and the position of the wreck was known. Conditions for a recovery would become favourable and Spalding was on the hook for a full-scale salvage attempt on the *Belgioioso*. With all expenses paid, it seemed like he had nothing to lose.

It appears the cooper George Small was first to reach Dublin after he was despatched with two of the smaller bells in early May. He was also tasked with building another bell in Dublin before Spalding's arrival. Charles Spalding and his nephew, Ebenezer Watson, followed later the same month in the hired brig *Renown*, captained by Joseph Bacon of Whitehaven. George Small appears to have completed his work in Dublin and then returned to attend the business in Edinburgh.

With the additional bell completed, and all of the divers' equipment aboard, the *Renown* set sail from Sir John Rogerson's Quay, Dublin, on 25 May for the wreck of *Comte de Belgioioso* lying on the Kish Bank. Having rounded the piles at Poolbeg, Ringsend, the salvage ship proceeded southward. On board were the captain and his small crew of Charles Spalding and Ebenezer Watson. Also travelling with the salvors was a somewhat curious observer.

Seemingly previously acquainted with Spalding, James Dinwiddie, a fellow scholar from Edinburgh, had achieved a generous measure of Mr Spalding's trust. Destined to achieve some notoriety, Dinwiddie the philosopher, burning with professional curiosity, joined the divers on the *Renown* and accompanied them on their expedition to the wreck in search of knowledge – and maybe a peek at some of the valuable cargo.

Not a philosopher in the sense that we understand today, Dinwiddie was more a scientist. He was a gifted mathematician and investigated and experimented in many of the sciences. He travelled widely, teaching and lecturing, and had been setting up a teaching franchise with the tutor Mr Henderson in Capel Street when Spalding arrived in Dublin.

Although some parts of the wreck were still visible above the water, it was a long way from shore and could not easily be seen. The sailing instructions given to Captain Bacon by the Lloyd's agent Black would have involved distance, bearings to prominent geographical features such as the Sugar Loaf mountain, Bray Head, and transits – where certain features were aligned on the land. It is very likely that Black accompanied the salvors to the wreck. It is certain that an accurate and detailed position of the wreck would have been recorded on paper by more than one person.

The *Renown* located the wreck site later in the day. The weather, however, appears to have taken a turn for the worse and the salvage expedition returned almost immediately.

Later accounts from Dinwiddie's own diaries, and contemporary press reports, gave a good general position of this shipwreck, but any confirmed positive position has remained a mystery to this day. Dinwiddie, an avid note-taker and diarist, recorded the position of the wreck as being '18 miles from Dublin, off the coast of Wicklow.' Another report indicated that the wreck was '2 leagues from shore'. One might well ask: how far was 18 miles from Dublin?

Captain Bacon and his ship of divers rounded the piles a week later, on 31 May, and headed southward to the wreck once more. Although familiar with the tidal conditions in the Irish Sea, the captain may not have been totally familiar with the tidal anomalies which exist along these sandbanks, also known as the Kish Bank.

Depending on the strength and height of the tides, the current, which flows over and across the banks, will normally flow in one direction with a certain speed, and as the height of the tide rises or falls the direction will alter and it will either weaken or strengthen – complicated. So, the adventurers might have sat over the wreck for a tide or two in order to familiarise themselves with its vagaries before making their first dive.

With the *Renown* firmly held in position over the wreck from several anchoring points, and probably attached to the wreck itself, they lowered the bell and began their dives. The first Low water tide of the day at the wreck site, on 1 June, occurred at six o'clock in the morning. The diving bell entered the water with Spalding and Watson inside at five o'clock, when the movement of the tidal water became slack.

The pair made three dives that day, each during slack water at the turn of the tide. The wreck lay in a general depth of 10 fathoms, but Spalding's dives to the bulwarks and deck of the vessel were 7–8 fathoms. The operations of raising and lowering the diving bell and decanting the replenishing barrels of air seems to have gone well at first and a satisfactory preliminary survey was completed. They removed some rigging and obstructions and reported that the main deck and entrance to the hold were open and that the ship's keel was off.

They remained on site through the night and rose early the following day to make their fourth dive, at six o'clock on Sunday 2 June. Being out of sight of land, and presumably the Almighty too, there was apparently no objection to attempting to recover treasure on the Sabbath.

The bell with Spalding and Watson inside was down an hour and a quarter. Three barrels of replenishing air had been delivered. Familiar with diving the area around the Kish Bank, I strongly suspect that this dive time probably exceeded the maximum time of slack water. One can rely on an hour at Low water slack during easy tides and a little more during neaps. During some exceptional conditions some additional time can be added.

After an hour and a quarter had passed, there was no response to signals made by the crew topside in the *Renown* to the divers below in the bell. It was later stated that the final barrel of replenishing air had not been received correctly by the divers and that the bell was then hauled up.

When the bell was landed on the deck of the *Renown*, the crew were astonished to see the bodies of the two men sitting upright on the plank but without any sign of life. Elementary attempts were made to resuscitate the victims, without success. The stunned captain and his crew recovered all of the divers' equipment and their own tackle and made sail for Dublin.

The inquest in Dublin and a volcano in Iceland

The jurors sitting on the subsequent inquest into the deaths of Charles Spalding and his nephew, Ebenezer Watson, at George's Quay, Dublin, returned a verdict of accidental death. The two men were later buried with significant ceremony at St Mark's church graveyard in Westland Row, where they still rest. The service was attended by well-known dignitaries who admired and had corresponded with Spalding regarding his scientific progress with the diving bell. As well as those already mentioned, these included some well-known Dublin merchants, city officials, the philosopher James Dinwiddie and Reverend Underwood.

The theories and suggestions as to the cause of the accident that were presented at the coroner's hearing and considered by the jury included 'Lack of air, when a replenishing barrel was purported not to have been sent down to the divers in a timely manner, due to the signal ropes becoming entangled' – in correspondence with James Dinwiddie, Charles Spalding's father, also Charles, held that the ship's captain was responsible in this respect; 'Poisonous gas entering the bell from the rotting cargo of ginseng' and 'Poisonous gas entering the bell from rotting corpses in the wreck.' There were no reports that the two divers had seen any bodies. It had been reported earlier that the putrid bodies in the wreck of the *Royal George* had affected the divers' breathing.

What the jury did not consider, and even if they had it is highly unlikely they would have understood its effects, was the eruption of a volcano in Iceland and the possibility that sulphur dioxide aerosols carried in the atmosphere had become lodged in the diving bell.

The divers, the coroner's jury in Dublin and the general public in northern Europe had not been unaware that their atmosphere had been considerably affected by a change in the weather. They were, however, seemingly ignorant of the extent to which the air they had been breathing had catastrophically changed since late May of that year.

At first, the remarkably fine weather was a portent for an unusually successful harvest. Farmers were jubilant, as were fishermen who could work their fields and catch fish from dawn to dusk. Soon, however, the weather began to get exceedingly hot and oppressive.

While Spain was suffering terrible storms, the British Isles was experiencing a great dry fog. Put more succinctly by others, it became a putrid season of foggy weather. Livestock died, crops began to fail and people fell ill. That summer also became known as the 'sand summer' and was the hottest on record, killing 23,000 Britons!

In Iceland, the volcano Laki had been spewing out poisonous gases containing sulphuric aerosols until it finally erupted at the beginning of June in the largest known lava eruption in history. It killed a large amount of the island's livestock and 9,000 people directly. A further 20,000 died as a result of failed crops and famine.

Enormous volumes of poisonous gases spewed out of Laki when its top finally blew off. Earth and poisonous gases mixed with the air when they were hurled high into the atmosphere, creating the deadly mixture that became known as the Laki haze. Air currents then moved the lethal concoction across northern Europe, affecting livestock, crops, weather and humans.

The downturn in global commerce that had begun in 1782, culminating in one of Europe's perennial financial bubbles, burst in 1783 and added further catastrophe to the already serious crop failure that year. Crop yields in subsequent years were adversely affected, so much so that the ravages of famine soon manifested themselves throughout Europe and were later suggested to have created the spark which ignited the French Revolution.

Deaths directly attributed to the event were in 2012 estimated at 6 million.

Although there was a surprisingly efficient postal system in Europe, a sailing ship would have to carry news of the eruption for it to get from Iceland to major European cities. As trade with Iceland was based principally on fish, and mainly seasonal, the actual effects of the eruption were witnessed first-hand, well before a global public knew what was happening or what was causing it.

It was not until 16 July that the intelligentsia in London began to suspect that something cataclysmic might be about to occur, and even then it was still not attributed to the earlier eruption of Laki. A contemporary report reads: 'Several astronomers and intelligenairs have given it as their opinion that the uncommon heat of the weather is owing to the approach of terrestrial eruption or an earthquake.'

Little did they know such an event had already occurred over a month earlier. Whether or not it was caused by the fallout from Laki or another volcano, the following report from Constantinople included similar observations on unusual weather: 'Plague rages with violence ... The raw misty weather which promotes contagion has continued for four weeks without interruption; a very unusual circumstance in this climate at this time.'

If the open diving bell, or any of the replenish air barrels that lay on the deck of the *Renown* that day, had been in a position to capture even a small amount of sulphur dioxide carried on the wind, such as that being spewed into the atmosphere by Laki, the consequence would have proved disastrous. When the bell was lowered to 7–10 fathoms, the air and any contaminants would compress and transform into a highly toxic gas.

Given that the quality of the air within the bell would have deteriorated significantly from the moment it submerged, the divers inside would likely have been overcome by the lethal mix of poisonous gas quite suddenly. The divers, however, also consumed the refills sent down from the *Renown*, so, as far we can tell, death did not occur until the last moments of the dive.

Understandably, it is unlikely that such a theory will ever be confirmed and what actually killed the two divers attempting to recover a treasure of the Devil's Metal will remain a mystery. During the escalating volatility of global finances at the turn of the twenty-first century, some traders labelled silver with the term 'Devil's Metal'. It is not clear if this was the first time that the metal attracted this description, but the term would seem to have more resonance with the biblical story of Judas, when he betrayed his Lord Jesus Christ for thirty pieces of silver.

The death of Charles Spalding was a significant event and was probably carried in every newspaper and booklet in Britain and . many more abroad.

His passing, along with that of John Day who had died attempting early experiments with submarines nine years previous, was immortalised in poetry in the form of Erasmus Darwin's 'Botanic Garden':

Oft shall she weep beneath crystal waves
O'er shipwreck'd lovers weltering in their graves;
Mingling in death the Brave and the Good behold
With slaves to glory and with slaves to gold;
Shrin'd in the deep shall Day and Spalding mourn,
Each in his treacherous bell, sepulchral urn!

Soon after Spalding's misfortune, and the departure of the *Renown*, an African diver and his family visited Dunleary. The curious extended family of foreigners, said to have been Moors, were set up with a diving vessel and all the necessary diving apparatus to salvage the wreck. After performing pandering diving feats for crowds of onlookers in the harbour over a number of days, the motley lot left Dunleary and headed for the wreck.

During this attempt, it is believed that the mast of the wreck was no longer visible. The new group had already been out to the Kishes in order to find the wreck and put a buoy on it. On their return, however, they discovered that their buoy had disappeared. Blaming the piratical marauders of that coast (between Bray and Wicklow) who had been continuing their depredations on the foundered ship, they had to search for the wreck again and secure its position once more. The Africans contended that the marauders had not only 'carried away their buoys, but cut away everything above the water's edge, mast and all'. They anchored their boat on all fours over the wreck and began their diving. By 'all fours' it is meant that four anchors were deployed in different directions in order to secure the diving vessel directly over the wreck and prevent any movement.

The African salvors recovered a considerable amount of rigging from the wreck and began to clear an access to the inside of the hull. Some of the items they recovered, however, did not belong to the ship. These included a great number of grapnel and grappling irons in the wreck, which were broken off and lost during attempts at plunder by the corsairs already alluded to. What success these men achieved is unknown.

Maybe due to some inexperience or the exuberance of their efforts to reach the treasure, a diving incident occurred and a fatality was narrowly avoided when a very daring Moorish diver free-dived the 7 fathoms to release the diving bell that had become snagged in the wreck. The weather eventually turned for the worst and stormy weather began to push in from the south. They let go and recovered their mooring, before weaving around the neighbouring shoals and making a run for Dunleary.

Quite surprisingly, they then seemed to have just disappeared from Dunleary and were last heard of in Wales, where they were reported to have attempted to sell the diving barge, which didn't belong to them.

Whether or not this latter attempt at salvaging the *Belgioioso* is related to salvage attempts by Dinwiddie himself, the man was not found wanting when it came to exploiting opportunity.

After Spalding's death, he quickly put together a series of lectures on diving using Spalding's own bell as a stage piece. Developing an interest in ballooning at the time, he must have also fancied his abilities as a salvor as he appears to have purchased Mr Spalding's diving bells when they were later withdrawn from auction. With the help of Mr Henderson, a tutor in Capel Street, Dublin – and by this time Dinwiddie's agent – they cobbled together a diving expedition to the wreck. Using a Scottish captain, a ship at Essex Quay and a foreign diver with some assistants, he mounted his own attempt at recovering the treasure. The underwriters, appearing to favour anyone who might show a capability of recovering their valuable property, were reported to have supported the diving operation, a fascinating account of which appeared in the newspapers.

The first reports by Henderson on the project that same summer mentioned pressure on finances. Their early diving on the wreck was nevertheless reported to have been favourable before the chance of fortune seems to have deserted Dinwiddie. He left Dublin and headed for England, leaving his agent and salvors short of money.

One might easily come to the conclusion that these two groups were one and the same.

A number of attempts to salvage the silver were made in the following months and years by other divers, including those by a Dutchman who seemed to have a good measure of success, recovering anchors and rigging, etc. that were brought into Dublin. Whether or not anyone reached the silver, and retrieved it from the wreck, is unknown.

No further mention was made of the silver until 1786. The Braithwaites from Whitstable sailed from Cardigan in the *Grace and Peggy* but were unable to persuade the Lloyd's agent to relinquish the contract, which they believed was already in place with other divers, to salvage the ship. They apparently returned to England empty-handed. This would suggest that the treasure of silver was still in the wreck at that time and remained there.

With the help of the cooper George Small, Charles' brother Thomas continued to improve the design of the diving bell and to experiment with a rigid hose for delivery of air under water – one that might deliver air pumped from above. Except in Thomas's case, the air pump would seem to have been below, in the bell.

Seemingly still in possession of his brother's generous contract on the wreck, Thomas arrived in Ireland after the Braithwaites left in 1787. Interestingly, he came to search for the wreck but seems to have had little success. He did eventually, however, return to his post in India as a surgeon with the East India Company, where he continued to dabble with bell-diving for pearls. He died there many years later.

It is interesting to note that, despite all of the notoriety attached to Charles Spalding, being a diver and improver of the diving bell, his brother Thomas, a surgeon with the East India Company, was credited in the news media for the construction of the diving bells in 1782.

He, along with an unidentified diver (possibly the aforementioned Mr Winer), seems to have been the first to explore the *Royal George* at Spithead.

It must also be without doubt that Spalding's brother-in-law, the cooper James Small, also played a significant role in the construction and operation of the oak-staved diving bells.

Two and a half centuries later – divers try again

Due to their locations on the main routes of travel in Ireland, the normal licensing hours of some public houses were altered, allowing them to open all hours in order to service the needs of genuine travellers. The owners of these coach houses, taverns, inns and pubs were considered to have sufficient bona fides to operate in accordance with the conditions and spirit of the waiver. The pubs were called bona fide houses.

Unfortunately or otherwise, depending on your point of view, as time went on the amount of customers grew and seems to have far exceeded any similar increase in the number of travellers. Consequently, many of the travellers became none the better for the spirit of the generous waiver. It so happened that upon exiting some of these bona fide establishments, it was not unknown for some unfortunate customers who were the worse for wear to suffer serious or even fatal injuries after falling under passing wagons or trams. Thus these public houses got such unfortunate names as 'The Morgue' and 'The Deadman's'.

The last in a long line, my father was a cooper with the Guinness brewery. He made barrels, big and small, which the brewery filled with stout. The barrels were loaded onto wagons and moved through the streets onto ships, trains and more wagons until they reached their destination. And, as you might imagine, the barrels suffered considerable knocking about and some began to leak. As the barrel was the property of the brewery, it was their responsibility to repair it.

This is where my father's skills were required once again. Being good at it, he was despatched on his bike with his tools and reeds. The side of the street, in traffic, on the quayside, in a ship or in the cellar of a tavern – he went anywhere a Guinness barrel leaked.

I remember him telling me about the time he was sent out to The Morgue in Templeogue on just such an errand. The Morgue was not only a bona fide public house, but a place where corpses sometimes reposed until they were collected for burial. Waking houses, some people called them.

Well, on one such occasion, while an unfortunate corpse was laid out in the pub, one of Arthur's large barrels was resisting the repairing skills of my father. Any attempt at simply upturning the barrel, thus upsetting the valuable brew, being firmly resisted, the large barrel remained in a leaky condition. This led to the drastic action of repetitively filling the glasses of a growing number of travellers and sympathisers, who consumed the contents down to the source of the leak as quickly as possible.

Evading all attempts at repair, the volume and level of the leak finally reduced until it reached the the bottom of the cask. As the leaky barrel was considered to be Arthur's responsibility, the cost of saving the brew and disbursing it to the growing number of clients fell to the brewery. Notwithstanding their financial loss, and the prospect of a severe dressing-down for my father and the tradesman to whom he was indentured, the finest wake ever seen in Templeogue was recalled by travellers for many years afterwards.

I also remember him telling me just how difficult it was afterwards to convince his gaffer that the kind of repair which was required was so difficult it had evaded all his skilled attempts and lasted the whole day without any success. That's the story anyway.

The man with the enthusiastic voice on the phone agreed. After we got around the mystery of the whereabouts of The Morgue we agreed to meet there the next evening. The Templeogue Inn is its more modern name.

That unlikely meeting was triggered by a small article I had written on the loss of the *Belgioioso* for Ireland's diving magazine, *Subsea*. The account of the loss, and the subsequent salvage attempts by Charles Spalding, attracted interest from a number of sources, including Keith Browne. And as it turned out, we were both simultaneously, but separately, corresponding with other enquirers.

We met in the snug over a pint and eagerly swapped what we both knew. I don't recall that we made any formal agreement to proceed as a team, we just began to phone one another with any developing information and continued to meet. And we still do.

Our search

After chart work in the comfort of the fireside chair, discovering that the sea was a much bigger place came as a surprise. Keith had initially solicited experienced help in the form of contract archaeologists. They produced a magnetometer and side-scan survey of the Bray Bank, which is a southerly extension of the Kish Bank. Their efforts produced almost zero results in the way of a shipwreck, but a real discovery was made after bobbing around on a heaving sea for hours on end – a profound understanding of seasickness.

East Indiamen were big, valuable and exciting ships, packed with men in the vanguard of the march of commercial civilisation, spreading their politics and commerce during adventures and quests for great wealth. The ships are long gone, but even today their wrecks are like no other and provide an irresistible lure for wreck-hunters.

Since Keith and I joined forces in 1997, our efforts to locate the *Belgioioso* on the Kish Bank have amounted to the discovery of fourteen shipwrecks there, as well as numerous pieces of wrecked ships. The total includes a small number of metal wrecks. We continue to be joined from time to time by club members, friends, my own sons and even JP, the well-known diver, and the monkey just hasn't got off my back since.

During early forays to the Kish Bank, we had the occasional use of a magnetometer, which produced a small number of hits – sometimes with interesting results. Followed up with sonar returns, and then investigations by divers, these produced numerous amounts of ships' timbers, crockery of various ages and design and an exciting early octant – a navigational artefact, not unlike its improved model the sextant – and a whole raft of other maritime curiosities.

Progress continued, with discoveries of one kind or another being made during almost every survey. We were using two magnetometers by then, which to my mind only amounted to twice the frustration these instruments can induce. We also had a hard boat and rib of our own. I remained a member of the diving club Marlin, which I had joined in 1981, and from time to time we were able to rope in some club divers to cover large areas of seabed. Their task was to help locate and identify small anomalies that the equipment had thrown up. This was hit and miss stuff at first, but by and large we got better at it and our successes brought a sense of achievement. We may never know, but it might have proved even more successful if the divers hadn't got so pissed off, diving on sand most of the time, and just buggered off.

A big leap forward followed after we acquired a side-scan Fisher 600. This piece of technology made a considerable difference to the number of finds and was a great boost to morale. The package is capable of detecting very small anomalies up to 75 metres (we used 50-metre scale) away on either side of the boat and instantaneously records their GPS position, depth, shape and size on a laptop in the boat. The software package that comes with the laptop is extremely versatile and enables details of the individual surveys to be recorded, presented as a whole and viewed in the comfort of your home.

The most exciting of these discoveries occurred early on, when we were towing the side-scan fish and it caught in something. We began to draw in the cable and could see that what we had caught was coming to the surface with the fish.

It could only be part of a ship's mast. Yes, it was definitely a ship's mast!

The level of excitement has never been higher in the boat since, but when the mast got to the boat we discovered the depths to which disappointment can plummet. If it looks like a mast and feels like a mast – it's not, it's a telegraph pole! It's true.

We were sometimes bored with the procedure they describe as 'mowing the lawn' – the long trawls up and down, towing the fish and trying to steer your boat on the newly adjusted course while waiting for sight of any little change or speckle on the seabed. Occasionally we digressed to more shallow water in an attempt at trying to restore our sanity.

Knowing, of course, that reports had indicated that the wreck of the *Belgioioso* was 10 fathoms deep, the occasional diversions were nevertheless welcome. During one of our earlier diversions, we hit on the wreck of the 638-ton full-rigged ship *Sir Charles Napier*. Built at Maramichi in 1841, this was by all accounts a beautiful ship. She was owned by the Liverpool merchants Locketts and was wrecked on the Kish Bank in 1857 while on a voyage to South America. The wreck lies close to two others, the 629-ton iron coaster *Vesper* (wrecked 1876), and the 5,230-ton steel ocean-going motor vessel *Bolivar* (wrecked 1947). There is also a number of wooden remains in the general area that can be seen on Infomar's multi-beam survey of the Kish Bank.

The *Napier* was identified by some of the crockery and the remains of the iron cargo that are still visible. These were very similar to the detailed description that was advertised when the wreck was put up for auction and sold by my namesake, the 'Widow Stokes', in Corn Exchange Buildings, Eden Quay. The *Napier* was subsequently heavily salvaged.

What remains today is a considerable part of the bottom of the ship, iron, brass, pottery, remnants of the cargo, some anchors, winches and part of the ship's capstan.

In the correct depth this time, another early find got us a little excited when sheets of copper were discovered. These sheets were of the prescribed dimensions used on ships of this period. Along with the copper on the seabed, there were some remains of very small handle-less cups – sake-size and with a Chinese-type pattern on! The crockery had no dates stamped on it, but the copper did have a stamp, tucked away within a fold of the metal.

When straightened out, and after a little detective work, the results were legible. As can see from the images in the book, a later, disappointing date was indicated.

Most of the artefacts in the images were discovered on the ridge and western slope of the Kish Bank, between latitudes 53.14.000 and 53.18.000N, longitudes 05.55.000 to 05.56.000W. As there was no shipwreck material among any of the finds that could identify them as being part of the *Belgioioso*, we began to extend our target area southward. This was seen at the time as just a necessary extension of the survey area, but it was becoming a task with daunting implications.

During the next six years, we covered a similar size swathe of seabed within the same longitudinal parameters. These ranged from latitude 053.14.000N to 053.08.000N. Surprisingly, even though this area of the Kish Bank contains areas that are equally shallow, these produced zero shipwrecks or wreckage. The undeniable implication is that, for some reason, ships did not wreck on the southern half of the Kish Bank but did on the northern half. The proximity of the broad expanse of the Codling Bank, when taken with other dynamics such as the direction of the wind and the state of tide and weather, may help to explain this anomaly – they struck there first. Or perhaps they are just covered over.

An area known as the Swash – a channel between the Kish Bank and the beginning of the Bray Bank immediately to the south and deeper than their general depths, thus allowing boats to pass through – was recorded as deep as 10 fathoms in the eighteenth century. This deeper channel has since disappeared, the water there is barely a couple of metres now, and the two banks have merged into one.

Given that we had concentrated in an area of 7–10 fathoms, the depth in which the *Belgioioso* was supposedly lost, we may have missed many other wrecks that lie on the top of the bank. We did at times, however, divert our attentions to searching for other historic wrecks and had some success. One of these was the emigrant American clipper ship *Pomona*, lost off the Wexford coast in 1859 with a terrible loss of life, and we bring that story to the reader in this book.

As the term the Kishes was at one time understood to include all of the sandbanks, from the Kish Bank to the end of the Codling Bank, which is at the same latitude as Newcastle in County Wicklow, we were compelled to extend our search even further south. The whole of the Kish and Bray banks have now been surveyed by us and our work continues on the Codling Bank.

Initial results for the Codling have revealed two shipwrecks, some anchors and isolated shipwreck debris. This bank is strewn in places with isolated rocks, which can give the impression of a wreck of some kind. There is nothing more frustrating than spending hours interpreting data, determining positions, only to dive on a bunch of isolated rocks – the exception being magnetometers.

While in this area, we again digressed from the task at hand and made some unscheduled runs over areas of secondary interest. The outer or eastern ridge of the Codling Bank is extremely shallow in places and has proven fatal for mid-channel and coastwise traffic alike. About midway along the eastern ridge, in a very shallow area, we located the remains of an old steamer. A considerable amount of steel sheeting is scattered around the area, with a large engine and boiler in the centre. The identity of the ship remains uncertain, but there is a strong suggestion that the wreck is that of SS *Adonis* (wrecked 1862), which was abandoned in a sinking condition off Bray Head and never seen again.

Further inside the eastern ridge, we located the wreck of the Scottish steamer *Lanarkshire*. Owned by Burrells of Glasgow, the 929-ton steamer hit the ridge in 1882 and was badly damaged. En route to Lisbon, she filled and eventually sank not far from the ridge without any loss of life. The remains have maintained the full shape of a ship and it is a wonderful clear, clean dive on a part of the coast that suffers from bad visibility. The *Lanarkshire* and the *Adonis* both appear to have been heavily salvaged and are missing propellers.

During another digression, we ventured into a very interesting anomalous abyss situated in another swash. This is the gap between the end of Bray Bank and Codling Bank. It was also an area known to have 'deceitful tides'. The general depth is 14 metre before it plummets, almost vertically, into a hole of 120 metres. Our divers had a look down to 50 metres, reporting a seabed of small stones and a very unusual amount and array of fish life. These included an unusually large number of cuttlefish!

The end of our search?

During the intervening years, the Marine Institute of Ireland teamed up the Geological Survey Office of Ireland and began a very successful and ongoing programme of mapping and surveying the seabed around Ireland. The working entity is known as Infomar. It is not an exaggeration to say that this programme has produced astounding results and has opened up a whole new future for Ireland.

One of the areas that has been surveyed is the Kish Bank, which was completed to a far superior standard in just a couple of days, compared to our twelve-year effort. Their results were far more comprehensive and detailed but, barring one or two exceptions, it included few additional shipwrecks in the same area surveyed. Courtesy of that organisation, an image of their survey results is included here, and many of their complete surveys are available free on their web site.

There is no doubt that as technology continues to improve rapidly, discoveries by amateur wreck-hunters like ourselves will also increase. Given the dwindling level of official resources, and the relative legislation that exists in Ireland today, this is bound to lead to increasing confrontation with official archaeologists.

Suppressing discoveries, abandoning to the elements those that cannot be recovered or conserved due to a lack of sufficient resources, is not an enlightened way to proceed. It is clear, however, that a new incentivised collaboration is desirable, one similar, maybe, to others that have already proved successful in other jurisdictions. Signs that are emerging are encouraging.

Into the Yawning Abyss

The loss of the emigrant ship *Pomona*, wrecked 1859. 424 drowned – 24 crew saved?

> Arranged side by side, they lay locked in the sleep of death, and the lifeless, which a few hours past were lighted up with life and animation, had become sickening objects, from which the heart recoiled ... the eyes seemed directed to that haven where shipwrecks are never known – where no dread is entertained of a tempestuous ocean, and where no unskilful mariner can cast them on the dreaded sandbank.
> (Narrative on the inquest held on 'Mrs Paxton, Female No.1' at Blackwater. *Wexford Independent*, 1859)

The *Irish Times* was launched in Dublin one month earlier. The new broadsheet produced a running commentary on the horrific unfolding details of the wrecking of an American clipper ship, the *Pomona*, on the coast of Wexford. It was very early days for the newspaper, which might have considered the gruesome facts of the shipwreck somewhat fortunate timing for circulation numbers.

His family ravished by disease and famine in 1848, the eleven-year-old orphan John Sisk entered the building trade and established a construction firm in Cork in 1859. This acorn would sprout into the world-class building company Sisk of today.

Three months after the *Pomona* disaster, John Maxwell was born in Liverpool and would be best remembered as General Maxwell and for his brutal suppression of the Easter Rising in Ireland and the execution of a large number of Irish rebels in 1916.

In all probability, Henry Lavery would never have made the acquaintance of the well-known deep-sea Captain Paxton. The only thing they had in common at the time was that they were both separated from their families. Joined by the same and separate tragedies, both men would die that day in different parts of the world and would never see their families again.

A hard-pressed and unwilling emigrant, Henry's business as a publican and wine and spirit merchant in Belfast had failed. He had travelled to Liverpool, where he secured passage to New York in steerage on the sailing ship *Pomona* in the hope of improving his situation. He left behind a wife and three young children – two girls and a boy.

The young boy, aged three when his father left for America, would become a world-class and prolific artist, and one of the renowned celebrity duo of Sir John and Lady Lavery. Marrying for a second time, Lavery partnered the beautiful Hazel Martyn Trudeau, daughter of a wealthy Chicago industrialist. Married twice before, it is said she and the family had fallen on hard times, but after persistent pursuit by John, and equally persistent refusal of permission to marry by her mother, she eventually became Lady Lavery.

Apparently in recognition of the part Lady Hazel Lavery played as a significant backroom facilitator between the Irish emissaries and London during the negotiations for the establishment of the Irish Free State, the fledgling state later commissioned her husband John Lavery to paint an image of a woman who would reflect and celebrate the new Ireland. John got the commission and Hazel got to be painted – again. Lady Lavery appeared on Irish bank notes until the 1970s.

A younger John Lavery may have referred to his father more often, and maybe more kindly, in private than he did in his autobiography *Life of a Painter*. Published in 1939, it carried on the first page the only personable reference to his father: 'In considerable contrast to Ruskin's father, who was also a wine merchant, he [Lavery's father, Henry] seems to have sold out and cleared out at an early stage, leaving his wife and children to fend for themselves.'

His remarkable frankness later in the book concerning his own uncharitable treatment of his unmarried sister, Jane, and her pregnancy, and his observations regarding the harsh conditions facing steerage passengers as she emigrated in search of the unborn child's father in the 1870s, are truly poignant. Her suicide soon after haunted him for years afterward.

One of the earliest marine maps of Ireland by Martin Wladseemuller, dating to 1513. It clearly shows the mythical island of Hi-Brazil and Achill, but omits the promontory of Erris and the 120-mile indent of Donegal Bay. (Courtesy of the National Library of Ireland)

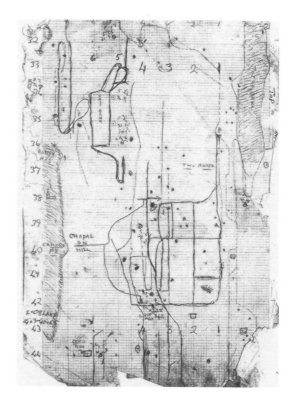

Fisherman's 'trawl' or 'snag' chart for the Arklow Bank and Blackwater areas on the coast of Wexford. (Courtesy of Martin Roe and the fishermen of Wicklow)

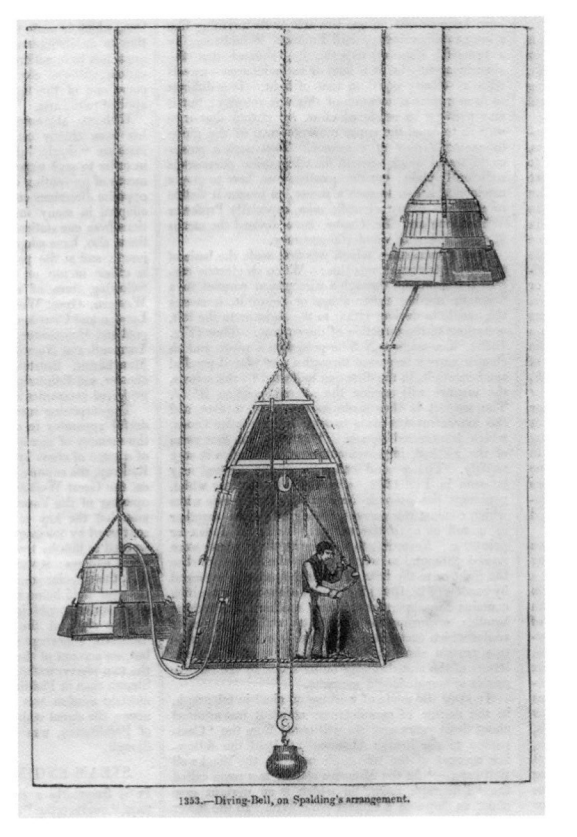

1353.—Diving-Bell, on Spalding's arrangement.

Left: An eighteenth-century diving bell used by Charles Spalding. (Author's Collection)

Below: Contemporary image of the wrecking of the City of Dublin Steam Packet Company's paddle steamer *Queen Victoria* under Bailey lighthouse at Howth, Dublin, in 1853. (Author's Collection)

Right: A representational figurehead of Queen Victoria from the paddle steamer of the same name which wrecked at Howth in 1853. Recovered by local fishermen, it is now on display at the Maritime Museum, Dun Laoghaire. (Courtesy of the Maritime Museum)

Below: Depiction of emigrants boarding paddle steamers at Liverpool. (Courtesy of the Maggie Land Blanck Collection)

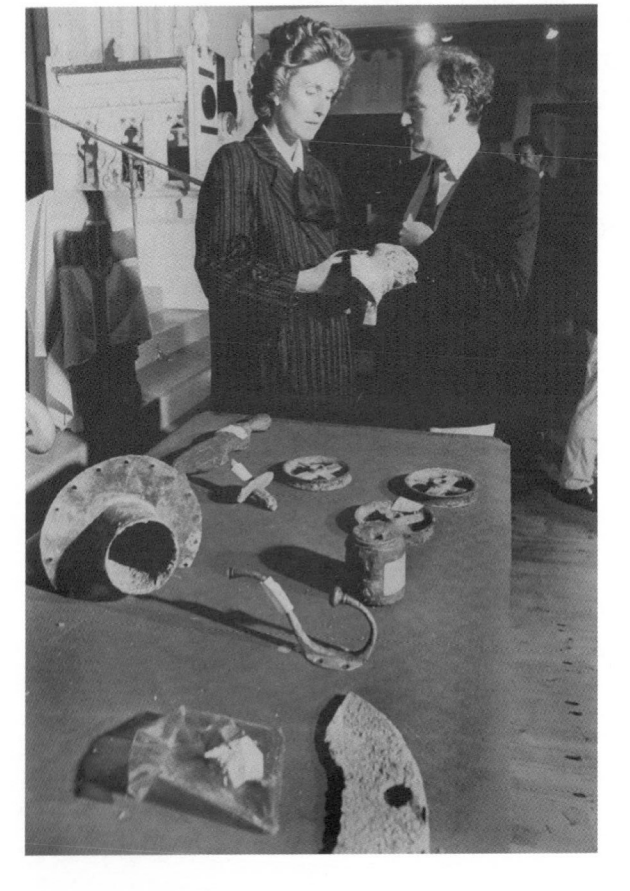

Above: Inflatable diving boat positioned over the wreck of the *Queen Victoria* in 1983. (Author's Collection)

Left: Irish Minister of State Avril Doyle receives artefacts and the results of the *Queen Victoria* wreck survey from the author and MSAC in 1986. (Author's Collection)

Remains of a snuff box discovered on the wreck of the *Queen Victoria*. (Author's Collection)

Frigate-like ship designed by ex-privateer captain William Hutchinson, dock-master in Liverpool. It is contemporary with and believed to represent the Indiaman *Comte de Belgioioso*, built and launched in Liverpool in 1782. (Courtesy R. S. Brown)

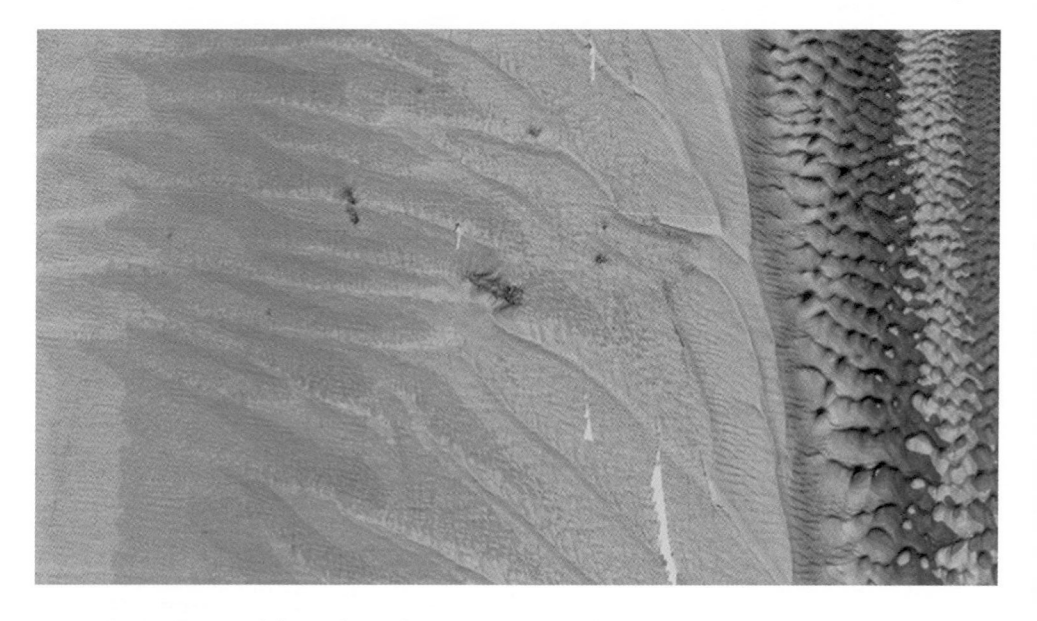

A mound of iron cargo, pots, faggots of iron and anchors in the wreck of the *Sir Charles Napier* from 1857. (Author's Collection)

Sonar survey of the Kish Bank. From right to left, it shows the wreck sections of the *Bolivar* (wrecked 1947), *Vesper* (wrecked 1876) and the scattered remains of a number of nineteenth-century timber shipwrecks. (Courtesy of INFOMAR)

Right: A collection of
mid-nineteenth-century
pottery recovered on the
Kishes of Dublin. (Author's
Collection)

Below: A print of the
American clipper sailing
ship *Pomona* commissioned
from the painting by artist
B. K. Cleare. Thanks to the
artist and the members of the
Wexford SAC for permission
to reproduce.

The old graveyard at Killila, just west of Blackwater village, where the Paxtons and Henry Lavery, victims of the *Pomona* sinking, were interred. (Author's Collection)

A depiction of emigrant passengers in distress and their ship flooding during heavy weather. (Courtesy of the Maggie Land Blanck Collection)

NOTICE TO MARINERS.
WRECK IN THE NORTH BAY OF WEXFORD.

NOTICE IS HEREBY GIVEN, that a Green Buoy, marked with the word *Wreck*, has been placed about 30 fathoms, N.N.W., from the Wreck of a vessel sunk in the North Bay of Wexford, about midway between Blackwater Bank and the Main.

The Buoy lies in 9 fathoms at Low Water Spring Tides with the following marks and Compass bearings viz :—

Blackwater Head, W. by N.

Cahore Point, N.E. by N.

Blackwater Bank Light Ship, E. ¼ N.

Marks.— A bush of wood on red clay cliff on with a Church in the distance North, and North Rock on Fort Mountain on with Clump of Trees on highest sand hill, South of Blackwater Head, W. ⅛ S.

The Mizen Mast of the vessel is standing about 20 feet above water and several spars attached to the wreck.

By order,

W. LEES,
Secretary.

Ballast Office Dublin, 7th May, 1859.

Above: The 'Wreck Buoy' notice to mariners, issued to describe the position of the wreck of the *Pomona*, wrecked in 1859. (Author's Collection)

Right: Figurehead from the American emigrant clipper ship *Pomona*, wrecked at Blackwater, County Wexford, in 1859. (Courtesy of County Archives, Wexford)

Recovered from the wreck of the *Pomona*, a wash bowl with decorative sheaves of corn. One piece of a matching bathroom set, it was part of the *Pomona*'s cargo. The Alcock Imperial crest was stamped on the base of the bowl and helped to identify the wreck. The crest has been copied and is shown in the bottom of the bowl. (Author's Collection)

Captain Otto Steinbrinck and the crew of *UC65* during the First World War. (Courtesy of the U-boat Archives)

The South Arklow lightship *Guillemot* before she was sunk in 1917. (Courtesy of the Guillemot Museum)

The crew of the South Arklow lightship *Guillemot*, 1917. It was sunk by *UC65* in the First World War. From left to right, back row: Unknown, Paddy Cogley, James Sinnot. Front row: Bob Roche, Captain Rossiter, Martin Murphy, Peter Gaddren. (Courtesy of the Guillemot Museum)

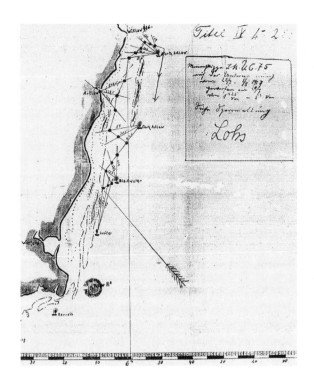

Commander Lohs' record of a mine-laying operation by *UC75* off the coasts of Wexford and Wicklow in 1917. (Courtesy of the U-boat Archives)

Johannes Lohs, commander of *UC75* during operations off the Irish coast in the First World War. (Courtesy of the U-boat Archives)

The minelayer *UC44* was raised and salvaged at Dunmore East harbour, County Waterford, in August 1917. (Author's Collection)

Photographs of propeller and stern torpedo tube on the wreck of *UC42*. Markings on boss confirm manufacturing details and the identity of the submarine. (Courtesy of John Collins and Tim Carey)

Left: Hard-hat diver P. Flaherty, based at Haulboline, Cork harbour, in the First World War. Flaherty was the first man to investigate sunken German submarine *UC42* after she was discovered in September 1917. (Courtesy of Tim Carey)

Below: Image of Broadhaven and Erris in a marine chart dated 1788. (Author's Collection)

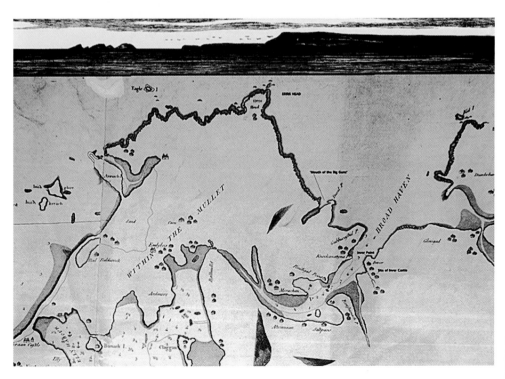

Above: Recoveries made by Leinster Divers from shipwrecks at Inver Point, Broadhaven, in 1986. The date of the wrecks ranges from the sixteenth to the nineteenth century. (Author's Collection)

Right: A wreck notice advertising the sale of the remaining cargo and hull of the sailing ship *Sinai*, Broadhaven, 1877. (Author's Collection)

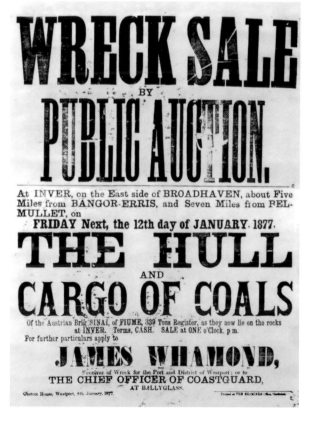

WRECK SALE
BY
PUBLIC AUCTION.

At INVER, on the East side of BROADHAVEN, about Five Miles from BANGOR-ERRIS, and Seven Miles from BEL-MULLET, on

FRIDAY Next, the 12th day of JANUARY. 1877.

THE HULL
AND
CARGO OF COALS

Of the Austrian Brig SINAI, of FIUME, 339 Tons Register, as they now lie on the rocks at INVER. Terms, CASH. SALE at ONE o'Clock. p m.
For further particulars apply to

JAMES WHAMOND,
Receiver of Wreck for the Port and District of Westport ; or to
THE CHIEF OFFICER OF COASTGUARD,
AT BALLYGLASS.

Custom House, Westport, 6th January, 1877.

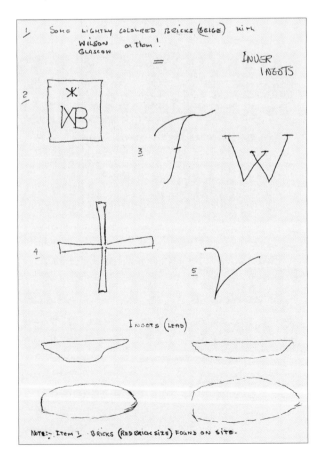

Above: A diver records cannon on a seventeenth-century wreck site at 'Mouth of the Big Guns', Blind harbour, Broadhaven, County Mayo. (Courtesy of Karl Brady and the Underwater Archaeological Unit, Department Arts, Heritage and the Gaeltacht)

Left: A sketch by the author of markings on lead ingots recovered from shipwrecks at Inver Point, Broadhaven, in 1986.

On the other side of the world, Thomas Paxton, a well-respected deep-sea captain from Williamsburg, was in command of the emigrant ship *Coosawattee*, berthed at Bombay. He had arrived in India in the beginning of January. The registered owners of the ship were J. R. Wilder & Co. and its agents were the Tapscott Line. She was due to turn around for New York, where the captain had arranged to meet his wife and their three children, who were sailing from England.

In the spring of 1859, the Paxton family booked cabin accommodation on the American sailing ship *Pomona* at Liverpool for the transatlantic reunion. What happened next was an unusual act of fate, or coincidence, which prevented any member of that family ever meeting again.

Emigrant ships and their companies

Almost as if there had been a spell of ill luck cast on the fine looking ships built by George and Thomas Boole of Boston in 1856, and on the name of Howland, the great American shipping magnate who partnered ownership in the vessels, both suffered an extraordinary series of losses over a very short time span. The most horrific of these was the wrecking of the *Pomona* on the east coast of Ireland, off Blackwater, County Wexford, on 29 April 1859.

Descendants of John Howland, whose name is synonymous with the arrival of the *Mayflower*, partnered many other well-known names in the shipping business. These included some of the greatest names in the sphere of American shipping merchants, such as Frothington, Ridgeway, and Aspinall.

Of a family with six other siblings, the shipwright brothers George and Thomas Boole began building their own ships in east Boston in 1853. The middle years had burgeoned with the growing industrial and emigrant trade, reflecting the huge growth in employment in the new world. There was also considerable growth in commercial shipping, both in imports and exports. The huge volumes involved required big ships quickly.

In 1856, the brothers' yard launched three large emigrant/freight clipper ships. They were the 1,181-ton *Pomona*, the 1,263-ton *Endymion* and the 1,322-ton *Plutarch*, named after mythological Greek gods or, in the case of *Plutarch*, the Greek essayist.

The three ships were owned by the shipping merchants Howland & Frothington. Howland & Frothington remained listed in the American registers as being the owners of the *Pomona*, but the Tapscott Line clearly acted as agents for the *Pomona* at the time of her loss. The third mate serving on the *Pomona* at the time of her loss, Stephen Kelly, gave a sworn deposition that the ship was owned by the DL Line. The situation regarding who owned and ran what was confusing, but was clarified later in the enquiry.

The three were all wrecked within a twelve-month period over 1859 and 1860. The *Pomona* was lost on the east coast of Ireland in April 1859, the *Plutarch* in December, off Ostend, and the *Endymion*, at first reported as a total loss, after being very badly damaged by fire at Liverpool in January 1860. Despite the initial report, the badly damaged hull appears to have been purchased and completely restored by its new owners, J. De Wolf of Liverpool. The ship appeared the following year in American and British registers and continued sailing until 1883, when she was abandoned and was believed to have been totally lost while carrying timber from New Brunswick to Liverpool.

Howland & Frothington had the misfortune to lose another Liverpool–New York packet, the *Roscius*, in August 1860 after she struck on Saint George's Shoals off Massachusetts. *Roscius* remained grounded and the crew and passengers were eventually taken off by a passing ship.

It was the golden age of the American clipper ships – speed, bulk cargoes and a quick turnaround for profit were everything. Shipwrights could turn out a bulky clipper for launching in six months. The fact that they were turned out quickly did not mean their construction was substandard. Quite the opposite; skills and materials were excellent, and so too were their insurance classifications.

The emigrant cargoes

It might first appear that there was a conflict of purpose with regards to the specific cargoes which these ships were designed to carry. As running ships was intended to be a profitable venture, voyages eastward, by the nature of migration at the time, were not calculated to carry large numbers of people but, instead, to provide mainly for bulk cargoes. The return was also bulk, but of a different kind – emigrants.

Among a variety of other cargoes such as grain and lumber, these big sailing ships went out with cotton for Liverpool and returned with hundreds of emigrants looking for a new life of opportunity in America. This meant that there could be little |concession to the comfort of the returning human cargoes as the outgoing bulk cargoes could not be accommodated economically below in lots of cabins or permanently divided spaces.

The conflict was easily settled by the shippers – whatever paid most would be shipped, so there was often a mix of general cargo and emigrants.

The issue concerning the transport of the emigrants was that the ships could not be, and were not, adapted solely for the comfort of humans, but also for the transportation of bulk cargoes of many kinds. Some were constructed more suitably for emigrants, but many had only steerage accommodation and, even if you could pay more, there were few cabins in these vessels.

Provision of food during the voyage was often optional. Provision of sanitary conveniences was abysmal. If you boarded in good health, you were lucky to reach your destination in a similar condition.

Things had moved on somewhat from the disaster of the earlier famine years and before, when conditions for travellers on ships were far worse and the journeys were purely a matter of survival. After mounting numbers of deaths from disease, and even starvation, governments intervened and forced ship owers to improve conditions for travelling emigrants. The measures were basic to begin with and often ignored once a ship was at sea. The move, nevertheless, was the beginning of a groundswell in the right direction.

It could be said that many of the major ship owners had become wealthy from their own, and ancestral, activities in the slave trade and their attitudes to human cargoes were being dragged screaming into a new era. The sheer number of competitors in the business helped to focus their attention, considerably.

Apart from the meagre statutory rations, of which you might frequently only get biscuits and water, the ship might supply additional food at a profit, or you could bring your own. The provision of meals was Dickensian, food being dished out to passengers from large cauldrons when weather conditions permitted.

Preparing and cooking food was sometimes franchised to a cook and groups of emigrants who may have brought their own food. All of the cooking was done on braziers or ranges up on the main deck in the 'houses' or 'cabooses' where the mood was often highly combustible. Weather conditions and the situation of the ship and its crew often dictated meal times, or the lack thereof. The ship's cook prepared food for the captain and the crew in a separate part of the ship.

Statutory regulations for commercial ships had not yet reached the point that the provision of a ship's doctor was compulsory, but many large shipping lines employed them. Their presence on a voyage, however, was not always obvious. With regards to the hundreds of steerage passengers in their care aboard any emigrant vessel, their duties would only seem to have been to ensure adequate ventilation and the maintenance of basic sanitary conditions. Just as with the cook, passengers were encouraged to provide their own doctor, who could receive free passage in return. In the case of the *Pomona*, there is reference to a ship's doctor, Dr Kelly. The *Pomona*'s doctor was also reported to have been Mr Fox.

Steerage, considered to have been the cheapest form of travel accommodation on a ship, is a term often considered within the context of advertisements displaying First Class, Second Class and then steerage accommodation. Even by then, the awful conditions still endured by steerage passengers continued to exercise lawmakers into legislating basic conditions for travellers, which was helpful but often ignored. The term had received such bad press that shipping agents were re-packaging it as Third Class.

The full range of advertised accommodation often gave the impression that the ship had considerable well-appointed space for all passengers, and that steerage or Third Class could only be but humane in such a well-appointed vessel. In these clippers, however, there was often only steerage available, and very few cabins for those passengers who were better connected and financially better off.

The fare was not subsidised. It might be paid by a landlord looking to get you off his land, or you might agree to an indenture agreement made through an agent on behalf of a prospective employer who would pay for the passage – and then recover it. Indentured servitude was disappearing, but still employed in some British and American colonies. The rounding up of labour at some of these points of disembarkation could be nothing short of kidnapping.

The policy and operation of migrant labour continues to be a trade in shame. On the plus side, some American counties were offering emigrants tracks of land for agriculture and the production of lumber, just as other 'New Worlds' were doing.

Passage in a cabin on a clipper cost about £18, and £7s 8d in steerage. Much cheaper could be had – at a risk. Expressed as a percentage of income, it is estimated that the cost of passage was actually reducing. However, it's interesting to note that this price hardly changed at all for the emigrants who travelled during the wave of mass emigration on assisted passage schemes 100 years later. So, relatively, you might say that it was far more expensive for an emigrant to reach America in the mid-nineteenth century than it was for one to reach Australia 100 years later.

The stark reality was that it was the wealthy who were travelling – the poor were fleeing, and these emigrant ships were appointed accordingly. That is, in a manner likely to maximise profit from their bulky cargoes, human or otherwise.

An emigrant's journey

Given the basic design of transport vehicles like carts and wagons, and the minimal road infrastructure, travelling to the likes of Liverpool from the interior of Ireland, or from the Midlands or Scotland, was a journey of endurance in itself and only the first step in a long trek in the search for a new life.

Emigrants travelled from remote areas by cart or barge, or even by walking to cities like Dublin. From there, they would take a sailing ship, or even a steamer by then, to Liverpool, experiencing their first taste of steerage travel. Then there was the wait, and the subsequent nights spent in the filthy hovels of Liverpool, before the arduous passage to America. And lastly, for those not seeking work at the point of disembarkation in the port cities, a final journey to the interior or west coast of America. Undoubtedly the journey required stamina – with children it must have been horrendously difficult.

If an emigrant had not already purchased passage, they had to do so at one of the ticket agents along the bustling quays of Liverpool. Steerage could mean different things on different ships. It might mean hastily reconstructed racks of communal bunks, hammocks or just a floor space on which to lay down with one's meagre belongings. Every aspect of many of these voyages was pure endurance, and many passengers did not survive the ordeal. Wealthy shippers who had learned how to pack humans during the slave trade continued with their inhuman attitudes and practises towards their fellow man – without the manacles. The provision of basic requirements like food and water, suitable sanitary conditions, access to fresh air and exercise suffered.

Hatches. A word, when used in connection with ships, that came to mean different things on different vessels and at different times. When used in connection with commercial sailing vessels, it meant a large rectangular hole in the ship through which cargo was lowered and then dispersed below. The term remains in use today. When the cargo had been loaded, the hole was sealed up with planks, made watertight with canvas and was said to be battened down. Entrance to below deck by this way could at one time be had by way of a temporary stairway. When deck houses were built on sailing ships, entrance to below decks could be had through a door inside and a permanently installed stairway.

In terms of those in steerage accommodation, reports that the hatches were battened down were meant to signify that access through the deck house to below decks was sealed or, in the case of no deck house, the hatch or hole to below was battened down and sealed up. Seemingly a very cruel measure, it was often reported that the terrified screams of those imprisoned below could be heard above the howling wind and the crashing waves.

Not being able to escape through the scuppers fast enough, the seawater would pile up on the deck and pour down through leaky planking. One can only try to imagine passengers' frantic but pointless search for any means of escape, which must have been terrifying. On the other hand, some that had experienced fair weather and a fast passage reported having enjoyed the voyage.

Battening down the hatches is a phrase often perceived as a cruel action by the crew. The suggestion is that they imprisoned the multitude of passengers below decks in order to help save their own skins. It undoubtedly occurred, but there are two sides to the story.

One is that, during foul and stormy weather, a captain and his crew needed full command of the deck, unhindered access to the rigging and an ability to operate the ship without having to care for panicked passengers on the deck. This would allow them to best weather a ship against stormy weather for everyone's safety. Large numbers of frightened passengers milling around on the deck of a heeling ship could be more than unhelpful, and could quite likely lead to injuries or even disaster.

On the other hand, the battening down was sometimes used to imprison large numbers of competitors for the often scarce lifeboats on a ship in peril. I am afraid that it is the latter which seems to have been the case during the *Pomona* incident and which became a major contributing factor to the massive loss of life.

One must also point out that there were a significant number of emigrant vessels, their owners and masters who made a respectable profit in the trade and managed to retain their honour without resorting to brutal practises against passengers and crew and the neglect of their ships.

The deplorable attitudes and treatment of passengers in steerage continued into the next century.

Point of departure

There were many ports dotted around the British Isles that handled ships and emigrants departing for America and beyond. By and large, Liverpool catered for the highest number of emigrants departing from Ireland and England, and many other places besides. Migrants who had shuttled to Liverpool from northern Europe joined the human sea of travellers, all trying to reach various parts of the world.

Waiting for passage, thousands huddled in the back streets and in the filthy unregulated accommodation of cities like Liverpool. Victims of unscrupulous agents and middlemen, they were often fleeced by merchants and purveyors of anything emigrants might require during a voyage. Waiting for passage, they were preyed on by thugs and shipping agents who were known to oversell non-existent accommodation on ships. Smuggling passengers was rife.

It was probably not a peculiarity of the Irish alone, but a practice in every country where making a profit overrides any other consideration, however the treatment of Irish emigrants by some of their own countrymen was particularly reprehensible. These were creatures who had set out as migrants and managed to reach these ports of misery and hope but had never left. Instead, they remained and exploited their fellow countrymen who followed.

The emigrants were in a city, the size of which they had never even imagined, in a land they knew nothing of. They had the good luck to find themselves in the company of a fellow countryman who would surely help them through the process – sure it was great. Paddy proceeded to take them around the different establishments, where they could purchase the necessary food, utensils and whatever else might be required for crossing the mighty Atlantic Ocean. And, finally, to help them convert their useless money into dollars.

All the while, Paddy's divvies from the loaded prices mount, along with his commission from 'Misther Tapscott'.

Emigrant shipping lines

The newspapers were full of them. Advertisements for passage commonly covered a whole page in a newspaper. Notices were plastered in every place of congregation, advertising passage to all corners of the kingdoms and beyond. Described as a shipping line, when Tapscott advertised all of the First Class ships he was running, that didn't mean that he owned all of them. It just meant that he was an operating agent for the owners in that city, and maybe he ran one or more of his own ships, which was the case with the Tapscott Line. So the company, Tapscott, Smith & Co. of Liverpool, was known in short as the T.L. Line (thus repeating the word line).

The Tapscott Line was by far one of the biggest in the business of shipping emigrants. Despite having offices in many countries, the company would seem to have gained something of a reputation for itself, being criticised at the time, and since, for its shady dealings. Given that there were enormous amounts of emigrants travelling and equally enormous amounts of money sloshing around, it is no surprise. The company's business reputation was almost global, and was well remembered for many years.

As shipping transferred from sail to steam, governments were entering the shipping business by sponsoring the migration of labour on 'national boats'. The move began a gradual improvement in onboard conditions for migrant passengers.

Shipping agents were not 'behind the door' when it came to overselling a ship, and their advertisements not only oversold the size of a ship but also the comfort that might be expected aboard and the length of the passage. They commonly stated that the passage might only take a couple of weeks when, in fact, it normally lasted nearly a month, and even several months on occasion.

Listed at the top of Tapscott's advertisement in the *Liverpool Mercury*, the next ship to sail with emigrants for America was the *Pomona* on 24 April. The *Pomona* was clearly advertised at more than 1,000 tons in excess of her actual size, as is her sister ship, the *Plutarch* – for which there was no departure date given. The ships were declared 'First Class Packets'.

For different reasons, gauging and recording a ship's size went through a number of administrative changes through the years. Despite the difficulty one might have in understanding the different reasons and arrangements for its calculation in different countries, the point to convey must be that the larger the figure of tonnage quoted, the bigger the ship is considered to be and, therefore, more likely to be safe and well appointed. Notwithstanding a ship's size being bumped up for this reason, such an association was often misplaced.

Attributed to journalistic error during a period prior to the ship sailing, and after she had been wrecked, the *Pomona* was quoted as being within a range of sizes that more than doubled the actual size of the ship. A range of weights from 1,000 tons to 2,500 were bandied about.

Upon completion in 1856, when the *Pomona* and *Plutarch* were registered in America, their respective tons burthen were recorded as 1,181 and 1,322.

Tapscott's advert also declared that if you could get a surgeon to take passage, he could have free cabin passage.

The law allowed the ship to be boarded 24 hours before sailing, thus negating the expense of the overcharge for a night ashore prior to sailing. The law is one thing ashore; on board a ship its application is at the prerogative of the captain. It was not unusual for a captain to prevent boarding until all cargo being carried was fully stowed away and, sometimes, not until the very last moment did he allow a scramble aboard.

Aside from hundreds of emigrants packed between decks, the cargo stowed on the lower deck of the *Pomona* was described as a valuable general cargo. It consisted of fabrics such as wool and calico. It also included a large amount of iron and steel goods, crates of tin plates and measurement goods. This last description was a complicated calculation involving the ratio between the weight and size of a cargo, still used today, which might have referred to the large amount of pottery goods that were being transported to New York. Other items include ironstone bathroom sets, kitchen and toilet ware, handless cups and saucers, jugs and many more items, which can still be seen in the wreck today.

Come that Tuesday, the remaining available space on all three decks of the *Pomona* was packed out with 448 persons, passengers and crew. This final figure is in excess of earlier reports, but almost universally accepted now. The true figure could very possibly have been greater.

The *Pomona* had three decks. The lowest, situated just above the bilges, was used to store any heavy cargo which had to be evenly distributed and secured. The space was often shared with the emigrant passengers. 8 feet above this deck was the main deck, where most of the passengers were housed, and possibly some lighter cargo. 8 feet above this middle deck was the upper deck. Under the masts there were two large saloon houses, one aft of the foremast and another aft of the mainmast.

These contained all the cooking fireplaces and utensils, and a saloon where the passengers gathered to eat or drink. Access was provided from the saloons to the steerage area below. The crew's quarters and some of the ship's stores were housed forward, in the area of the fo'c'sle. Below this lay two huge piles of anchor chain in the bowls of the ship and, attached above, the ship's anchors and the boasted new design of patent winches.

In the stern adjoining the poop, there was another raised house and an aft saloon. Space on the port and starboard side provided cabin accommodation for First Class passengers, which were described as state rooms. The central area provided cooking facilities for the captain and crew. Accommodation for the captain and its officers was situated in the aft end of the ship, beneath the poop deck. Above, the ship's steering and navigating equipment was fixed to the deck in an exposed position, aft of the mizzen mast, in the stern of the ship.

It was advertised that the *Pomona* would sail from Liverpool on 24 April, but she was delayed for a further three days. In this case, it is likely that Captain Merrihew allowed passengers to board on the Tuesday evening before sailing, as it was reported that the ship cast-off on Wednesday 27 April at 5.00 a.m, with the advantage of a high tide. It was later stated, though, that departure did not occur until the later time of 1 p.m. This is contentious as the ship is unlikely to have sailed against a tide unless it had been towed well out into Liverpool Bay. High water in Liverpool on 27 April was at 07.30 a.m.

SSW

Some things in life seem certain, and others are not quite so. It is certain that a ship bound for America from the west coast of England must first exit the Irish Channel and clear the coast of Ireland. To do so, it would exit through the North Channel, to the north of Ireland, if bound for say, Canada. Alternatively, as in the case of these clipper voyages to Boston and New York, they would exit south, through the Irish Sea and the St George's Channel. This southern exit proved to be the most treacherous for a large number of sailing ships.

Having left Liverpool Bay, unless the weather is exceptionally thick or the wind contrary, the north coast of Wales will remain in view until the north-western tip of Anglesey is rounded and Holyhead passed on the port side until it finally disappears to the stern of the vessel. The most direct course, which would see a sailing ship through the gate of the St George's Channel and past its craggy sentinel known as the Tuskar Rock, was roughly SSW.

Given the vagaries of weather, it was not at all certain that this course could always be maintained. As sure as one can be, given the winds that were blowing on 27 April 1859 – fresh, ESE and later, from the less favourable direction, SSE – these should have proved favourable enough to see the ship safely round the Tuskar. Scarcely 60 miles away, without a change in tack or course direction, the ship should have made excellent time. The journey down the channel, however, was always a question of how far westward a ship would drift or 'crab' before it got to Tuskar.

It is often the case when these winds increase in intensity and back easterly during poor visibility, as they did for a time during the early morning of 28 April, that a ship can be driven dangerously more westerly than has been anticipated by its navigators. This fact has certainly been a major contributing factor in the loss of so many vessels on the extended series of shallow sandbanks that exist off the coasts of Wicklow and Wexford.

Fatally compounding the problem was poor visibility. If the watch can see the danger in time, they might be able to avoid it. In order to help mariners with this, light buoys, lighthouses and warning bells were being established in danger areas. These were a great assistance to mariners, but in order to benefit from the light you must be able to see it, and then identify which one it is. It is of no assistance to be able to see a light so poorly that you cannot identify it. It is of no assistance to be able to see a light well, but unable to recognise its meaning! And what if you don't see the light at all? Well, if there is a bell and you can hear it, it may be of help. Hearing it above the noise of a howling storm is difficult.

The optimistic outcome from a course SSW set in from the tip of Anglesey was to beat down the channel, identify the Tuskar, and then turn right for America. It is not as simple as that of course, especially if you hadn't spied the Tuskar before turning right. The measures taken in that event were, if practical, to bear off in a safe direction – usually south to east – and to reduce speed and sound the lead. When the light or lighthouse was eventually seen, or when it was estimated beyond doubt that the Tuskar Rock was cleared, a new course westward could be set.

Sounds simple, but so many times vessels missed the light, did not reach the latitude of the light or did not see the light and ended up embayed or wrecked in Wexford Bay. In order to alleviate this problem, an additional floating light was established off the north end of the Blackwater Bank. Critically, the light did not appear until 1857, only months prior to the disaster.

Although the additional light at the Blackwater Bank was of indisputable value to mariners, it initially led to unforeseen problems, similar to those encountered here. What the authorities were aspiring to was a string of guiding lights with distinguishing signals, situated at intervals along the outside of these sandbanks from Dublin to Wexford. However, 1859 was still early days and the technology of reflected light was not what it is today, and they weren't particularly reliable either. It was also made clear that mariners themselves must become familiar with reading the lights.

How it happened

Appointed by the Board of Trade (BOT) to conduct the subsequent enquiry into the loss of the *Pomona*, the nautical assessor Captain Harris was not inclined to express unqualified confidence in the evidence given by the only survivors from the disaster. Lamenting the few reliable witnesses to have survived, he reported that, 'In this case for the most part they are illiterate seamen, devoid of all responsibility, and ignorant of the lights or position of the ship. We can therefore only form our conclusions from the evidence brought before us.'

It was nevertheless accepted that the *Pomona* did not pass Holyhead until four or five o'clock on the evening of 27 April, a full 12 hours after the stated departure time for leaving Liverpool. This would seem to suggest some delay in the Mersey, or some other difficulty that may have delayed the ship that was not mentioned.

Some form of disagreement between the captain and a member of the crew arose at this time and was brought up at the enquiry, with some suggestion that the captain called him down to 'lick him'. This was an old form of punishment involving covering parts of the body with salt and allowing goats to lick it off. The goats, of course, just kept going. By then, the meaning had probably changed to that of a non-literal 'flogging' – commonly administered as a telling off or a deduction of pay. The mention of this indiscretion was dismissed and declared to be the business of a separate discipline enquiry.

The timing of the ship's progress would have been more in conformity if later testimony, putting the departure time at one o'clock, was correct.

The wind was fresh and favourable, coming from the comforting direction of SE, and all bode well for the *Pomona* to make a quick passage through the St George's Channel. It was so favourable that the captain remarked that they would reach New York in seventeen or eighteen days.

The journey down the channel continued well, and many of the passengers were reported to have been in a celebratory mood. The night wore on, and some of the passengers retired, but a large number, cheerfully inclined, had congregated together in the saloons and were singing and dancing up to a late hour, there being both a fiddler and a piper on board.

The report reminded me of my own emigrant voyage in the Irish Sea – hardly a voyage, more of a rough crossing. The tears you've caused to flow are left on the quayside, and at sixteen it's a huge adventure in search of the elusive golden opportunities abroad. The opportunities manifest in the hardest work you've ever imagined. The ship swayed and all the big men with their brawny arms and open-neck shirts crammed the bars, singing and swaying. The beer in the glasses slopped and spilled, and the crew soon gave up on the increasing level of vomit sloshing around in the toilets.

The funny thing is I didn't get seasick then, and despite all the rough days on the sea since, it just never happened. I don't know why that should be so, but I do have the greatest sympathy for those who can be prone to seasickness, for I have often seen some reduced to a terrible state of incapacity as a result.

One of the few ranking crew members to survive the sinking of the *Pomona*, the third mate Stephen Kelly, later relied on for some accuracy in recounting events, told the enquiry that a light was seen ahead at around 11 p.m. What was reported to have occurred next didn't make complete sense and led Captain Harris to his previously mentioned remark concerning the accuracy of witness statements.

Uncertain whether the light seen was that of the Tuskar or some other, the ship was hauled northward and eastward, away from the light. The manoeuvre, supposedly intended to claw the ship away from danger until daybreak, when they could confirm their position, was maintained until four o'clock in the morning. The weather then blew up considerably more violent and easterly and thickened with rain until the captain finally changed course and headed west – not for America, as he supposed, but for the coast of Ireland, only a few miles away. The ship, and the 448 souls it carried, never reached America – only twenty-four managed to scramble ashore on the east coast of Ireland.

The evidence as presented led to confusion. However, statements indicated that a light was seen and the ship turned north away from it, and eventually west – straight for the coast of Wexford. The mariners had confused their lights and their actual position. A more simple summing up of events was that the *Pomona* sailed down the channel on a course SSW until it reached the Blackwater light, confusing it with the Tuskar Rock, then turned west, directly for the coast of north Wexford.

Assembled from the testimony of the third mate, Stephen Kelly, and the coherent recollections of the few reliable survivors, Captain Harris secured an answer to the interminable question – was the lead sounded? The conclusion was that it had not. He nevertheless deduced, and reported, that the ship was 'properly found and seaworthy'.

The National Lifeboat Institution took issue with this particular aspect of the findings. Although the statutory number of lifeboats, seven, were on board the *Pomona*, they claimed this number to be totally inadequate, being insufficient by at least thirteen for the number of passengers being carried at the time. The boats in question, and others like them in widespread use, were also described as not being real lifeboats but sham lifeboats.

Any reasonable person might assume that the blame for causing the ship to become a wreck might be spread proportionally between the violence and thickening of the weather, the lack of visibility, and the negligence of the master and his crew. Interestingly, these BOT reports always endeavoured to determine the state of the weather at the time of an incident, but never to attribute it as a cause of the incident. It was almost as if a captain and crew should be capable of managing all and any weather conditions they might encounter.

After the enquiry was concluded at Wexford, the committee for the BOT concluded unequivocally 'that the ship was lost by default of the master'.

Captain Harris, a man bestowed with determined and singular views, gave the enquiry the benefit of his simmering opinion as to the cause of shipwreck.

While the Lloyd's agent, Francis Harper, a man with thirty years' experience of many wrecks, was explaining the series of events that in his view had led to the disaster –'mistaking the lights, the tide and the weather etc' – Captain Harris intervened impatiently, claiming that this '... has never been the story. No vessel is ever lost but from one of two causes – mistake of lights, or unknown set of tides.'

Frustrated by the same old excuses offered on such occasions, one presumes that Captain Harris might also have thrown in faulty compass. In this case, the accuracy of the compass was not called into question.

Stranded on the Blackwater Bank

The *Pomona* struck the Blackwater Bank about 5 miles south of the Blackwater lightvessel. The water to the outside of this bank is 40–50 metres deep and rises quite quickly to the bank in some places. However, where the ship struck, the gradient occurred over a longer distance of about 2 miles before it reached the depth on which the *Pomona* grounded. This is approximately 4 miles from Blackwater Head. Sounding the lead in such circumstances would quite likely have given sufficient notice of travelling in the wrong direction.

The crew would have been first to notice. The impact would not have been like striking a rock – a sudden and audible crash and a violent stop. Gaining on the sandbank, the ship's progress through the water would have gradually slowed through the mounting sand until she finally took the sandy bottom and lurched over to a halt. Despite that, it was reported that the *Pomona* grounded heavily. The inexperienced and those asleep below might have been slow to realise that the ship had stopped and heeled further over. Inexplicably, the cook, Michael Mulcahy, later stated that he went to his bunk for 2 hours after the ship first struck!

In hindsight, the ship's predicament at this time could be viewed in differing ways. If the ship had grounded elsewhere, on a part of the bank that was as shallow but over a wider area, she may have become totally stranded and unable to get off. If the vessel then held together, a good many of the passengers might have been rescued when the weather abated. The same result might have been achieved if the captain had decided to deploy his two large anchors and chains when she first took the ground.

The prospect of saving the ship and the passengers must have weighed heavily with Captain Merrihew at this time and the alternative of not deploying the ship's anchors and waiting for the next high tide, which might lift the ship and let her get off, must have been uppermost in his mind.

The ship was stuck fast and remained that way through the night. The passengers rushed up on deck and for a short time a wild scene of terror and confusion ensued. The captain and crew eventually 'restored something like order'. There were almost 400 passengers below, and this is the last comment made about the emigrants as a whole until their lifeless bodies began to drift ashore when the ship began to break up.

The statements are confusing on the central issue of whether or not the passengers were battened down below decks. Not addressed in any detail during the progress of the enquiry, it must have been at this point that the passengers, though not all of them, were battened down. This would have been accomplished by securing access to the central hold and the exits from steerage through the deck houses. Despite a general belief that this was indeed the case, the cook Michael Mulcahy referred to some women coming up from steerage and the third mate Stephen Kelly stated that the pumps were manned by some of the male passengers. These may have been those who had already been topside and never returned below.

Even though the shore was only about 4 miles away, and low-lying with the exception of Blackwater Head, it can normally be seen from where the ship was stuck on the bank. They were almost at the safety of the shore but could not see it or be seen from it.

The wind howled and the rain sheeted across the pitch black sky. Nothing could be done but to wait for daylight.

The wind and rain intensified. The sea bashed through the bulwarks and over the deck of the ship. With the vessel working dangerously on the bank, and the water pouring through the decks all through the night, one might have difficulty understanding the full extent of the terror experienced by those who were confined below for the next 12 hours.

Around ten o'clock the following morning, Captain Merrihew gave the order to cut away the main and the foremast. This was a procedure that was quite common in such circumstances, reducing the action of the wind on the boat and avoiding the dangers created by the leverage of the huge swaying masts. The top of the mizen was lost, but the lower part was retained in the event of the ship floating off and providing for a jury rig later, or for a possible rescue.

The measures were insufficient, however, and failed to prevent the sea from continuing to lift and pound the ship on the sandbank. Despite perceptions of moving sandbanks along this coast, this one hadn't moved for centuries, except around the bones of shipwrecks. The pounding and cracking of the hull continued. The ship was badly damaged below, and the pumps were by then permanently manned in an effort to keep the level of the water in the ship from rising.

The masts had already been cut away, High water had come and gone, but the ship failed to get off. Quite unexpectedly, but probably helped by the strength of the current over the bank during the falling tide, the ship began to break free from the clutches of the sandy bank. She then began to move over the bank and was blown easterly towards the shore and into deeper water.

Again, Captain Merrihew was presented with a difficult choice. If the large clipper continued to be blown helplessly towards the shore, it would eventually ground again and almost certainly become a total loss. But how far from the shore would it ground again? It must also have occurred to him that they would quite likely get much closer to the shore and some of the passengers, at least, might have a better chance of being saved.

A similar incident occurred the following year and, although there were fatalities, it had a more fortunate outcome.

The full-rigged *Lydia* of Liverpool struck the Blackwater Bank near the spot where the *Pomona* foundered. In this case, the ship was blown on to and then over the bank and grounded closer to the shore. A small boat put out from the stranded ship but was swamped in the surf, drowning her three occupants. The remaining nineteen aboard were saved when rockets eventually got a line to the ship.

Ten years on, again in the same place, another large American clipper, the *Electric Spark*, was run ashore. She became a total loss, but with very few casualties.

The captain's motives may have been entirely honourable when he chose to make an attempt at saving the ship, and, who knows, maybe the passengers as well. Unfortunately, his actions condemned the ship, and almost every passenger aboard, to death. What followed that day was probably the most regrettable aspect of the entire period of this disaster, and one not fondly remembered in the history of shipwreck on the coast of Wexford.

At the break of day, those on the deck of the stranded vessel could now see the shore and those who had gathered on the shore could see the large sailing ship grounded on their doorstep. Word was immediately dispatched to the lifeboat men along the shores of the county. With the relatively short distance to the shore and the land now visible, the captain reportedly ordered his crew to launch the remaining lifeboats.

Two of the seven lifeboats on board the *Pomona* had already been washed away during the storm. Three more were staved in during attempts to get them out. Some crew were lost during the operations, one of them being Michael Hayes from Wexford – so near and yet so far from his homeland. Only two remained when providence and hard work lent a hand.

There are quite a number of ballads commemorating the lore of shipwreck on the coast of Wexford. The ballad 'The *Pomona*', collected by Joseph Ranson C.C. in 1937, was published in *Songs of the Wexford Coast* and the following verse is just one that is critical of captain and crew and their action during the tragedy:

> With her rigging and her bulwarks and her steerage torn away,
> Wasn't that a dismal sight to see in Wexford Bay?
> 'Twas in that dreadful crisis her captain stood amazed;
> With cruelty he bound them down to meet their watery graves.

The stern of the *Pomona* slipped off the sandbank, and the action of a favourable tidal current and wind began to drag the remainder of the ship into deeper water. Whether or not it was because the ship was filling or that the captain was making an attempt to save her, he gave orders for the anchor(s) to be let go. It was suggested that the reason for this manoeuvre was that the anchors might bite and then hold the ship. Swinging on the anchor, she might then have come round and back onto the bank again, gaining some additional time for a rescue.

Considering the conditions, and where the remains of the ship lie today, 2.5 miles from the shore and 1.5 miles from the inside of the bank, having sunk at her final mooring, this seems to have been an over-optimistic assessment of their predicament. The distance from the bank was too great for the length of available chain, as was the strength of the easterly wind.

Testimony and reports differ as to whether one or both anchors were let go. In either event, one or both anchors ploughed into the sand, the chain(s) ran out and the ship held. As the *Pomona* had gained almost 2 miles on the shore, the depth under her hull had reduced again. She might have drawn almost 30 feet by then, which meant the same measurement existed beneath the ship. There is 60 feet over the wreck today.

It was reported that there were forty men on the pumps when the first of the two remaining lifeboats was lowered. Recounting this moment, and with surprising clarity and conviction of fact, Stephen Kelly's declaration reads 'At 1.30 p.m. a long boat got out, when the cook, steward, boatswain and three others left in her.' This boat set out from the stricken vessel with only six persons in it. It reached the shore, where it overturned in the surf, drowning four of its occupants.

The passengers' cook, Philip Mulcahy of Waterford, who had been in the job for less than a week, and the boatswain, Richard Long, made it to safety. It was later reported that the cook testified 'the ship's crew gave no thought to saving the lives of the passengers'. No clarity, however, was given to which part of the crew he meant by this – the crew in his boat, the crew that followed in the remaining lifeboat or the crew left behind?

The crew that left Wexford later on the paddle steam tug *United States* gave sworn depositions to the American Consul upon their arrival in Liverpool. The involvement and obligations to both jurisdictions, American and British, in such circumstances are interesting.

With only one remaining lifeboat, Stephen Kelly, in his sworn statement at Wexford the day after he was brought there, told what happened next: 'Myself, fifteen of the crew, and passengers, left the ship at 2.30 p.m. in the whale boat and landed at Blackwater. I expect the remainder of the crew and passengers are all drowned.' The last sentence is odd, as it is in the present tense – and those left behind were almost certainly all drowned by the time he made this statement.

Stephen Kelly gave a sworn and signed statement to the Collector of Customs, Mr Cochlan at Wexford, that was published in several newspapers verbatim. He, and the remainder of the surviving crew and passengers, travelled to Liverpool on the steam paddle tug *United States* before the official enquiry began. The fact that key witnesses could depart so easily from such a disaster without being formerly questioned by the appropriate authorities was found to be unacceptable by the subsequent enquiry, which recommended measures to be put in place in order to prevent its reoccurrence.

Now regarded as the official and accepted total, the number of survivors in this boat stands at twenty-two. Reports published in Liverpool on 4 May announced the arrival of, 'the third mate, nineteen of the crew and four passengers'.

The last moments of the big ship, and all those trapped in her, were described by Mulcahy, at the inquest of 'Mrs Paxton, Female

No.1': '... The last boat had not long got off when the vessel with all on board sank into the yawning abyss which opened its gaping jaws to swallow this multitude of poor creatures ...'

Additional testimony put the final nail in the coffin of any doubt: '... No effort was made to save the women and children, the sailors were too busy saving themselves ...'

The inquest proceedings on the body of Mrs Paxton, and the other bodies lying in the boathouse at Ballyconnigar, began on Saturday 30 April. It sat all day and reconvened after services the next day. The testimony submitted by third mate Stephen Kelly, and the passengers' cook Peter Mulcahy, was revealing in that it suggested that the departure of the two lifeboats had been under quite different circumstances and had occurred within a short time of each other.

Mulcahy's view was that, 'The captain preserved great calmness, but the chief mate seemed desirous of abandoning the vessel.' His testimony also suggested that the first boat was an organised attempt by the captain to get a boat to the shore in order to raise the alarm, and that the second was a desertion at a time when 'the bulwarks being then crowded with passengers half stupefied'.

It has always been difficult for me to attribute cowardice to any man in such circumstances, as one will remain unsure what might overcome the otherwise normal function of the mind at such a time. However, despite Mulcahy's view that the bulwarks were 'crowded with passengers', the fact that there was no further mention of thronging passengers on deck would lead one to believe that the hatches and exits from below deck had indeed not been open, or opened, in time. If they had, it would have given those below that last and maybe hopeless opportunity of saving themselves. The low body count after the initial stages of the sinking would seem to confirm this.

Such actions can only be condemned.

Mulcahy's boat was the only other lifeboat to get away from the sinking ship. It managed to get through the surf and landed safely on the beach at Ballyconnigar. The local inhabitants had already begun to assemble on the sandy pebbled shore after the first boat had overturned and spilled its occupants into the raging breakers. The locals immediately began to render assistance to the survivors who had reached the shore from the second boat. During late afternoon and evening, the remaining few bodies were extracted from the surf on the shoreline and brought to the local boat house.

This appears to have been the extent of the rescue and recovery during this initial stage of the sinking and its aftermath, and unbeknownst to the survivors and the rescuers this was the last contact with any living person from the *Pomona*. With the two from the first boat and this second group of survivors to reach the shore, it represented the total number who survived the wrecking of a large modern ship. She had been carrying 448 passengers and crew.

The small number of victims and survivors who had gained the shore in the initial stages of the aftermath were mostly members of the crew, along with some passengers who had been in cabins. Barring a few, maybe, it didn't include any of those who had been battened down.

What transpired between the crew who remained on board and those who escaped was not recalled with any certainty. The separation would suggest only two possible situations. Firstly, that it was agreed and amicable, and secondly that it wasn't. Captain Merrihew, with the first and second mate, remained on the sinking ship. As we will discover, it would appear that they might then have gone below out of the storm, perhaps in an effort to comfort the passengers and to wait with them in the hope of a rescue.

After the aftermath

It was quite common after such incidences for accusations of excessive alcohol taking by members of the crew to fly. This case was no exception. Reports appeared in several papers suggesting that the captain had been drinking with the merrymakers. Today, sharing a seat at the captain's table for food and drink is considered an honour. However, the captain and his fellow diners aboard the liner *Costa Concordia* later became the target of hatred in 2013 after the ship struck a reef and sank while they dined.

Accusations of drinking reached ridiculous proportions in the *Maine Temperance Journal* the following June, when it stated that a statement had been received by them from the mate J. P. Harwood accusing the three First Class officers of being drunk in their cabins, and that the ship sank and went down in their sleep. A surviving crewman by that name is not mentioned in any roll. The findings of the BOT enquiry did not arrive at the view that any of the crew had been drinking. They did however condemn the crew for deserting their passengers.

The weather worsened and no further bodies, dead or alive, appear to have come ashore at Ballyconnigar, or become visible around the sunken ship. The ship did not sink straight away, but was reported to have sunk within an hour of having come off the bank, damning all those below decks to a watery grave. The actual moment of the sinking was described in testimony by the ship's cook, Mulcahy, and makes frightening reading.

News of the catastrophe had spread almost faster than the coastguards could deliver it, up and down the length of the coast. The lifeboat station at Rosslare to the south, and the Collector of Customs, Mr Cochlan, asked Mr Devereaux – owner of the steam tug *Erin* based at Wexford – to tow the lifeboat the 10 miles to the wreck. They, however, could not set out in the prevailing conditions and could do nothing more than keep up steam and stand-to at Rosslare until the weather abated.

The lifeboat at Cahore was hopelessly situated 10 miles to the north and was transported to the beach at Morriscastle, nearly opposite the stranded ship. The lifeboat men launched several times but were beaten back time and again by the force of wind and the height of the breaking surf. The situation remained hopeless until the next morning, when the weather began to settle.

The number and category of the few victims that were washed ashore that day, at Ballyconnigar and beyond, was telling. The bodies of four crewmen had been tossed out of their boat earlier, and there were the bodies of cabin passengers. The bodies of the cabin passengers, Mrs Paxton and her three children, Thomas, Hanna and Lizzie, were recovered at Ballyconnigar and Ballynesker, which is a little further south.

It is sometimes the case that truth is stranger than fiction, and so it was on this day. Mrs Paxton, wife of the deep-sea captain Thomas Paxton, had died with her three children. On the very same day, her husband died aboard his ship, the *Coosawattee*, anchored in Bombay. The entire family was wiped out at sea in one day.

A regrettable action during any tragedy, it was reported that the body of Mrs Paxton was stripped of her fine clothes when it was washed ashore at Ballyconnigar. The accused was the local woman Ann Kirwan and, along with her complicit husband Thomas, she was promptly convicted of the offence at Oulart Petty Sessions. Both were sentenced to six months with hard labour.

The sentence might seem severe, but when one considers extreme cases of stealing from shipwreck, where the accused could be arrested, put before the court and hanged all on the same day, maybe the Kirwans didn't do so badly?

What struck me about this incident was what wasn't stolen from Mrs Paxton's body. Undoubtedly Ann Kirwan had committed a repugnant act, but the woman did not steal the beautiful pair of gold earrings still being worn by Mrs Paxton, nor the large sum of money and other items of value found later on her body by others. Exactly what she stole with the clothes, if anything, was not made as clear as you might expect. An issue with Mrs Paxton's gold watch arose, but it proved difficult from the reporting to determine exactly where this was first recovered, and by whom.

Stealing clothes from shipwreck victims was not unknown in Ireland, or anywhere else for that matter. In fact, the whole episode was badly reported and the fact that one newspaper was copying another verbatim did not help.

Newspapers reported that Mrs Paxton had been carrying a large amount of money on her person and the suggestion was that this was the target of the Kirwans. We don't know this to be certain, as on 4 July, long after the Kirwans were convicted, newspapers were reporting that Mrs Paxton 'was interred respectably, for a large amount of money was found on the person of Mrs Paxton'.

The ruling as reported in the 18 May 1859 edition of *Freeman's Journal*, which was copied from the *Wexford People*, is also worth noting:

> Despoiling the Dead – At the Oulart Petty Sessions held on Tuesday last, Thomas and Ann Kirwan (husband and wife) residing at Ballyconnigar, were charged and found guilty of robbing the dead body of Mrs Paxton who was drowned in the ill fated ship *Pomona*. Six months imprisonment with hard labour.

Other newspapers reported that they were found guilty of stripping the body – a noteworthy difference? It just seemed from the reports which covered the incident that some antipathy existed between the office of the constabulary and the local citizens. Wexford being Wexford, maybe this should not be unexpected.

The Petty Sessions ledger did reveal a constant stream of charges being brought against local people in Wexford at the time. Offences such as having no harness on a horse, spitting, loose car, drunkenness, trespassing, etc. seem very petty indeed.

The ledger also reveals that Anne Kierwan and her husband Thomas appeared at Oulart court on 10 May 1859 and were prosecuted by witnesses, Patrick Malone, and Constable John McNulty. The same charge appeared against husband and wife, which was withdrawn on one page and then re-entered with a slight differences.

Addressing the pair, the clerk read out the charge: 'On the 29th of April 1859, at Ballyconnigar, you had on your premises several articles of shipwreck goods – one gold watch and rings – some wearing apparel shamefully removed from the dead body of Mrs Paxton, when cast ashore at Ballyconnigar from the ship '*Pomona*' wrecked there.'

The reader will quickly note the pair were charged with having the goods, but not for removing them from Mrs Paxton's body.

They were found guilty and were sentenced to six months hard labour. Fastidious record keeping, but what the ledger had no facility to record were any statements made by the accused. Exactly what happened in the surf during those dreadful hours will have to remain a little uncertain.

The ledger also reveals that the Kirwans were not the only ones to appear at Oulart for stealing from shipwreck. On 2 June, William Shiel was charged with wrongfully carrying away or removing wreck, contrary to the provisions of the Merchant Shipping Act 1854.

The body of a gentleman of middle age was also recovered, as was that of a young man estimated to be twenty-five years of age. The middle-aged gentleman may have been Dr Kelly (first reported as Dr Fox), the ship's doctor whose body was also said to have been recovered at this time. Barely visible, a six-month-old infant was also recovered on the shore. Which of the bodies was Henry Lavery is unknown, but it was nevertheless recovered to the boathouse at Ballyconnigar, where he was waked with others.

Henry Lavery was subsequently identified by one of his family, who travelled to Wexford. His wife died three months later and the children were farmed out to relations for rearing – literally, in the case of his son John.

Henry Lavery was buried with the other victims at Killila cemetery, a very small enclosure atop a small hill immediately to the west of Blackwater village.

During those first recoveries, the body of a grey-haired elderly woman was tossed around in the surf a couple of miles further south at Curracloe. After a confrontation of sorts, some local men supposedly refused to help in recovering the body until they were paid. The body was recovered by a local constable and a gentleman.

More than a month later, identification of items found on a body that came ashore on the same popular holiday beach indicated that it was that of Captain Merrihew. He had a 1,000 dollar bank note on him – believed to have been worthless!

Reports of the inquest held by coroner Dr W. C. Ryan on the captain's body appeared on 6 June. It is held by local people that divers reported having seen the body of Captain Merrihew still bound to the mast of the sunken ship.

At first light, and after the weather moderated, the steam paddle tug *Erin*, based at Wexford port, set out for the wreck with two lifeboats in tow. I have no doubt that the rescuers knew that the *Pomona* had already sunk and harboured little hope of recovering any survivors from the wreck itself. Even so, the description of the scene they came on was pitiful. Hovering over the wreck, all that could be seen of the large ship were the remains of its mizzen mast, still attached to the submerged clipper ship. And still attached to the mast, fluttering in the breeze on a fresh morning, was an American pennant.

There were no bodies, alive or dead, to be seen anywhere. It must have been a terrible feeling for all the would-be lifesavers as they hovered over the wreck beneath them, knowing that it must have contained hundreds of passengers within its wooden walls. The tug and lifeboats returned to Wexford without saving or recovering a single creature – but entirely pleased with the execution of the boat.

Criticism of some local inhabitants appeared in almost every newspaper. In the case of Ann Kirwan and her husband, it was severe – a brute in human shape. This was a climactic comment on the actions of just a couple of local people, which reflected badly on the whole community and caused eternal regret. It is often the case that regrettable actions by just a few will sometimes overshadow greater and noble acts. On that day, and during the days and weeks that followed, a considerable number of victims and personal items were recovered by local inhabitants. These acts, and the reverence shown to the victims, can only be seen as admirable.

It seems clear that there were few on the deck of the *Pomona* when she finally sank. Those that got away were, by and large, crew and some cabin passengers. Helped by the ongoing work of the salvage divers, when the ship began to break open, the bodies flowed out of her. The victims who were not recovered during the immediate aftermath of the tragedy came ashore, or were picked up along the whole of the east and south coast of Ireland during the months to follow.

It was reported that 7,000 emigrants had already travelled that season, and the loss at Blackwater represented 5.5% per cent of them.

It was common for confusion to present in tallies after the loss of an emigrant vessel. Record keeping was not always accurate, and overselling accommodation was prevalent, as were stowaways. This case was no exception. Once again, many newspapers just reprinted what had gone before in others.

The *Liverpool Mercury* of 3 May 1859 published an account of the disaster, along with a passenger list. They also listed the names of the three passengers and twenty crew that made up the survivors. One of the surviving crew was named, John Meehan – passengers' cook. James Mulcahy, also reported to have been the ship's cook, was not listed here.

The passengers

The *Pomona* had 393 passengers on board when she left Liverpool, including sixteen married males and twenty-six married females, 148 single males and 164 single females, thirty-two children between the ages of one and twelve and seven infants.

When one totals the number passengers, 393, with the reported number of crew on the *Pomona*, forty-four, the figure amounts to 437.

The enquiry held by Arthur Walker JP, John Walker JP, and the nautical assessor for the BOT, Captain Harris, at Wexford on 7–9 May delivered the totals: 400 emigrants, forty-four crew and four others (possibly stowaways).

The undisputed figure of twenty-four survivors puts the total number of victims at 424. The discrepancies in themselves are not large, but where there is confusion, doubt will remain.

Despite it having been the worst emigrant shipwreck disaster on the coast of Ireland, and all the hullabaloo it created in Wexford – with depositions, inquests, the BOT enquiry, extensive salvage, shock and horror at the all the bodies washing ashore and the accusations of their mistreatment – the Harbour Commissioners for Wexford made absolutely no reference to it in their minutes. It was an incredible event but it did not create an obstruction to the harbour. There was nevertheless an issue concerning the lights within their jurisdiction, and, perhaps, a common sympathy.

But no, the minutes read as if the commissioners had been exclusively preoccupied by the day-to-day running of the harbour, pilots' expenses, the obsession with charges for ballast and their evasion, and so on. Neither was there a mention of any donation made to the lifeboat, or for the burial of the victims. It appears as if they had just hoped all mention of the disaster would go away.

Wreck-hunting and the law

As I have already admitted, our small band of diving enthusiasts can only be described as wreck-hunters. Despite the fact that this description has a popular image, we do not search for forgotten shipwrecks willy-nilly, or for brass mementos or profit. We chase lost and forgotten history and 'the story'.

These days, our hunting is determined by a number of factors. Given that all of our group, bar one – I being retired from the nasty habit – have to work for a living, it is a part-time hobby. Our activities are also regulated by the vagaries of the weather, available finance and the laws of the land. Much as we would love to have a Ballard or Odyssey-like budget, ours remains a comparative shoe string.

Given our age profile, the type of diving that can be comfortably accomplished now is well below the 50 metre range. This keeps us, by and large, in the more shallow inshore areas and gaining ground on the bus pass. What we have going for us is well-grounded enthusiasm, an intelligent approach to research and survey work and a deep interest in maritime history.

The notion of hunting for shipwrecks seems exciting and, in practice, it is. However, the practice is restricted by legislation, most of which is welcome. The implementation and tailoring of it suffers from attitudes and the restricted funds available to professional archaeologists, who are constrained by ever-diminishing departmental budgets. There are few votes in archaeology, which makes it difficult to compete for a share of the national cake – taxpayers' money. It has become less troublesome to adopt the position that if something cannot be searched for, recovered and or preserved according to 'best practice', it is best left where it is.

The laws in Ireland differ considerably from those of our nearest neighbours, the UK, and the difference continues to be a source of heated discussion and argument between those active in the jurisdictions.

The legitimate view taken by the professionals is that when artefacts are removed from the seabed without record, the scene of a shipwreck and their context is lost forever. This is undoubtedly true. The alternative, which is also true, but denounced, is that a shipwreck will continue to decay and crumble in its underwater environment until its contextual value is almost completely obliterated. It is also true that the contextual value of the varying aspects of a ship's construction, and the artefacts associated with it, may in some cases have already been de-contextualised by the original violence of the wrecking. This could include such factors as a torpedo, a reef of rocks, or simply years of abrasion, trawling and previous professional salvage. There is also the argument centred on the age of a wreck, and the archaeological value that might be retrieved from shipwrecks of, say, the Victorian period, or after is questionable. The history of ships, areas of shipbuilding, and the maritime commerce of this period and onward is so well preserved and documented in many cases that preservation's for preservation's sake may be unwarranted.

To my mind, discovery now is better than the uncertainty of possibly no discovery in the future. There are no waves of criticism breaking over the operations of Odyssey Marine for instance. The USA seems to handle any amount of historical discoveries quite efficiently. Is it just a question of money?

How it works in Ireland at present is as follows. The over-arching '100-year-old rule' means that any shipwreck – not the age of the ship – that is 100 years old is protected and a licence must be obtained if you wish to dive to it. Chronological exceptions are made in the case of certain vessels such as the *Lusitania* and the First World War German submarine *UC42*, both of which were wrecked off Cork and deemed to warrant an exclusion or protection order, for whatever reasons.

Divers and researchers like our own little group, or even a diving club, will first identify a shipwreck of interest. We then apply for a licence to use detection equipment to search for it. Having found something, we must then apply for a licence to dive and look at it. In order to identify or date the wreck, we might recover a piece of pottery or something else than can be dated – this too needs a separate licence, and if it's done without permission you must explain why. These licences may then be granted on an annual basis.

Any intention to excavate the wreck – well you can whistle for that one. This requires a considerable amount of consultation with the authorities and a pile of paperwork. It can also be prohibitively expensive. Divers are discouraged from retrieving artefacts, any that do break the surface must be handed over to the appropriate authorities.

In other words, you may, after a very lengthy and expensive process, have discovered a very important shipwreck or artefacts but be entitled to nothing. The position of professional archaeologists is understandable and often final. However, a balance in everything is desirable, and can often be progressive and rewarding.

Notwithstanding all of the above, I understand that the underwater archaeological unit attached to the department of Arts, Heritage and the Gaeltacht is chronically understaffed and under-financed. Despite this, our own small group has been fortunate to have received excellent advice and guidance from this unit. I would, nevertheless, feel comfortable arguing that more should be done to encourage amateur wreck-hunting. When found and recorded, considerable leeway should be given to the mapping and recovery of some artefacts from some shipwrecks for local display. Finding suitable areas of display may of course present some difficulty, but this is not an insurmountable issue.

Beachcombers or wreckers?

Each tradesman smuggled or dealt in smuggled goods; each public-house was supported by smugglers … each country gentleman … dabbled a little in the interesting traffic; almost every magistrate shared in the proceeds or partook of the commodities.

G. P. R. James.

It was 2013 and spirits were flagging. Our search for the *Comte de Belgioioso* had anchored us for years. Almost all the areas of interest had been explored and we were finally coming to the cloudy end of the barrel. Despite an unwillingness to submit, it was time to start considering a new target. Preferably, it would be one of historic interest, in easy reach, and a shipwreck that had not been previously discovered.

A notice inviting tenders for the salvage of the wreck of the *Pomona* was advertised and posted in Liverpool. The salvors arrived at the site of the shipwreck surprisingly quickly, within a fortnight of it going down. The men were led by the diver Richard Blower and, according to a statement made by him, he arrived at the wreck 'on board a steamer sent by the United States Steamboat Company to look after the wreck of the *Pomona*'. Blower was an experienced and able diver and was assisted by Joseph Rodrigeaux. They travelled from Liverpool to the wreck by tug, carrying all their diving apparatus and towing two barges.

Blower's actual purpose at the wreck is confusing. Reported to have been engaged by the United States Steam Tug Company (not, it is important to note, '... Steamboat Company'), he was the first diver into the wreck and proceeded to recover crates of goods from inside of it. It remains unclear what, and how much, cargo Blower actually retrieved. The first dives to the wreck attracted controversy after there was disrespectful treatment of the trapped bodies inside the wreck in various stages of decomposition. In order for the divers to penetrate the wreck, the closely packed bodies were removed, some in terrible condition, and were then allowed to float around the bay.

During the enquiry, Blower was asked about the hatches and access to below decks. He described how the hatches had no fastenings on and that there was free access to below. He quickly added that when a ship goes down, the pressure will build up inside the ship and can blow off any closed hatches. Whether he knew it or not, he was assisting in the implication that the hatches could have been open before the ship sank, thus relieving the owners of blame for the deaths of the passengers – essentially murder. Who was to know different?

Such an assumption, of course, is ridiculous. This was no sudden sinking! There is no possible reason why all of the passengers should stay below decks, in a ship that was about to sink, while all of the doors and hatchways were open! They weren't on deck at the time of sinking because they couldn't get there. It was their night to remember.

After some discussion among officials, arrangements were made for the provision of coffins and a diligent recovery of the bodies got under way. So expeditiously, in fact, that the head of a very tall male corpse was removed in order to fit it into one of the boxes! Despite the terrible scenes that faced the helmet divers, the salvage work continued and a considerable amount of the cargo was retrieved and shipped to Liverpool, where it was later auctioned.

Early consideration was given by the owners to a proposal to raise the wreck but the idea was abandoned after mature consideration. The wreck of the *Pomona* was later auctioned and sold.

As is quite often the case, we were not going to be the first divers on the wreck. There was, though, a lot to be discovered from the wreck of the *Pomona*.

Just a small wall pier overlooked by a nice old pub, Cahore had been a favourite seaside holiday place with my own family for many years. When we stayed there, it was impossible not to read about or see references to shipwrecks in the local pubs around, such as in the aptly named Windjammer. The pub overlooking the pier, the Strand Inn, is a favourite and has quite lot of news articles and photos to browse, including details of the *Pomona* tragedy.

The gravity of this incident has been underrated until very recent times, when a large inscribed stone was erected in the village of Blackwater to commemorate a disaster that was responsible for the largest loss of life from a single shipwreck on the coast of Ireland.

Cahore's jutting dog-leg pier is one of two halves. The area in the lea of the cliffs to the south, and tucked between rock features that extend from the shore into sea, had always been a haven for local fishing boats.

A short stone pier was eventually constructed in the early Famine Years, and then added to about sixty years later. The pier was used to land and load coal, lime, salt, fish and sundries. This had previously been done at local beaches all along the adjacent coastline. The smacks and early coasting steamers have long since disappeared and, being an exposed short-stay harbour – more just a pier now – it is only used by the occasional fishing boat. It is, nevertheless, extremely popular in the summer time with holidaymakers and their pleasure craft. It also provides a platform for swimmers, and small children fishing for crabs.

Some early enquiries along the coastline in the vicinity of the *Pomona* disaster led me to the nearby Roman Catholic church in

Ballygarret, where local people believed that the pews in the church were constructed from the timbers of the *Pomona*. The practise of recycling bits of shipwrecks from around the coast of Ireland was common and, in some places, still prevalent.

This kind of recycling has always occured, even in more modern times. For example the MV *Ranga*, wrecked at Dingle, County Kerry, in 1982, gave up equipment and brass fittings to many of the local people.

An interesting example I am more familiar with is the deck timbers recovered from the wreck of the Norwegian motor vessel *Bolivar* when she wrecked on the Kish Bank off Dublin in March 1947. During what was described as the worst winter on record, the timber was brought ashore by Mr Homan of White Cottage on Killiney Strand, and, according to himself, this was used in the re-flooring of nearby Shanganagh Castle, which later became an open prison. A cargo of hides went into the repairing of footwear and making lady's handbags for the local inhabitants from Dublin to Wicklow. The brass portholes adorn divers' homes throughout Dublin, and the ship's bell found a home in one of the most prestigious boat clubs in Ireland – the National Yacht Club, Dun Laoghaire. This demonstrates how there is always a home for such artefacts.

The timbers in Ballygarret church are certainly ship's timbers, and I believe they are from the wreck of the *Irrawady* (wrecked 1856), which wrecked a bit closer to Cahore.

As with the case of the unfortunate woman and her husband at Blackwater, timbers, ship's fittings and valuables from shipwrecks were always seen as fair game, particularly in remote and sparsely populated areas all around the coasts of Great Britain and Ireland. They are, in essence, no different than the *Pomona*'s anchors, which were later recovered by local fishermen and displayed in Kilmore Quay village. Although flotsam and jetsam was, and still is, seen as fair game, the law remains quite specific on the matter – the stuff belongs to someone! This could be the owner of the ship, owner of the cargo or the owner of the land onto which it has been washed up. This does not take away from the fact that a person(s) can become eligible to claim for recompense if they have assisted in the recovery and saving of any such items.

Outcomes to claims under maritime law can vary widely.

Tenants and farmers used the fruits of their beach combing to erect shelters for animals and to build barns and homes. Examine door frames, sills, and rafters in any old house still standing within a mile of the coast and you are liable to find shipwreck timbers. Part of the Wooden House restaurant pub in Kilmore Quay was a total add-on, with the deck house from the nearby wreck of the *Neptune* in 1860 being used. To be true to balance, I must add that there was a wreck sale in this instance, and I believe real money changed hands.

There is an important point to be made here nevertheless. The conditions that prevailed among the rural populations around Britain and Ireland in the nineteenth century, not only prior to these middle years but well after, were still harsh. Many had to scrape an existence from what surrounded them, and they often found themselves in conflict with landlords and agents of the Crown. Many of them were referred to as wreckers and were lumped in with smugglers in the same breath. The two were sometimes the same but, more commonly not.

Quite unjustifiably, the description smuggler has been inextricably bound with that other coastal occupation – that of wrecking. The term wrecker, and the men and women who may have carried out the practise of wrecking ships, continues to be confused and intertwined with that of smuggler. The term suggests that they were people who might have purposefully set out to wreck ships, when it actually referred to any of the people who descended on the wreck of a ship and helped themselves to whatever they could. It might also seem to be true that their deprivations were, on occasions, at the expense of any potential survivors. I contend that such acts, if they occurred at all, occurred in a very small number of cases.

More commonly however, the men and women who descended on the scene of a shipwreck were local and did all in their power to assist any survivors. Those who were lucky to survive a shipwreck had usually come ashore before any of the valuable cargo or flotsam from the ill-fated vessel. After initial attempts at rescue, and any care that could be given to survivors, the rescuers may have helped themselves to whatever cargo and valuable bits of timber that were washed on shore.

Unfortunately, a witness can come on a situation at the wrong moment and, even then, newspapers had to sell and paper doesn't refuse ink. One doesn't have to go far along the coast of Wexford to discover old accusations made about the misconduct of local inhabitants at the scene of a shipwreck. These were later withdrawn when discovered to be false.

Ordinarily, the act of plundering a vessel wrecked on or near the shoreline, where bodies and valuables came ashore, had nothing to do with the practise of smuggling and remains a popular coastal occupation to this day. In 2007, the large container ship *Napoli* wrecked on the coast of Devon. Its cargo was looted for days by local people, and many others who came from much further afield for free pickings. Such cases are not common today, but neither is this an isolated case.

To define wrecking as the act of taking valuables from a wreck that has foundered near or close to shore seems fair and accurate. It is, nevertheless, a somewhat different interpretation to that of an older and misconceived understanding of the term, and a view still held by many, which posits that wrecking is the deliberate attempt to lure a ship onto a dangerous coastline, where it might become disabled or wrecked.

Such views became entrenched in areas, particularly where outside law – uninvited agents of authority – was unwelcome.

Wrecking may have occurred in this way and may, on some occasions, have been caused by the very same coastal folk or smugglers. But it did not occur in any organised way again, being more a situation of opportunism. Nor did it occur to any significant degree in this form around the coast of Ireland. Despite this, the view was held in 1783 that mariners and merchants needed further protection from the depravations of these types of landsmen. Included among additional measures was the following reaffirmation of the existing laws: 'It was a capital offence to put out any false lights with intention to bring any ship or vessel into danger.'

The practise of smugglers signalling to a brig or schooner hove-to offshore should not be confused with any otherwise serious attempt at wrecking. The result of the one would jeopardise the future of the other.

There had been so much reported on the *Pomona* tragedy that I had always assumed its remains would have been long since rediscovered by local divers. It seemed to me that such a great tragedy would obviously have drawn the curiosity of divers in modern times, particularly those divers that resided in the surrounding counties.

At first it seemed I was correct and we soon learned of a local group who were very active in the area. After we made enquiries and met up, it transpired that these local divers did spend a lot of time looking for the *Pomona*, but had found another wreck in the process – the steel coaster *Clara*. Lost in 1933, she had never been dived by modern divers, meaning that there was still lots of brass goodies on her. The lads just got stuck in and never got around to locating the remains of the *Pomona*. Their interest in an old wooden wreck would seem to have just waned after that.

A project with encouraging possibilities was beginning to emerge. We knew the wreck was close to the shore and had not been relocated in modern times. It was found many times by fishermen when their gear caught in it, but apparently they didn't know what it was. One exception might be the plate with the ship's name *Pomona*, held in the Wexford County Archives. There are several old nets and pots stuck in the wreck today. Two anchors were recovered by trawlers many years earlier and are believed to have been those deployed by the *Pomona*.

Fishermen are one of the first points of contact when researching the whereabouts of a wreck. When their old snag charts are cross-referenced with seabed surveys such as those by Infomar, the results can be quite surprising.

The fishermen's two anchors are certainly of the period and both were mounted in the fishing village of Kilmore Quay. The larger of the two was moved to the museum in Gorey in recent years.

The American

Patrick Karnahan lives in California. He is a musician and songwriter with the Black Irish Band. For a bit of diversion, he fights forest fires – huge ones in the mountains. Just as in our story, the chances of him and I ever crossing paths were miniscule. In fact, I still haven't met the man, but there's still time.

Being an American vessel, there were considerable connections between that country and the *Pomona*, its crew, agents and divers, and the victims of the tragedy. Most have already been alluded to. But another unusual, and pleasantly surprising, connection later emerged.

While surfing the internet, I discovered a modern ballad dedicated to the loss of the *Pomona* and its victims. It is performed by the musician Patrick Karnahan and the Black Irish Band. The piece is accompanied by this brief account, written by a fellow musician of Patrick's, who describes how the Californian songwriter had come to learn of the incident:

'The 'Wreck of the *Pomona*' was inspired when Patrick visited a museum in Gorey, County Wexford. On the third floor of the old castle museum there is a bow figure on the wall. It is an Indian maiden with a food basket (*Pomona*). Alone, Patrick viewed the figure, as lightening flashed about the room. He had read about all the Irish emigrants who died tragically. He walked out shaken and very disturbed. After, he ended up on a mountaintop at sunset, overlooking the Irish landscape, where he wrote the ballad. Patrick has always believed that some songs just have to be written, people's lost voices must be heard, and they must not be forgotten!

One can see how the figure was misinterpreted, but the Indian figurehead is more probably meant to represent Pomona, the mythical Goddess of Plenty.

After reading, listening, and looking at the performance, I was hooked. The performance can be viewed here – https://www.youtube.com.

The other members of our team were already convinced that this was a shipwreck worth having a go at, if only to preserve the story, and we were sure we might also be able to satisfy a musician in a far-off land and place the ship firmly back in the memory and lore of the Wexford people.

My next step was to make contact with Patrick. The reason for this was to seek permission to use his ballad and video. What I had in mind was that, at some point, the museum at which he first learned of the *Pomona* disaster might, along with some images and underwater footage, be able to place it on a loop at the exhibition. Quite unselfishly, he agreed without any reservation or any request for royalty payments.

We are still in contact and I keep him up to date with developments. He remains interested in the progress of our findings and this story.

The research began in earnest during late summer 2013. Fortunately, there was quite a lot written and recorded about the incident. The tragedy occurred recently enough to be covered extensively in a wide range of newspapers in several countries, including local Wexford papers. There is also a wide range of written material available on the history of the ship, its construction and its owners. Until recently, builders' drawings of the *Pomona* and her sister ships were for sale on the internet from an auction house in the USA.

As divers in search of the wreck, the most valuable material was a detailed description of its position submitted to the *Wexford Independent* by those aboard the tug *Erin*. Also published was 'A Notice to Mariners' by the Ballast Office in Dublin, describing the position of a buoy placed on the wreck, along with the bearings giving its exact position. All in all, the information was deliciously precise and proved to be accurate. It's not often the ducks line up so conveniently.

The wreck buoy notice gave three bearings recorded to geographical positions on the coast of Wexford, and one to the contentious Blackwater lightship. The lightship was later withdrawn, so its position had to be rediscovered. The bearings were all plotted on a modern hydrographic chart to produce the last known position of the *Pomona*.

With a good estimated position in the cocked hat, the next step was to get a boat there and survey the surrounding seabed in that area. We normally operate from two boats. One is a RIB, used mainly for diving, and the other is a twenty-six-foot Sea Ray. This is a covered boat which is probably more comfortable in Florida, but is nevertheless a more suitable platform for operating the electronic survey equipment than the RIB.

Unfortunately, and probably one of the reasons why this wreck has remained undiscovered for so long, its position has remained difficult to get to. Not too far from the shoreline, it lies almost midway between the only two decent launching and departure positions – one at Arklow and the other at Wexford port, nearby Rosslare – a distance of about 40 miles. This makes any journey to the wreck a round trip of 40 miles.

Never ideal, but a much closer position to launch and work from is the slip and pier at Cahore. However, as we would only discover later, due to recent storms this had silted up and would not take our survey boat except just at the top of the tide – for about two pints.

Keith and I travelled on the initial recky to Wexford. I made the 2-hour journey from Dublin to Arklow on the Friday afternoon by boat and met Keith, who had driven. We over-nighted in the Arklow Bay Hotel.

I always harboured an impatient disregard for the sniffing of the cork ritual, believing that the practise of tasting the wine, and sniffing the cork, was just for show – bolstered by the fact that I had never seen anyone return a bottle of wine. We had dinner in the hotel restaurant that night, and my buddy Keith sent back not one but two bottles, one after the other – deservedly. My lesson in sniffing rotten wine complete, we ordered a third. This little rascal didn't escape, and cried out for company when it began to expire.

Refuelled, we left the marina and headed down the river not too early the following morning. It took about an hour to get to the estimated position. We had prepared a plotted grid chart covering approximately 1 square mile, with the estimated position of the wreck being at its centre. Towing our side scan, we covered the easterly half in jig time, resulting in some small but unconvincing shows. The weather deteriorated and we returned to Arklow.

We packed away the gear, had a coffee and Keith returned to Dublin by boat. I left by car and we met up again, a couple of hours later, at Dun Laoghaire. We had failed to locate the wreck but we had another half of the grid left to survey.

Infomar, an organisation representing a collaboration between the Marine Institute of Ireland and the Geological Survey Office of Ireland, have been surveying and mapping the seabed around Ireland in recent years, producing the most fascinating cutting-edge surveys. Most of their survey results are online and available to the general public. It is a facility we had been monitoring, but there were certain areas of the coast that had not yet been completed. Our area was indicated as being one of these but, nevertheless, we decided to ask. Bingo – they had just completed it and kindly sent us a copy of their results.

Dragging the cursor over the digitised copy the sonar survey, the lat/lon figures reeled before finally coming to rest at our estimated position – bang on! There it was. Almost exactly on the position that was announced in the Notice to Mariners 154 years earlier – the anomaly was almost clearly visible. I say almost as, at first, it would not have been immediately noticeable to just anyone. You would have to be looking for something in that precise area. It was, however, unmistakeable to us. It was wreckage on the seabed.

With the ever so slightly adjusted position under our belt, we made a return visit to Arklow and then on to Blackwater, just as before – but without the wine tasting this time. There was no need to deploy any of the survey equipment; the sonar on the boat indicated an anomaly straight away. The wreck was inside the half square mile not yet surveyed.

Given the amount of wreckage that makes up the site, it is not a boast to claim that we almost certainly would have located it on the next run.

It was mid-September when we eventually returned to Arklow. Refuelled and all planned up to make our first dive, we left the following morning. We intended to make two dives – one in the morning at the slack on High water, and a second on Low water slack. We were carrying eight diving cylinders and five people, not to mention all of the lead and equipment. Four divers and a charming new ginger-haired friend, David, a neighbour and friend of Keith, made up the team. There was a lot to carry for 20 miles in the sun-loving Sea Ray, so we split up. Two went by car with some diving cylinders to Cahore, and the remainder went by sea with the remaining equipment. We would pick up the two boys and additional equipment on the way at Cahore and continue with the full load the shorter distance to the site.

We duly arrived at Cahore and prepared to pick up the remaining members of the team. This was not as easy as first thought. Storms had deposited sand on the seabed near the pier and made coming alongside very uncomfortable – negative clearance! After a few expletives and some dodgy manoeuvring up to the pier, we managed to get the boys on and beat a hasty retreat with a shiny propeller. We were four divers and one ginger cox'n. I dived with the well-known diver JP and Keith dived with another of the group, Philip de Leon. The volunteer boatman, by then known only as Ginger, had two conditions of service – a swim in the noddy over the wreck site, and a pint in the Strand Bar back in Cahore. He had company for one of them. It came to our attention that, as the site is obviously a grave for some unknown number of victims, there is a question of reverence here – this was duly noted.

The visibility in the water was terrible, and very little was seen by our eyes. John had brought a GoPro camera, and I swore it recorded a different dive than the one we had actually been on! What it was able show in very bad conditions was amazing when compared to what I had remembered seeing with our eyes.

We returned to Arklow, dropping off the boys for their pint in the Strand Bar en route. Coming alongside proved just as tricky the second time, the boat unexpectedly bouncing the bottom. Nudging up as close as we dared, the boys had to jump off the bowsprit on to the harbour wall. They would sup up and return by car to Arklow. They did and, what do you know, they were late.

With lunch behind us, we returned to Blackwater to make our second dive. Paired up as before, the visibility somewhat improved. We were able to make out the patent winches and chain haws pipes. We could also make out remains of the cargo of iron and a scattered variety of pottery.

Recording its position, we removed a piece for identification. It was a white glazed bowl, 14 inches in diameter. Printed on the base was 'Imperial Ironstone China – John Alcock'. Stamped on the base was 'Ironstone China – John Alcock, Cobridge'. It was part of a wash stand set, and we dated it to within ten years of the ship going down.

A considerable amount of timbers was also showing on the wreck and in the sand. There was a 2-metre-high mound, approximately in the middle of the wreck, which is topped with nets. I came away from the site under the impression that despite some marvellously intact sections of the wreck, it had suffered extreme pulling at, even to the point that there is some evidence of explosives being used on it at some point.

Once more we returned to Arklow and left the boat on the marina, making the rest of our return journey to Dublin by car. We had found the wreck, identified it, and recorded it on film – a good day's work.

A week or so later, we assembled some of our research material and with the large bowl, and an account of the dive and our findings, we submitted them to the Department of Arts, Heritage and the Gaeltacht. This, incidentally, is another requirement that comes with the granting of a licence.

In 2014, we applied to the department again for a licence to revisit the wreck, and to do a camera survey of the wreck. This was granted and we returned to the site in early summer. The cause of our delayed return was the extraordinary conditions that existed in the Irish Sea earlier in the year. It would not be overstating to say that, for months, clarity in the water was zero. Comments by those living near, on or from the sea were all similar – they had never seen such a prolonged spell of bad water and were at a loss to understand it, as were we.

Eventually it cleared, and we returned once more to Arklow in *Fourpence*, our covered Sea Ray.

You might well ask what's in a name?

The names given to boats never cease to amaze me. Having access to thousands of names in my database of shipwrecks, you can clearly see a pattern to the choices made over centuries. These range from contemporary monarchs, a member or members of a family, saints, historical figures of note, geographical features, mythical figures, and terms of endearment or endeavour. *Mary and George*, *The Brothers*, *John and Joseph*, *Sir Charles Napier*, *Dublin Bay*, *Neptune and Jupiter*, *Lovely Jane*, *Le Nouveau Destin*, to name just a view.

Despite being a diminutive monetary sum, *Fourpence*, the boat's name, was derived by two young men in the employ of financial giants.

In more modern times, as the numbers of pleasure boats have risen, the names of boats have become less significant and more light-hearted, but no less interesting. If one takes a walk around a marina, it is easy to see that the owners of all the bobbing sirens have christened their adventures with cryptic, but not so hard to interpret, meanings. Most are female names, many a sop to the missus for spending so much on a big boy's toy, and many others are an expression of adventure and escape. Pop stars have become popular, Elvis to name one. I had to double-take when I spied *Marina Lou*, the marina's floating toilet. Behind every name lies an interesting little story.

The topic of names brings to mind the day some friends and I were fishing over the wreck of the *Queen Victoria*, at the Bailey, Howth.

We had been diving on the wreck earlier in the week and left a buoy on it. When we returned to fish over it at the weekend in my half-decker *Venture I* (there was also a *Venture II*, followed by a couple more unnamed ones) we hauled up on the buoy and tied up to the wreck. As the Bailey is a notable landfall for the bay's yachters as they pass from their clubhouses in Dun Laoghaire over to Howth, and from Howth to Dun Laoghaire for lunch at the weekends, we would seem to have been in their way on this particular occasion, possibly necessitating a minor adjustment to their course.

A skipper on one of the yachts radioed the coastguard to announce, 'This is *Penny Wise*, *Penny Wise*,' alerting them of his observation that there seemed to have been a boat disabled and in distress at the Bailey. Sounding confused, the alert skipper further added, 'They seem to be fishing!'

I just couldn't resist and picked up my own handset to notify the coastguard of the situation. 'This is *Pound Foolish, Pound Foolish*, we are that boat fishing at the Bailey, but we are not in any trouble. Over.'

Our rib is named *Ouzel* – You'll have to work it out yourself!

To conclude our story

The next visit to Arklow went off without incident. We operated the same scenario of refuelling and proceeded onward to Blackwater the following day. The visibility this time was far better and we were able to make an updated report on the condition of the wreck. The conditions were perfect – the weather was fine and tides easy. You could comfortably dive the wreck on an extended slack water, and just surface wherever you liked. Ginger was once again on station, keeping one eye out for us to surface and the other on opening time.

The dive was flawless except for one thing. During my ascent, an old chestnut dropped out of the tree. Some years ago, I hurt my ear quite badly while diving in the Red Sea, and it took some time before I could dive again. Since then, my ears had a habit of clearing at different times, and, in the case of the bad one, sometimes with great difficulty. The result was usually disorientation and then a feeling of nausea. In the extreme, such as at Blackwater that day, when Ginger arrived to pick me up, he and the boat seemed almost vertical. It's just a case of waiting for things to normalise, or closing your eyes and holding your hand out. Future diving might be like eating the elephant – a bit at a time.

We wrapped up, travelled back to Arklow in lovely sunshine, swapped individual observations of the dive – nothing compares. The few pints afterwards, however, do come close.

It is the intention of the group to apply for a licence once more in order to make another couple of dives on the wreck of the *Pomona*. Our hope is to verify some questions about anchors, whether there was one or two, the extent of the cargo remaining, how much hull structure is still intact, and so on.

Until then, adieu.

P.S. I have since had the pleasure of meeting Patrick Karnahan, during his recent return to Ireland.

The Drowning Command

In terms of shipwrecks, vessels that were sunk by an act of aggression during the First World War, or any war for that matter, fall into just one single, and very separate, category of loss. There is no need to examine any complicated coincidence of weather, the durability of a ship's construction or the possibility of a negligent crew. There is only one indisputable cause – an attack by man against a ship and those who happen to be on board her at the time, with the sole purpose of sinking it.

The repeated assumptions that America declared war on Germany during the First World War as a result of her citizens and ships being attacked by Germany's U-boats – for example the *Lusitania* incident – remain misguided. The suggestion that the sinking of the *Lusitania* was a Machiavellian plot contrived by the British authorities is a separate and equally mistaken suggestion. In terms of conflict and war, and the naïve belief that a set of rules governing the rules of engagement will prevent the use of all measures necessary to achieve victory, or the fact that the *Lusitania* was carrying arms, are neither here nor there. The U-boats were at first restrained in this regard as a result of American diplomatic protests lodged against Germany for such attacks, and against Britain for its blockading of Germany. America was not minded to enter the war at this earlier time, and when she finally did it was for different reasons.

This has not been the first or the last time that war was has been pursued for reasons that were not accurately recorded. We have since become much more aware of this type of media management, which has reached new heights of sophistication today.

American citizens died crossing the Atlantic when their ships were attacked by U-boats both before and after the *Lusitania* incident in 1915. Despite the nature of this inflammatory incident, America did not enter the war until a full two years later. America was conscious of the fact that at that time it was still early in the conflict, and Britain could still be victorious. And besides, orders for all kinds of war material were doing very well, thank you. Politicians were also well aware that political opinion in America had not yet reached a point where it would abide sending troops to die in Europe over a squabble between empires.

For more pragmatic reasons, America was just not ready – militarily, industrially or morally – for an open-ended war with unknown ramifications in Europe.

Last, and probably not least, the ground rules had not yet been agreed for its prosecution and conclusion – who would pay for what and who would get what? Repayments for the debts accumulated by Britain for the prosecution of this war are still being made.

By 1917, the position had changed dramatically. The war had dragged on another two years and it had become apparent that Germany, though it might not achieve a total victory over France, might agree a favourable armistice. On the other hand, her war industries were making impressive technological advances with submarines and had put in place an advanced programme of mass production. Given more time, Germany might ultimately have succeeded in overwhelming the Allies.

What German naval commanders had not allowed for was the extent of political interference on behalf of manufacturers in the production of naval armaments. These were often in conflict with requests by naval commanders and stymied the completion of more suitable vessels and armaments.

A German invasion of Britain might never have been possible or desirable at the time, but victory in France or a favourable armistice would mean the embargo and the blockade of Germany's mercantile and still intact naval High Seas fleets would have come to an end. The results might have meant new alliances and a European power emboldened by success. Unbridled manufacture of advanced weaponry would have followed. This presented considerable possibilities for expansionist policies. A hundred years later, one might be tempted to assume little has changed.

A year of living dangerously

The battle which took place around the British Isles between the Allies and Germany's U-boats, between January 1917 and the spring of 1918, decided in great part the outcome of the First World War. The situation was one of unparalleled danger, the like of which would not present itself again until the Battle of Britain during the Second World War. Britain was already experiencing serious difficulties with supplies and war material, and it was Germany's intention to choke off all shipping traffic to Britain before America could deploy its enormous resources.

Germany's second campaign of unrestricted submarine warfare was announced in February 1917 but had already begun weeks earlier. The policy of unrestricted warfare was not confined to the sea, but also extended to the use of gas and biological warfare, for which they were prosecuted when the war had ended. These acts were admitted to during the war crimes hearings that took place in the International Court of Justice in The Hague. Effectively, Germany was attempting to leapfrog Britain's blockade with her own blockade of Britain, while at the same time planning to over-run the Allies in France. Ships and supplies were not only reaching Britain from her dominions and America – almost unrecorded is the large part Ireland played in keeping Britain supplied. The reasons for this omission might seem to have been deliberate but, simply, Ireland was not considered a separate country to Britain – it was Britain. One doesn't hear of how coal from Wales, timber from Scotland or grain from Kent saved the war. Same goes for Ireland.

America eventually began to roll out her war machine, and in a stroke all German hope of achieving unfettered access to the Atlantic was dashed. Just as in the Second World War years later, America's mobilisation, and the might of the military machine which she brought to bear, became massive and proved unstoppable. The land war across Europe remained in the balance until the spring of 1918, when the outcome became inevitable. The German High Seas Fleet remained bottled up and the overall success rates enjoyed earlier by its submarines began to diminish after May 1917.

Further research now shows how Germany's apparent failing fortunes, which continued into the spring of 1918, were not reflected in any reduction in the number of attacks on shipping in the channel between Ireland and England, known by many as the Irish Sea or the Irish Channel. The latter is meant to include all of the water, that is the North Channel, the Irish Sea and the northern part of the St George's Channel. Neither was it the 'quiet lake' that some in the Admiralty labelled it when shipping companies and mariners decried the lack of escorts. However, because of the utter havoc and destruction that were perpetrated in these waters by German submarines during the First World War, it is fully deserving of the nickname U-boat Alley.

Entries in the online database of shipwrecks for Ireland, irishwrecks. com, show that for the forty-eight months prior to the commencement of the First World War there were eighty-nine shipping casualties recorded in the area known as U-boat Alley. During a similar time span after the outbreak of the war, there were 718 entries. These included all losses and attacks by U-boats. For our purpose, U-boat Alley includes the coastline from Antrim to Wexford, and also includes areas such as the North Channel, the Irish Sea and the St George's Channel.

Following the announcement of Germany's second unrestricted U-boat campaign in February 1917, the wrath of its under-sea boats was unleashed once more. The full range of Germany's submarines attacked enemy ships in the alley and in the entrances to it. By this time, the larger ocean-going U class, the coastal UB class, and the minelayer UC class all had improved armaments and excellent radio communication capabilities. Improvements in the latter proved to have unforeseen or miscalculated consequences.

While on patrol, commanders of German submarines were not shy making radio contact with their base, but in so doing their transmissions were being detected by the British Admiralty. Progress is a two-sided coin, and the Admiralty were also becoming increasingly proficient, even down to identifying individual submarines. Their capacity for interception and decryption of German naval communications was later described as their greatest secret.

Although the smaller boats were rated coastal, they undertook cruises that were remarkable. They routinely circumnavigated the British Isles in all kinds of weather, with cruises sometimes lasting three or four weeks. A more fitting description for these voyages might be 'attack missions'. When the larger U class began to turn up off the east coast of America, the range and capabilities of these ocean pests both surprised and disturbed the most senior British and American naval commanders.

Successes for the different German submarines operating in the alley at this time varied. Some commanders seized every opportunity to attack all kinds of enemy vessels, while others achieved little success, seemingly a reflection of their inexperience or capabilities.

Submarine and U-boat are words that conjure up impressions of daring adventure, danger, heroism and even glamour, just like the romantic tales of pirates. After the first few days in a stinking metal tube, the glamour soon went out of it. At first they pretty much had the open sea to themselves and just disappeared when there was any sign of danger.

Submarines soon proved to be a dangerous way to travel through inhospitable seas. If you weren't running for shelter from the terrible weather that can prevail in the North Sea and the North Atlantic, you might otherwise be trying to avoid the growing numbers of increasingly capable enemy vessels tasked with destroying you.

Iron tubes that housed between twenty and eighty submariners, in cramped conditions, and in some terrible seas, proved a terrific strain on their crews and some of the more successful commanders were invalided out of active duty. This was an effect of the U-boat war that was not peculiar to German submariners. Allied naval personnel suffered too, particularly sailors who served on U-boat hunters, and 'Q', or 'Mystery Ships'. These played at being normal mercantile sailing vessels or plodding steamers, or by lying helpless and waiting for a submarine to show and challenge them – if they were lucky. Otherwise, just bang! An unseen attack was terrifying and resulted in a mad scramble for survival if, once more, you were lucky!

Of particular interest in respect of the alley, were the UC boats – submarines that laid mines. These submarines also carried torpedoes both inside and outside of the submarine. The forward torpedo tubes of these minelayers were fitted externally on the pressure hull but were operated from within. The stern torpedo tube formed an integral part of the pressure hull and was also operated from within. Spare torpedo tubes could be carried externally, aft of the forward torpedo tubes. Reloading the forward tubes could only be carried out when the boat was on the surface. It was known for a spare torpedo to be carried within the sub, probably for the stern tube.

Their compliment of arms consisted of: eighteen mines in six chutes; three torpedo tubes (two forward, one aft), all preloaded with a spare for each; 22-lb gun permanently fitted forward on the deck, and a machine gun carried internally that could be mounted on the conning tower. When the torpedoes that were pre-loaded on departure had been fired, the spare torpedoes stored externally behind the outer tubes and, on exceptional cruises, inside the submarine, were then reloaded. This type of rearmament could only be accomplished when the submarine was on the surface. Their most important feature was stealth – these submarines could lay mines and sink ships without ever being seen.

This was also the case with the mines in the top of their chutes, if they needed to be reset for any required change in operations. In order to accomplish this rearming or adjustment, relatively calm water was required, and these operations were sometimes carried out in remote bays and at night. Reports of the presence of enemy submarines in such bays may have contributed to the abundance of ridiculous propagandist accusations that were spread by naval intelligence concerning the assistance given by German sympathisers around the coast of Britain. What they really meant was around Ireland.

Mine-laying by German submarines was carried out at predesignated target areas, where they were laid across known shipping routes in very particular places at very particular times. The movement of important convoys and some particularly important ships seemed to have been known to the Germans, who tried to anticipate events with their nasty eggs.

There were a number of UCII boats and other classes of submarines operating in the alley during this period, but the minelayers presented so great a threat that the authorities felt compelled to take additional and exceptional measures, in order to put a stop to their advance.

The first of these mine-laying submarines out from the elaborate submarine base at Bruges, Flanders, and into the alley was *UC65*, commanded by Otto Steinbrinck. Born in 1888, Steinbrinck entered the naval service in 1907. He specialised in torpedoes and, like other notable aces, artillery. His first submarine command was *U6*, followed by *UB10*, *UC65* and *UB57*. He was withdrawn from active duties in January 1918 due to exhaustion. He played a significant role in German industry before and during the Second World War, as did other ranking officers, and was sentenced to six years' imprisonment by the Allies for membership of the Schutzstaffel

(SS). He died through ill health and a sickness which required an operation in 1949, just before the expiration of his sentence.

UC65 began sinking ships in the alley on 8 February 1917 and retreated from there at the end of the first week in May. During these cruises, Steinbrinck sank or damaged a total of forty-two ships.

Between 1914 and 1918, he sank 206 ships and damaged twelve more. 106 of these were while he was in command of *UC65*. Some of these war incidents occurred in the Alley and are the subject of further account here.

On 1 March, Steinbrinck sank the ship SS *Drina* off Skokham Island, near south-west Wales. At 11,484 tons she was one of the largest sunk in the alley and it was controversial. There was more than one explosion and it is conjectured that the ship struck a mine first and was then torpedoed.

At first she was claimed to have been a hospital ship. There were approximately 334 on board; 189 of these were crew. There were fifteen casualties listed. The *Drina* had been a hospital ship in 1915 but had been decommissioned from this role and was carrying passengers and cargo at the time of her sinking. Such incidents involving ships that had been naively or falsely considered off limits by virtue of being considered passenger ships, such as the *Lusitania* and the RMS *Leinster*, were grist to the mill for the propagandists. The incidents were highly controversial and attracted false reporting. There was only one kind of reporting during the First World War – that which was allowed by the authorities.

Fiercely critical of the Gallipoli campaign, and of how censorship was having a detrimental effect on the prosecution of the war, a letter was penned by Ellis Ashmead Bartlett, a journalist with the *Daily Telegraph*, in 1915. It was addressed to the British Prime Minister Herbert Asquith, but was seized and confiscated by military intelligence while being carried by an Australian journalist, Arthur Murdoch – father of now-famous Rupert. The incident is just one example of how total censorship was during the First World War.

Historical confusion was added to when it was announced that another huge ship, an actual hospital ship in this case, was damaged by a mine on the same day – the *Glenart Castle*, 6,824 tons. Though another report claimed it had been sunk in the English Channel, the damaging mine was said to have been laid by *UC65*. Seemingly stretching imagination, this was nevertheless true. The hospital ship

Glenart Castle struck a mine off Lundy Island on 1 March 1917, but was only damaged and didn't sink.

A year later, the *Glenart Castle* was sunk by *UC56* in the English Channel on 26 February 1918. The commander of *UC56*, Captain Wilhelm Kiesewether, was pursued for war crimes. Due to the similarity in the submarines' numbers, confusion persisted.

Attacks on hospital ships or anything acting in the service of the injured and sick has quite rightly attracted criticism in every war, even up to the present day. During the First World War the lines were deliberately blurred and many transports could variously be classified as a hospital ship: one carrying medical personnel, Red Cross volunteers from America, injured soldiers, medical supplies, painted white, not painted, etc. There were a number of such incidents which have come to light, and it is now known that munitions and war material were being shipped from America among any of the above.

The organisation of the Red Cross was criticised during the Second World War for harbouring spies among its personnel, and continues to be viewed with a jaundiced eye by some nations. The latest victims are the nongovernmental organisations (NGOs) that are believed to have been infiltrated by opposing forces and have seen some of their members kicked out of war zones.

The *Drina* lies 200 feet deep and the issue of clarifying some of the controversy surrounding the attack, for example, which submarine sunk her and exactly how the ship was deployed, has been the work of the diver and author of this excellent website devoted to the event: http://taffthehorns.com/One-Dive-to-HMHS-DRINA-Sadly-sunk-on-St-David-s-Day-1917-off-Milford-Haven-Rules-of-engagement-of-Civilian-Vessels-had-taken-a-sinister-cruel-change-.

The ship that disappeared

Steinbrinck continued with his attacks in the alley during the remainder of March and the following incident took place on 28 March. Although this was a highly unusual and violent attack by *UC65*, it did not result in any loss of life. Defying any clarity, the disappearing news was dramatically announced in newspapers and posted in Dublin Port.

There were at least two types of vessels whose activities were otherwise ordinary but became unique during the period of the war. The first of these was fishing boats and their crews. Despite a naval war in progress, and a very real possibility that fishermen might encounter a U-boat, they nevertheless had to earn a living and people had to eat. So, they continued practising their livelihood unless ordered by the Admiralty to stay in port. Fishermen were totally unprotected on the sea and they paid a heavy price in terms of their fishing boats being sunk by enemy submarines, casualties and loss of earnings. Although their livelihood was badly affected there was, surprisingly, little loss of life. Their injuries and losses, no matter how minor, did not minimise the terror.

The second were lightships. Without any means of propulsion, these vessels were permanently moored offshore and these, too, lacked any means of defence against an attack. Their job was to provide a light for the guidance and protection of mariners and ships.

Notwithstanding the dangers inherent in such conflict, they did not feel unduly vulnerable. It was understood by all that these vessels were neutral and should not perform any war duty, except to provide light for any ship travelling on the sea. German submariners generally kept to this understanding, probably due to the fact that the lightships were of as much benefit to them as they were to their enemy, as well as for some additional reasons.

There is little recorded on this important aspect of the war against submarines, and much of it was kept secret at the time. American naval forces in Ireland were not always kept in the loop. However, though seemingly unaware of the earlier sinking of the south Arklow lightship *Guillemot*, the commander of Queenstown-based USS *Wadsworth*, Joseph Taussig, was nevertheless privy to the agreement when he remarked in the 8 June 1917 entry of his diary that, 'They still carry out the agreement which makes lightships immune from attack, but I am sure this is because the submarines use the lightships for their own navigation, and locating them.'

He seemed to be unaware that the Admiralty had already been interfering with the lights when he prophetically continued 'otherwise the submarines may become a victim of its own trap at a future date'.

Only a few months later, Taussig discovered how the lights were interfered with. While attempting passage back in to Queenstown, he discovered that the lights at Ballycotton and Kinsale were not lit.

The lights provided navigational aid but, crucially, they were also used as a target bearing for the U-boats in order to position themselves for an attack and lay their mines in the correct positions. However understandable it might have been, the British authorities contravened this apparently unwritten agreement when they fitted lightships with communication equipment and hydrophones in order to detect and relay the positions of the enemy submarines to naval intelligence.

It was King Louis XIV who probably gave birth to the light-keepers' eternal motto 'For the Safety of All' when the great entrepreneurial lighthouse builder Henry Winstanley was kidnapped by French privateers during construction of the Eddystone lighthouse in 1697. Having learned of the capture, the French King ordered his release and is accredited with the message: 'I am at war with England not with the world.'

Even though the practice of submarine watch inevitably placed the lightships and their crews in extreme danger, there is no evidence that the lightship crews refused to cooperate, even if this had been a free and legitimate choice. There is also a small number of recorded incidents where lightship crews rescued German submariners.

By 1918, those submarine commanders who had been so confident in their own capabilities and had sensed victory had grown tired and worn out. One by one, they saw their comrades fail to return and despaired of politicians. The enemy had learned all the tricks and were on the offensive. The smell of defeat was in the air when Commander Ernst Hashegan wrote:

It is though the very sea had gone over to the enemy; it seems as if electrified, so violently do attack and defence rage upon it. Every wave is a foe. The coastal lights are false: the sea marks treacherous. They listen-in for us, to hear the distant beat of our screws; and feel us with electric fingers along the sea bed.

There were very few cases of a German submarine detecting a lightship attempting to warn a nearby ship in danger of attack and then attacking or sinking that lightship.

The first deliberate, and almost unique, example of this type of attack on a lightship occurred on 28 March 1917, when *UC65* sunk the *Guillemot*, the south Arklow lightship, off the coast of Wexford in almost identical circumstances to the *Diamond Shoals* incident the following year.

The later incident occurred off the coast of America, when in August 1918 the motorised *Diamond Shoals* LV 71 was sunk after it had used its radio to warn ships of a submarine in the area. *U140* promptly boarded her, put off the crew in a boat, and sank the lightship.

At this time, it appears that the two lightships mentioned are the only two examples of lightships being attacked and sunk by a German submarine during either the First or Second World War. It is possible that other cases may come to light in non-English speaking countries.

Out of Zebrugge, Otto Steinbrinck was in command of *UC65* and his attack missions in the Irish Channel began on 24 March, at around the same time a fellow commander, Johannes Lohs, was cutting his teeth in the North Sea in *UC75*. Steinbrinck's trail of destruction did not end until he left the alley at the beginning of the second week in May. He had sunk forty-two ships.

Some individual commanders were chalking up considerable success around Ireland, and their crews may have been experiencing similar exuberance to the U-boat crews that followed in the next World War, who were reported to have described their own period of high success rates as their 'happy time'.

On 28 March, *UC65* sank ten ships, including the *Guillemot*. Among these losses was the *Dalgali*, a 724-ton Norwegian steamer sunk off Arklow. Although Norway remained neutral during the First World War, her fleet of ships was treated with merciless severity by German submarines. After unrestricted warfare was declared on 1 February, the likes of Norway's sailing ships did not stand a chance. Norway's mercantile fleet of sail and steam suffered far worse than any other neutral, including America. She lost almost a thousand ships, amounting to a million tons.

The *Dalgali* was sunk by gunfire from *UC65* after the crew were allowed to escape in the ship's boats. They reached the Irish coast safely.

With just one boat being able to inflict so much destruction, one could easily understand why their enemies might be moved to alarm, and to concerted efforts, in order to put a stop to such high-performance submarines.

UC65's log entry reads that Steinbrinck and his crew boarded the *Guillemot* at 6.10 p.m. on the 28th and found no secret material on board. After questioning Captain Rossiter and his crew of light-keepers, he put them off in the lightship's longboat and then placed charges deep in the hull. The lore of U-boat commanders instructing the survivors of their handiwork, useful for knowing which direction to steer for safety, and even how and what time they were likely to catch a train, was supposedly repeated in this case.

The bombs exploded, but the stoutly built lightship failed to sink. After repeated shelling from the submarine's deck gun, she finally disappeared, as did the submarine – leaving the lightship's crew alone, and with a considerable distance to row for shore.

The only reporting of the *Guillemot* incident was the following disappearance notice that was posted in Custom House in Dublin, and reported in the 2 April 1917 edition of *Freeman's Journal* under the heading 'Lightship Lost': 'The south Arklow lightvessel has disappeared'.

Otto Steinbrinck relinquished his command of *UC65* in July 1917. The boat was subsequently lost in the English Channel on 3 November 1917, when it was torpedoed by HM submarine *C16*. Her commander, Klaus Lafrenz, and four of her crew survived.

The first lightship that was lost because of the war was the *Corton*, off the west coast of England, when it was struck by a mine laid by *UC6*. The sinking was not intentional and was due to a drifting mine that became entangled in the lightship's mooring chain. Nevertheless, it resulted in five deaths. Two of the lightship crew were rescued. A similar occurrence involving the East Dudgeon lightvessel took place during the Second World War.

Revenge for the loss was claimed when *UC6* was detected with hydrophones by the crew of the Kentish Knock lightship and was sunk after it was ambushed with a mine-net in June 1916.

Lighthouses were also attacked during the First World War when it was thought they were passing on information regarding the position of the enemy. For similar reasons, it was claimed, they were attacked again during the Second World War.

As Jim Blaney recalled in his excellent article for the in-house Irish lights magazine *Beam*, Rossiter (senior light-keeper on the *Guillemot*) was both praised and admonished over the loss of his vessel. Praised for his bravery in warning the ships of the lurking

U-boat and reprimanded for disobeying Admiralty instructions! As these instructions to the light service were secret, the Admiralty's reported view on the matter is hard to comprehend.

It is clear, however, that visual signalling was reported to have been forbidden, though electric signalling by telegraph was not. The men were duly awarded their medals and torpedo badges.

Signal by radio from light installations was quite correctly suspected by German submarine commanders to have been practised. Commander Hashegan, in *U62*, crept up on the Caernarvon lightship a few months later and might just as easily have destroyed it and its keepers for what he had seen – true or not:

> Cautiously we creep up to the lightship, aft in the cabin a light is burning. No doubt they are sitting there, the old sea dogs over the grog and cards, or perhaps they are entering in their logbooks all the calls for help they are receiving on their wireless aerial that day ... Neither do we trouble these Lightship folk; sea marks, so to speak, are neutral. They show the way to friend and foe.

Lightships and installations were attacked again during the Second World War for much the same reasons, but inconsistently. The international code of agreed understanding, which should have kept lighthouses and light-keepers safe from attack during conflict, was broken during both world wars and mayhem reigned.

Diving the wreck of the south Arklow lightvessel

Divers from the Marlin SAC visited the wreck in 2006 and 2007. Locating the remains of the *Guillemot* was not difficult as she was quite close to her position marked on Admiralty charts. She was sunk on the spot where she had been anchored and has remained there ever since.

The divers devoted two summers to locating her, assessing the lie of the wreck, depths, and the times of slack water before making a series of 50-metre dives to the wreck.

As is quite often the case, the visibility in the water off the coast of Arklow was very poor during the dives. At 50 metres, a lot of lamp light was required to find your way around the wreck. The divers did manage, however, to inspect the whole length of the wreck. They reported there was very little of any superstructure still remaining above the deck, but that she was completely intact down to the keel and sat almost perfectly upright on the bottom. Significantly, they also reported seeing the hull piercings caused by the gunfire from the submarine.

I was not present during the dives on the wreck in 2007. I had just retired and moved to a new home which, coincidentally, is perched on the east side of Tara Hill, overlooking the Arklow Bank. During one of the days that the divers were down on the wreck, I happened to be observing the divers' boat through binoculars from my terrace. After about 40 minutes, I noticed that the boat had drifted away from her original position and continued to drift. I also knew that the slack water had ended and the tidal flow had recommenced. The divers had not got back into the boat. Something was wrong and I made a dash for the Arklow lifeboat station.

On the way, I made telephone contact with the station and they informed me that the lifeboat had been launched. Before I reached Arklow, however, the emergency had been handled.

The dive boat *Quickspin*, a 26-foot Offshore, was being handled by someone who was relatively unfamiliar with the boat when the engine stopped and couldn't be restarted. It took some time before the cox'n discovered how to switch to the spare battery, but he eventually got it done and a potentially regrettable incident was luckily averted.

Deep into the conflict, Germany was experiencing a shortage of valuable metals and, reflecting some desperation, orders were given to submarine commanders to seize quality metals from arrested vessels. While it was reported that the crew of *UC65* attempted to remove the lightship's very large bell, they apparently failed to do so and it is believed to be still in the wreck. The Marlin divers did not locate the bell of the *Guillemot* on this occasion.

There was no loss of life in the *Guillemot* incident, and the German government later paid reparations for the loss of the lightship.

A new *Guillemot* was completed after the war and took up station off the Irish coast. She was eventually withdrawn from service and docked in cement in Kilmore Quay harbour, County Wexford. Having spent a few years fastened in concrete as a local maritime museum attraction, she was later undocked and cut up.

Commander Lohs confronts Guinness

The next ace into U-boat Alley was Johannes Lohs in command of *UC75*. Lohs was born in 1889 and entered the naval service in 1909. He took command of his first submarine, *UC75*, in March 1917 and patrolled off the east coast of England. He arrived off Cork in May 1917, where he sank three sailing ships, one steamer and seven fishing boats off the Staggs. On his homeward leg, in a disputed incident, he sank the sloop HMS *Lavender* off the coast of Waterford.

The sinking of the fishing boats is interesting as it highlights a particular policy adopted by some U-boat commanders. This was not one of cruelty, which is sometimes vehemently argued, and there were very few casualties. It was instead, I respectively suggest, strategic. By creating such mayhem among fishing boats, it subsequently tied up some of HM naval resources. There were also some reports that fishing boats possessed radio.

In any event, there is no doubt that many fishing boats were converted and armed. Some even held onto their painted registration numbers. Some were fitted with radio communication gear and hydrophones, crewed by naval personnel, and patrolled these same waters. An attack on fishing boats was also an attack on the supply of food, an issue just as important to Britain as the supply of arms.

Commander Lohs may have gained some small victories during this patrol, but he might also have been much more successful if he had just been a little more patient. America had just entered the war and had despatched her first destroyers to Queenstown. If Lohs had not revealed himself by sinking the fishing boats and forewarning his enemies of his presence on this occasion, he might well have successfully laid his mines in the path of the approaching and unsuspecting destroyers. Sinking or damaging any of these American symbols of the new military alliance might have dealt a severe blow to morale.

Lohs had a habit of being in the right place at just about the right time though, and just missed altering major events of the war on more than one occasion.

Another similar event occurred at the end of May, when *UB64* sank ten fishing smacks out of Kilkeel while they fished off the Isle of Man. The two incidents are a little unusual in that there were so many fishing boats involved. One wonders what was going through the fishermen's minds as the surfaced U-boat went from smack to smack, sending them to the bottom with bombs and gunfire. Words must have been said!

Johannes Lohs patrolled again in May/June 1917, mainly focusing on the south-west coast of England. He began attacking vessels in the alley in July, resuming again in August and October to December and hitting twenty-three vessels.

In August, letters began to arrive at the world-famous Guinness brewery in Dublin. Their barrels had washed up along the shoreline on both sides of the alley, and the finders were looking for reward, or recompense for their trouble in saving the brewery's porter from the sea.

The barrels had got there after Commander Lohs in *UC75* sunk the cross-channel Guinness steamer *W.M. Barkley* on 12 August. Dublin Port had previously been closed due to submarine activity in the alley, but was temporarily reopened again to allow some ships to leave. This included the *Barkley*. Its crew were not to know, however, that this particular submarine hadn't gone away.

Lohs had been lying in wait off the Kish lightship about 5 miles from Dublin. He had seen the steamer approach in the distance, and as the light faded, he positioned his boat for a surface attack. It was later revealed that the lights on this side of the ship had not been darkened. The crew of the *Barkley* did not see the submarine and took no evasive action. The Guinness steamer was torpedoed aft of the bridge, on the starboard side, and sank soon afterwards.

The Guinness ship was armed and had a trained gunnery crew, but the gunner was below doing his washing and making tea with a man named McGlue. Able Seaman Thomas McGlue survived the attack and later gave a marvellous account of the sinking and his brush with a German submarine commander. The account appeared in an article titled 'Recollections of the *W.M. Barkley*' that appeared in the Guinness house magazine *Harp*.

Describing how, if not for the barrels of Guinness, they wouldn't have had enough time to get into a lifeboat, the account may have lent support to the company's famous slogan 'Guinness is good for you'.

Four of the crew were in the lifeboat when Lohs came alongside it. He questioned the survivors as to the ship's identity and cargo, and eventually gave them directions for shore. McGlue's recollections marvelled at the encounter with the submarine, describing it as 'as big as a collier' and marvelled at Lohs's linguistic skills – 'Sure he spoke better English than I did.' Captain Edward Gregory from Arklow and four other crew members were killed in the attack.

Diving the wreck of the *Barkley*

Despite some fanciful notions that wrecks can move, the remains of the *Barkley* lie exactly where she was sunk by Lohs, about 7 miles east of the Kish lighthouse. Its association with the world-famous Guinness brewery has attracted a few hardy divers in recent years. At almost 60 metres, however, the wreck is beyond the diving range of ordinary sport divers and has proven to be a wreck on which a number of regrettable incidents have occurred, including some quite serious ones.

Despite my own self-imposed depth limits, a number of other adventurous divers have visited the wreck. They report that there is considerable silting up of the hull and all of her wooden superstructure has disappeared. The wreck has been imaged by Infomar.

Not likely to ever usurp the Guinness name and brand, might it be likely that Diagio, the new owners of the famous brewery, could be tempted to sponsor a search of the wreck, if only to recover the only bell missing from their fine collection of the brewery's maritime mementos displayed in the Guinness Hop Store museum? A few years from now the wreck will come under the protection of the National Monuments Act's '100 year rule' and special authorisation will have to be sought for such a mission.

Commander Lohs and the town of Arklow

Referred to earlier, these mine-laying submarines provoke particular interest in the methods they used to lay their mines. Relying on the unchanged positions of the lightvessels in the Irish Channel, U-boat commanders like Johannes Lohs were able to lay their eggs across the busy shipping lanes. When stationed near Ireland, he navigated the east coast inside the notoriously dangerous Blackwater, Arklow and Kish sandbanks, placing his mines across the safe channels between them that were used by ships to enter or leave harbours – including ships carrying munitions from the port of Dublin and the extensive Kynoch production facility at Arklow. For this purpose, Kynoch steamers used both Wicklow and Arklow harbours.

In a tribute to their navigation perhaps, or just the draught of a submarine, there are no recorded incidences of a submarine becoming stranded on any of these sandbanks.

In order to place mines in the best possible positions, Lohs used the lightships for bearings. The mines were laid during darkness and at High water. His knowledge of these dangerous waters would seem to have been comprehensive.

The Kynoch munitions works, situated on the north shore at Arklow, blew up on 21 September 1917, killing twenty-seven employees. Testimony at the subsequent inquest, and a belief by townspeople which remains to this day, suggests that the explosion was caused by a round fired from a submarine. Submarine commanders knew this vast munitions works was there, and from the record of his patrols Lohs certainly demonstrated that a submarine could get within range of the complex.

Commander Lohs recorded details of his patrols on charts where he indicated his routes, hits, geography and marine conditions, comments, etc. During his July patrol, he laid his full complement of mines across all of the access channels to Arklow. Interestingly, Lohs' records indicate that bearings were taken from the south and north Arklow lightships in order to lay these mines in the correct positions. Was this south Arklow lightship a replacement for the one sunk by *UC65* four months earlier? If it was, was it replaced in the same position?

There are few records of vessels being damaged by these mines at this time. Nevertheless, he didn't return to Flanders empty-handed and sank three steamers in the area with torpedoes. The steamer *Lynburn* sank near the Arklow Bank when it struck a mine on 29 August. The *William Middleton* was badly damaged and towed to Rosslare, County Wexford, after she struck a mine in the St George's Channel on 28 September.

Local people in Arklow still believe that the Kynoch munitions works on the north shore of Arklow town was blown up by a shell fired from a German submarine offshore during the First World War. Other than testimony of mysterious lights shining on the road above the factory moments before the explosions and the sound of a whoosh (presumably from a projectile), there was no supporting evidence for an attack by a submarine.

That was it until 1958, when the coaster *Anna Toop* grounded on Arklow Bank. It was soon pulled off by a trawler from Arklow, only to sink in deeper water. Divers from the Liverpool Salvage Association investigated the wreck. Not being able to find it, they hired the same trawler that had pulled off the *Anna Toop* to help locate the wreck. During the trawl, they snagged something. One of the two divers, a man – the other being a female diver, which was very unusual at the time – dived to the snag, surfaced, and stated that it was not the *Anna Toop*, but a First World War submarine!

This account was related to me by a man who was a sixteen-year-old deck hand on the same trawler at the time, going on to work for the Liverpool Salvage Association very soon afterwards. While there, he clearly remembered seeing the file on the *Anna Toop* and the diver's report of the submarine. Needless to say, the file disappeared.

The story hit the newspapers and cemented belief in the earlier tale describing the supposed attack on Kynoch's by a submarine. The mysterious wrecked submarine was supposedly located once more by a very colourful early scuba diver named Manuel de Lucia, but never since. Needless to say, when contacted by me, Manuel was unable to supply any details whatsoever as to the whereabouts of the wreck, but he did say that it had twin screws and rails.

In as much as such stories can be enhanced when relayed in a pub, this one was told to me in complete sobriety by the boy, who was a retired man by then.

There is no submarine, from either World War, reported missing in this area. Such reports on naval intelligence has not prevented submarine wrecks turning up where they have been least expected.

Commander Lohs, the *A.H. Read,* and the largest liner in the world

Lohs's knowledge of Liverpool Bay was equally impressive, as can be seen from his contemporary diagrams of mine-laying across the heavily patrolled Liverpool bar in the Queen's Channel. These sunk the Liverpool pilot-and-examination vessel *A. H. Read* on 28 December. The loss of the *Read* was terrible. There was a total of forty-one men aboard the steam cutter including pilots, radio operators, examiners, and apprentices and only two survived.

The mines, however, may have been intended for another target – the world's largest liner turned troop transporter on its first voyage from America in its new role.

Lohs had observed some very large vessels in the area, but narrowly missed the giant *Leviathan*, the German-built ship which had formerly been named the *Vaterland* prior to being seized in New York. Every possible precaution had been taken to get this symbolic liner, packed with thousands of American Doughboys, safely across the Atlantic and up the Irish Channel, and over the bar into Liverpool. A hit would have been an enormous propaganda coup for Germany, and a terrible blow to the morale of the Allies.

As with *Lusitania*, the departure of the huge ship would not have gone unnoticed as it slipped out of New York, and the U-boats were immediately alerted to expect its arrival on the far side of the Atlantic. Packed with American troops, she marked the beginning of the new strategy of troop transportation to Britain and, increasingly, to the west coast of France – directly into the land war.

The end of Lohs

Lohs commanded *UC75* in the English Channel during early January 1918 before taking over *UB57* from Steinbrinck. His old boat was later rammed by HMS *Fairy* off the Belgian coast in August in an incident, like so many others, described as controversial.

In command of Steinbrinck's old boat *UB57*, Lohs continued to chalk up considerable successes, not least in U-boat Alley, when he returned there in February 1918. Lohs and her crew were lost off Flanders in August 1918 when their boat struck a mine.

There was considerable U-boat activity in the alley during the First World War. The two U-boats commanded by Steinbrinck and Lohs were particularly successful. They were highly decorated for their achievements and their memory was celebrated by their countrymen for many years after.

British Intelligence tackles the minelayers

The minelayers represented a threat like no other. If they had grown in any number, they could have saturated the waters around Britain and Ireland with mines without ever being seen. On the other hand, they experienced an extremely high attrition rate. They were plagued by losses, some of which were due to being struck by their own mines exploding beneath their hull. These casualties were categorised by some as having occurred from 'unexplained or unknown' reasons. 'Unexplained' covers a multitude of things. Sounding a little like Donald Rumsfeld, an examination of the following incidents, which occurred in Irish waters, might help to explain the unexplained.

Off the entrance to a port that was disgorging a large amount of war material, the first of these occurred when *UC44* supposedly struck one of her own mines off Waterford on 4 August 1917. Captain Kurt Tebbenjohanns and two crewmen escaped through the conning tower and reached the surface. After some time together in the water they separated. Tebbenjohanns was eventually rescued by local fishermen, the two Power brothers and another named McGrath. The other two submariners were not recovered and are believed to have drowned.

Tebbenjohanns was whisked off to Britain, interrogated, and later revealed the full crew list. He also provided the explanation that, immediately after the ninth mine was released, something struck the submarine and there was an explosion. Admiral Hall, however, claimed that the British had laid a trap for the submarine, which they had been expecting. They had supposedly transmitted the false announcement that they had swept up mines laid by an earlier UC boat and that it was, in fact, one of these unswept mines that had sunk *UC44*.

The minelayer was almost immediately raised by Commander Davis and his crew into the nearby harbour of Dunmore East. The two other submariners that had escaped with Tebbenjohanns from the stricken submarine were Bahnster and Richter, both engine-room crew. Tebbenjohanns stated on 7 August, while in custody in London, that there were 'two or three others' who escaped with him through the conning tower. Richter's body supposedly washed up later and was buried at the nearby village of Duncannon, situated across the Waterford estuary on the opposite side and to the north-east of

Dunmore East. His body was later reinterred in the German military cemetery at Glencree, County Wicklow.

The details surrounding the dead German crew of *UC44* are mystifying. The bodies in the submarine were seen by American officers stationed in Queenstown during a visit to the wreck while it was still in Dunmore East harbour. The Admiralty stated the bodies, totalling twenty-eight, were respectably buried at sea. It is difficult to understand why, when they were ashore, they were not buried there. How the body of machinist Richter was recovered, and came to be buried at Duncannon, is not known. I discovered his name at the German cemetery in Glencree some years ago, and traced him to *UC44*.

When *UC44* was brought into Dunmore East, it was reported by visiting American naval personnel that the bodies of the deceased submariners were still in it. The Admiralty appears to have conceded this by stating that these men were later buried at sea. Admiralty instructions, probably naval intelligence, were in keeping with this practice. Why, once the bodies of the submariners were taken ashore, they couldn't have been buried there has not been satisfactorily explained. Naval tradition and all that aside, it can only be assumed that their presence was being concealed and the idea of 'out of sight out of mind' was being followed. It was, after all, Admiral Hall's urgent priority to keep all knowledge of the submarine's disappearance, and the reasons for it, secret.

UC44 yielded some very valuable intelligence before it was taken back out to sea again, sunk, and later dispersed. She was also said to have been dispersed once again, many years later. Notwithstanding statements that the remains of the submarine had been blown up and scattered, the engine from *UC44* was later reported to have rested for many years in a commercial garage in Duncannon and then, finally, under tons of rubble in the back of the harbour, where it is still believed to be.

And then along came *UC42*

The second case of a minelayer lost in similar circumstances occurred around the same time *UC44* was being salvaged. Relocation of the wreck had eluded researchers and divers for so long that many began to believe such a wreck never existed.

An almost simultaneous event, this next loss involved *UC42* in the mouth of Cork harbour. The command at Queenstown were taken completely by surprise when this submarine was discovered lying on the seabed on the afternoon of 31 October just 2.5 miles outside the entrance to Cork harbour.

Once again, as confirmed by British authorities, this was another minelayer that had struck one of her mines in an attempt to lay them across the entrance to Cork harbour. It was reported by navy divers that five of the mine chutes were full and that the first chute was empty. The implication is that it was the last mine out of the first chute that didn't behave and struck the submarine.

The presence of a German submarine so close to the entrance of this large British naval base, where thirty-eight American destroyers were deployed, was considered by Admiral Bayly to be quite extraordinary. The U-boat was first detected by patrol boat *P55* when tapping or signalling noises were heard coming from the disabled submarine lying motionless on the seabed. The sounds detected coming from within the submarine were said by some of the Royal Navy listeners in their patrol boats above to have resembled Morse.

The sub was depth-charged twice and then dived on. Parts of her were that were retrieved indicated that she was *UC42*. The hatches were said to have been open, considerable damage to the stern was described and some of the submariners were assumed to have died trying to escape. The Admiralty later presumed the bodies of the sailors were still inside the submarine. There was no mention of what became of the other two mines, or of any floating bodies on the surface.

The only mention of the discovery of any bodies appeared in the most unlikely of places.

In a letter written on British government stationary and signed 'P. Flaherty, 24 The Beach, Queenstown, Ireland', Flaherty, a diver, confirms that he examined *UC42* on 2 November 1917. He states that '... her stern is blown off just a little before the after planes.' He also described, in unusual detail, the naval uniform on the body of a sailor 'laying outside the wreck that followed me'. This was supposedly caused by his own movements through the water. Other than the damage stated, he also wrote that the rest of the submarine was intact. The diver signed off with his name, and his address at 'HM Dockyard Haulbowline.'

Confusion existed around the remarks that the stern of the submarine was blown off when it appeared that it wasn't. This can be attributed to interpretation – the stern, the submarine's outer casing and the attached protruding ancillary equipment were missing, but the pressure hull would seem to have remained intact. The propeller(s) and shaft, and stern torpedo tube, remained structurally intact.

The diver's letter also contained the address of Messrs. Stillwell & Sons, 42 Pall Mall, London SW1. This was an interesting firm of Admiralty agents whose archival material for this period of the company's history is held by the Royal Bank of Scotland group and is closed until 2017.

Contained in the *Navy List* for 1939, the following gives a good description of this company's functions:

> By the absorption of the business of Messrs Stilwell & Sons (Navy Agents since 1770), the Westminster Bank provides a special Navy Branch, devoted to the banking requirements of the Royal Navy and Royal Marine. Officers and ship's crews are thereby ensured of the facilities they need in the drawing of officer's pay from the divisional paymasters, the management of claims for salvage, slave bounty and prize bounty, the drawing of half pay, unemployed full pay, and pilotage allowances, and the preparation of the Annual Return required by H. M. Paymaster General Office etc.

The addressee may be someone quite different and Stillwell & Sons' address may only have been included to let the reader know that he, the diver, can also be contacted through their offices.

There were twenty-seven or twenty-eight fatalities when *UC42* failed to resurface. Naval correspondence began to fizzle out between Queenstown and the Admiralty after reports that the submarine was still buoyant and enquires as to whether it should be moved. An unknown number of her mines and torpedoes were subsequently reported to have been removed by American and British naval personnel.

After initially warming to the task of raising *UC42*, enthusiasm began to wane in favour of focussing on the intelligence being retrieved from the already raised *UC44* at Dunmore, which the Admiralty considered to be 'more important'.

Although it became the Admiralty's stated intention to send a team from HMS *Vernon* to destroy *UC42* on site, we now know that *UC42* was not blown up and that it never budged an inch. The only way that the body of the German sailor might have got out of the submarine was through one of the hatches.

UC42 was relocated in 2010 during a resurvey of the Kinsale gas field pipeline. Local divers quickly identified her and the news broke in January 2011. She lies relatively close to the gas pipeline, whole and in surprisingly good condition. The stern of the wreck is damaged, but to an untrained eye it does not resemble the 'completely destroyed' or 'blown off' reports sent to the Admiralty which suggested the damage was caused by striking her own mine. She is also in shallower water than had been reported.

The thing about this new breed of minelayers was that quite a large number were lost inexplicably – that is, either mysteriously or during the process of laying their mines. The most acceptable theory in some cases is that the mechanism controlling the release of the mines' anchors was faulty. Understandably, there were also a number of claims by German submariners that the mines were being sabotaged during or after production. As Robert Grant in *U-Boat Hunters* put it '... the UC boats had a mysterious tendency to blow up'.

Suggestions of conspiracy are nearly always dismissed in these instances, but there is no good reason for not considering it in this case. Admiral Hall was a master at creating the fertiliser that nourished a plethora of conspiracies, which was a valuable weapon in itself – confusion. There is evidence that, in a number of cases, it was the third mine – the last one out of a chute – that exploded when released. These were the the only mines that could be adjusted from the deck of the submarine before or after going to sea.

These were two very similar incidents and they occurred in a relatively short period of time, and in close proximity to each other. *UC44* was lost off Waterford in August and *UC42* was lost off Cork in September.

There was yet another, which was also somewhat connected. *UC33* changed commanders at the end of July 1917 and began cruises off Cork and Waterford with Alfred Arnold in command in August. She used torpedoes to sink the British steamers *Akassa* on 13 August and the *Spectator* six days later. Seven sailors were killed. Her patrol was previous to that of *UC42* but followed that of

UC44, which was ashore in Dunmore East at the time. There is no indication as to what damage her mines caused.

UC33 returned to the same area in September, and again it remains unclear what damage her mines were responsible for. Three men were killed when on 26 September 1917 she attacked a convoy and torpedoed the oil tanker *San Zeferino*. She then surfaced and shelled the still floating oiler off the Tuskar lighthouse, County Wexford. In response, the submarine was shelled and rammed by Royal Naval escort *PC61*. This escort vessel was commanded by the Antarctic explorers Joseph Stenhouse and Frank Worsley.

The P boats were armed patrol sloops, but a number had been converted to Q boats, denoted by the addition of the letter C, and sometimes called PQ boats. These were specially constructed as small mercantile coasters. They had reinforced bows for ramming and were heavily armed. During interrogation, Arnold later stated that he was not confused as to the identity and purpose of this escort.

Arnold confessed that his submarine was unable to dive and escape being rammed by Worsley as the submarine had snagged one propeller while laying mines off Waterford a couple of days earlier. The second gave up at just the wrong moment. He also told his interrogators that his submarine was badly holed and sank with appalling rapidity. Captain Arnold also believed that the propeller had been damaged when the submarine hit the bottom earlier.

The captain and his navigating officer, Steuermann, had been in the conning tower at the time of the attack by *PC61*, and both were blown by compressed air to the surface from 40 metres. They were in the water together for a while before Steuermann died and Arnold was picked up by the escort.

Coincidentally, *UC33* had been damaged a few months earlier for the same reason as the loss of the other two – striking one of her own mines. Prepared as negatively buoyant, the mines should not have travelled to the stern of the vessel after they were let go. They were supposed to have dropped below the boat immediately. In just two months the Admiralty eliminated three of these valuable submarines and captured two of their even more valuable commanders.

Arnold was taken to Milford Haven and then to London. He was questioned in both places and considered to be unhelpful. He nevertheless got off some letters to his wife and comrades, which included yet another letter to Commander Pasquay at Brunsbüttel.

Once more it included obscure references to his own his crews' 'belongings at home' and that there should be 'no difficulty in arranging for them'.

All of the UC boats damaged or sunk by their own mines in 1917 were built in the Vulcan Hamburg yard. There were no such recurring incidents after the loss of *UC42*.

I am going to stick my conspiratorial neck out here with the following suggestion. When *UC44* sank and Tebbenjohanns was brought ashore, cables flew between Dunmore, Cork and London, and the commander was whisked off by train and on the night mail-boat to Britain to meet his interrogators.

A survivor of the sinking of the RMS *Leinster*, assistant purser Bill Sweeney, remembered that Tebbenjohans had been transported and accompanied by a British officer on the RMS *Leinster*. While the two were drinking in the saloon during the crossing from Dublin to Holyhead, the ship's commander, Captain Birch, learned of the liberty being enjoyed by the two and headed straight down to the saloon. Having already being attacked by German submarines, Captain Birch was none too happy to see them enjoying the company's hospitality on board his ship and threatened to confine the two of them if the submariner was not placed in irons immediately.

After the war, Tebbenjohanns recalled for *Westward* that he was confined in a special cabin after he gave his word of honour not to escape – it wasn't locked and the officer (one of two) returned to the saloon. Tebbenjohanns suspected that the *Leinster*'s captain may have been smarting, quite justifiably, after the torpedoing of her sister ship RMS *Connaught* a few months earlier.

While he was in London on 7/8 August, Tebbenjohanns penned at least two letters. These would have been heavily censored letters with agreed text, sent through the auspices of the Red Cross. Their translated transcriptions are now on file at the PRO, Kew. There is also the possibility that he never penned these letters at all, and that they are a fabrication.

The first of these was to his father, Friedrick Wilhelm, sent on 7 August, outlining his ordeal and asking his parents for more clothes etc., some which were still at his base in Brunsbüttel. He suggested that he would write to the base and inform his superiors that his parents would be collecting his belongings. This latter part, of his first letter, was apparently in preparation for what was to follow in the second.

The second letter was to Lt Commander Pasquay at Brunsbüttel, dated 8 August. In this, he once more outlines his ordeal and the loss of his boat and crew. Apart from other obscure references, such as not having paid his taxes or bills, and making good on an omission of thanks for a gift of books, he continued with the following suggestions for a visit by his parents to the base, in order that they might collect some of his belongings:

> I have requested my parents to arrange to fetch personally, if possible, the things which I left at Brunsbüttel. May I ask you to see that great care is taken in unpacking the box, so that there is no accident, as there are some eggs at the top. I have not yet thanked Messrs Goedard for the gift of books. Can this perhaps be done from your end?

I don't know beyond doubt if these letters were actually sent as written and recorded above, or if they were received in Germany.

Tebbenjohanns must have been short of clothes and personal possessions as he lost these while trying to escape from his submarine and during his time in the water. Accustomed as officers on both sides of the conflict were to their creature comforts, it is nevertheless a preposterous notion that a submarine commander who had just lost his boat and crew, and had become a POW, was remotely interested in broken eggs in his foot locker in Germany! Equally, I don't know what was meant by the other obscure references to taxes and books, or Goedard. One might read all kinds of messages into his unusual remarks.

Given his own experience, however, I strongly suspect that his reference to 'eggs at the top' was a clear reference to the mines at the top of the chutes in these minelayers! Mines were often referred to as eggs, and the author of this letter was trying to warn his comrades about what had caused the loss of his boat – it had been no accident.

As it was the mines and not the submarines, with the exception of those with unexplained damage to their engines, that failed to operate as designed, it would appear to me that this is where a problem lay. There were three operations to make a mine active. It must first be released and sink successfully. The mechanism which controls the release of the arms clasping the mine to the anchor must operate correctly. A successful release will then pull a pin, arming the mine while it rises to the surface.

It would appear that in inexplicable cases of sunken submarines, the mechanism controlling the release of the mine from the anchor had been activated while it was still in position in the top of the chute, but remained safely together until it was dropped. When it left the chute, the arms came free immediately and the mine parted from the anchor. Being positively buoyant, the pin was pulled, arming the mine, but the mine was then carried to the back of the boat, where it struck and detonated.

Given the number of these incidences, and sticking my neck out a little further, the claim by others that a series or batch of these mines, or the adjustable detonating mechanisms, were sabotaged while being manufactured or installed is a very plausible one. As both sides employed agents and activists, one might further conjecture that British naval intelligence were desperate to conceal the cause of the explosions, and the identity of a valuable accomplice, and thus actively pursued the policy of no survivors when they gave their Nelsonian nod to some U-boat hunters.

Desperate for results, the Admiralty encouraged the activities of submarine hunters such as the decorated Godfrey Herbert, aka 'William McBride' of *Baralong* infamy, in order to defeat the very real threat to commercial and naval shipping that had emerged with the new minelayers and submarines in general. Herbert transferred to Queenstown around July, just prior to these incidents, and apparently just after sinking *UC66* on 12 June in the English Channel. The submarine was depth-charged by Herbert in his specially adapted trawler *Sea King* and supposedly disintegrated after the detonation of her own mines.

The 'kill' was not awarded to Herbert until after the war, but the cause of the sinking, from which there were no bodies and no survivors, remains in some dispute.

When Herbert arrived at Queenstown he joined up with an old shipmate, another successful Q ship commander named Stopford Douglas. Both were under the command of G. Heaton DSO, head of the mine-sweeping flotilla.

Not overjoyed at the prospect of serving under Admiral Bayly, Herbert nevertheless rose to the task at hand and was remembered by the Admiral in glowing terms in his book *Danger Zone*: 'If the whole future of the war with Germany was to rest on anti-U-boat contests, here was the type of mind which could render invaluable aid at headquarters.'

Godfrey Herbert DSO commanded an armed merchant cruiser during the Second World War and died in Rhodesia in 1961.

There were, of course, two survivors from these UC submarine incidents, Captains Arnold and Tebbenjohanns. Both were confined for the duration of the war. As it happens, extensive material has been retained on file in the National Archives in Kew regarding prisoners of war and transcripts of their interrogation, etc., including those of Tebbenjohanns and Arnold.

Among the record of questions and answers by the two commanders, the revelation that officers could serve out the remainder of their confinement in a neutral country came as a surprise.

The fact remains that there is very little first-hand testimony to substantiate whether or not these submarines were sunk by their own mines, and, if so, how. The only contemporary record is that penned by Tebbenjohanns in his letters and his list of the crew. Unsurprisingly, little is known about either man's role in civilian or military life after their release.

After the *UC42* incident, no additional UC boats were reported to have been lost by striking their own mines during mine-laying operations. A significant number of the UC boats built at the Vulcan yard in Hamburg also suffered from unusual engine problems, prompting Robert Grant in *U-Boat Hunters* to pose the question: 'Could sabotage have played a part?'

The German minelayers mounted a two-pronged attack during 1917. One of these was in the Irish Channel, and the other along the south coast of Ireland. Despite the havoc they caused, they did not prevent an American build-up, or Britain receiving essential supplies.

Laying mines was a two-way street, and the Americans became better at it. They eventually laid thousands of them across the North Sea and the English Channel, ultimately severing Germany's access to British waters and the Atlantic.

Diving the wreck of *UC42*

Don't ask me how, but I just knew that the Admiralty reports summarising the fate of *UC42* were not accurate. What set me thinking were the station reports and the information contained in the logs of the different patrol vessels that were involved in the submarine's detection and destruction – they didn't match some of the prominent naval intelligence summaries. I copied these in the National Archives at Kew, and they described the destruction of a submarine off the entrance to Cork harbour in September 1917. They were at odds with some of the Admiralty's own summations of the incident.

It's a credit to British intelligence and record keeping, or the lack of it, that so many researchers were eluded by the details of the incident. More than a few doubted that the submarine was there at all.

Almost ensuring that it would never be found, the reported position of the wrecked submarine recorded by the Admiralty's Hydrographic Office offered a significant discrepancy from the record of position reported by the patrol and diving vessels. Given the significant amount of contemporary activity and record regarding the detection of this minelayer, depth-charging it, the diving on it by hard-hat divers at the time and subsequent removal of documents and equipment, there is insufficient latitude to assume a simple clerical error had occurred.

Using the bearings reported by the patrol vessels that stood over the disabled submarine at the time, we plotted our own estimated position and made a number of forays out of Crosshaven, Cork harbour, in search of it. Crosshaven is also home to the oldest yacht club in the world, the Royal Cork Yacht Club, and it is where many of the officers stationed at Queenstown during the First World War socialised. This would have including those from the mine-sweeping flotilla that detected *UC42* just off the mouth of the harbour, off Roche's Point, in 1917.

As the seabed can be quite rocky in the general area, the only device we felt might help us to detect the wreck was a magnetometer – a mistaken assumption. Armed with not one but two of these completely frustrating devices, we began 'mowing the lawn'. Natural magnetic anomalies aside, anyone who has used them will know just how frustrating varying results can be if the depth and speed is not kept uniform, or if the fish rises or falls, or if it comes nearer to rocky outcrops – and so on. If it's blowing a near gale and your head is not what it should be after a late night in Cronin's, you should go back to bed.

Other equally frustrating results can be produced on the turn. It so happens that the area we concentrated on was, broadly speaking, the correct one, but it was also an area through which the pipeline to the Kinsale gas field passed. Given that we were getting these anomalies in an area where we believed the pipeline to be, we ignored the results on or close to the turn.

To cut a long story short, we did find odd bits of naval debris but failed to locate the wreck. I turned most of my key research material over to local boatman and diver Billy Birmingham in 2009 with best wishes for any future wreck-hunting he or his friends might like to pursue.

In 2010 a resurvey of the Kinsale gas pipeline took place and the wreck of *UC42* was detected with a commercially operated side-scan. It was not in the precise area we had covered, but it was damn close. The wreck was dived almost immediately by a group of divers from Cork, who produced some great images of the wreck, and that was that – almost.

It was certain that word of the find would travel and the wreck would soon be swarming with divers. Not in itself a problem, but I had heard through the grapevine that there was still explosive material in the wreck and, given its proximity to the Kinsale gas field pipeline, it was more than just possible that an exclusion order might be placed around the wreck. The presence of any deceased German sailors in the submarine was another matter to consider. A preservation order was later placed on the site.

Burning with curiosity and with an unseasonal lull of calm weather upon us, we seized the moment. Seven or eight members of the diving club headed down to Crosshaven on the morning of 30 January 2011. We chartered a local angling boat and skipper. In such matters it's hard to surprise locals, but on this occasion the skipper was more than surprised to learn where and what we were headed for. He had heard nothing of the discovery on his doorstep. We brought our own GPS and guided the boat to the location. The journey out under the old military forts guarding the entrance to Cork harbour was short enough. The marks were good and we had no trouble locating the site. We all dived together and had a good old mooch around the new wreck.

Now, when I tell you that January in Irish waters does not make for a comfortable dive, it is a statement that really doesn't do justice to the severity of the cold I felt that morning. Of course, all jazzed-up to the gills, we didn't pay much heed before the dive. Getting out was a different matter. It was an angling boat and the skipper's boarding ladder was more akin to a step-ladder hanging out of the *Titanic*.

Delighted at finally hauling my limp body over the gunnels, the skipper redeemed his dwindling reputation when he produced broad-rimmed mugs of soup, broad enough for me to plunge my frozen finger tips into – I don't normally wear gloves and I don't normally dive in January these days. The numb finger tips tasted gorgeous for most of the journey back to Crosshaven.

Lying relatively close to the pipeline, and in surprisingly good whole condition, the stern of the wrecked submarine is damaged but does not resemble some Admiralty reports on file that suggest she was completely destroyed after striking one of her own mines. The outer hull, a lighter gauge metal than the pressure hull, has almost completely disappeared, leaving the inner hull totally visible and remarkably intact. I assume the remains of some its submariners are still within the hull.

A contrasting opinion was held by the diver and researcher Eoin McGarry, who suggests that this damage is consistent with what one might expect to be caused by a mine. He also stated that the foremost mine chute is empty, and that there are mines in the other five.

The possibility of subsequent salvage of mines aside, this concurs with other Admiralty reports. There were no sign of torpedoes, although the tubes remain closed. Quite a number of the mines remain and seem to be filled with this pale putty-like substance. I am told this is the explosive contents of the mine. Gas and high explosives!

What this immediately reminded me of was the story of the diver who walked into the Great Outdoors store in Cork many years ago to have his diving cylinder refilled. While waiting for the fill, he parted with the story of how he stumbled across the wreck of a submarine during his work laying the pipeline to the Kinsale gas field. He recounted how the mine chutes were filled with cement!

Since writing, it has been reported that this submarine wreck will be dismantled, recovered or destroyed because of the exposed mines in it and the danger presented by divers tampering with them while in such close proximity to the gas pipeline. It would also be nice to see an attempt made at investigating for any remains of the submariners that may still be inside.

Epilogue

The Flanders command had two gruesome reputations. One was for their destruction of a huge amount of shipping by a small number of exceptional commanders. And one can't help wondering if the outcome of the war might have been different if there had been more of them.

The other was its high attrition rate. The command suffered the loss of so many boats and crews that it became known as *Abs aufkommando* – the drowning command.

The Well-Head of All Pyrates

The smuggler is a person who, though no doubt blameable for violating the laws of his country, is frequently incapable of violating those of natural justice, and would have been in every respect an excellent citizen had not the laws of his country made that a crime which nature never meant to be so.

Adam Smith.

The descriptive name of Broad Haven is given to an area off the north shores of Erris, which is one of the most extreme promontories of Ireland and is situated on the north-west coast of Mayo. This wild and beautiful place was recorded on maps as far back as the fifteenth century, when it was described as Brede Haven. Variations such as Bread Haven and Braed Haven appeared later. In the seventeenth century it was recorded by the Dutch cartographer Jacob Aertz as Brodhaven, and thereafter as Broad Haven, Broadhaven, and Broadhaven Bay.

One of the earliest maps of Ireland, 'Tabula nova Hinernie, Anglie et Scotie' in Claudius Ptolemaeus' *Geographia: Strassburg 1513*, clearly outlines Clew Bay and Achill but does not show definition for the promontory of Erris, or the large indent of Donegal Bay. This general part of the west coast of Ireland is labelled 'Cormadella'.

'Corma' was known to the Greeks and the ancient Celts as a beer made for the lower classes from grain and some honey, a brew that gave headaches. 'Della' or 'Delta' could be a diminutive of several Greek words with different and some obvious meanings. Not well-known for grain production, why this area should be singled out for beer-making is not clear – was it exported from there at one time? The monks were there, and were certainly good at it, but they were prevalent in a number of other places too.

Probably meaning the same as it does today, the evolved version of the name Broadhaven is in wide use throughout the British Isles and would seem to have Dutch or Scandinavian origins, where the specific older combination 'Brede Haven' is still in use. Steeped in ancient archaeology and mythology, 'Erris' itself is derived from Iorras and Lar Ros, meaning 'a western promontory'. It was also known as Invermore in the sixteenth century, meaning a large estuary. This might have referred to both the Blacksod and Broadhaven bays.

As well as English, there are records of Spanish, Dutch and Danish ships visiting and wrecking in this area. A number of other place names dotted around the promontory would also seem to have been derived from the influence of visitors from other countries. *Carraig na Spana* abound, but it is also known that the Dutch and the Danes exploited the rich fishing grounds in their busses off the west coast of Ireland, well before the British and the Irish who lived along there. An unlikely exception were the fishing boats that came from Rush and Skerries on the east coast of Ireland.

Having been in Ireland since the ninth century, it is all the more surprising that there is not more record of the Danes in this part of Ireland.

Danish Cellar, an area in the cliffs at Erris Head, and *Cuirdin Min* (the Dutch Rushes), a plant growing on the cliffs of Erris, also point to outside influence. The places that have kept their Irish names can be quite revealing, such as the one indicated at the entrance to Blind harbour on Bald's map on the north face of Erris. Written as Bealagunnamore, or Cannon Mouth, it is right on the money and is the very place where divers located the wreck site of a seventeenth-century ship and a number of large iron cannon.

Appearing to be an old Irish place name, Gub A Vruni is one that presents some difficulty interpreting. Seemingly a mixture of Irish and an Anglicised interpretation of an Irish word or name sound, such as 'Rooney' or 'Roney', and the 'bh' replaced with the same sounding 'v'. The name Rooney is synonymous with the lore of wrecking in this area. The 'Gub' referred to is an area known now as Brandy Point. It is the next point north of Inver Point, where there was supposedly a ship with barrels of brandy wrecked. Father Sean Noone in *Where The Sun Sets* gives its older name Gub A Vruni, and the translation 'Wreckage Point'.

As use of the letter 'V', but not the sound, is extremely rare in the Irish language, there may be reason to suspect that it may have some connection with the Spanish Armada wreck believed to be at nearby Inver Point, and the German-Italian word name Bruni, from Bruno, loosely meaning 'brown person'. Bruni also has history in the Scandinavian countries. It could also simply be because the land is boggy and brown at this place.

The description suggested by the name or term Broad Haven can be assigned to two places in the same area. One, Broadhaven Bay, is meant to describe the whole expanse of water, from the sheer and inaccessible cliffs of north Erris across to Kid Island on the opposite and northern side of the bay. For some reason, the Stags, a dramatic feature of high rocks which emerge from the sea a couple of miles further eastward and opposite the entrance to Portacloy, are traditionally included in any description of Broadhaven Bay. The small Kid Island denotes that sharp geographical turn eastward into a vast expanse of sheer cliff face which runs for about 30 miles to Sligo and can rise to 900 feet (GSI) in places. This impressive east–west geological feature of high cliff coastline diminishes after the broad estuary of Killala Bay.

The outer bay of Broadhaven can be a haven for ships on the Erris side seeking respite from south to south-west winds, and on the north side, off Dun Keeghan, from northerly winds. However, both anchorages are not to be relied upon for holding a ship during any appreciable winds, owing to the slatey or rocky nature of the seabed. With certain exceptions, given its almost complete exposure to the west, this area cannot provide any unqualified safe haven for ships.

Instead, Broad Haven, when used in two words without the bay, meant a large harbour of refuge within the bay. This other haven spans the waters between the coast at Inver on the eastern shore and that at Ballyglass. The waters are significantly deeper in some places on the western side of the Haven. Tucked in behind the headland of Erris, and orientated north–south, the area provides almost complete protection from winds emanating from a wide range of directions. However, winds in a narrow window between the north and north-west can present a threat to ships driven in or sheltering here. It was also known as 'Broad Haven harbour'.

Situated on the eastern shore of Broad Haven is the small harbour of Inver, essentially just a small, but safe, bay with the scant remains of Inver Castle at its eastern end where the Owenduff river flows into it. Opposite an ancient grave mound in the sand dunes, Inver Castle was situated in a slightly elevated position above the shore. It was a structure of great extent and strength, and at one time it was considered the principal fortress in Erris. It was owned by the Burkes, the home of the Barrets, and then the Cormucks, Cormicks, McCormucks or McCormicks, and then the Shaens. Sometimes called Inver Bay, it can give shelter from the northerly winds to relatively large boats.

The waters within this broad haven can provide protection from storms from almost all directions, and the area is known to have been used by native and foreign mariners alike since records began. Importantly, it is quite suitable for loading or landing goods from ships and for repairing ships.

Referring to the totality of Broad Haven, it was considered that its estuary and bay could provide a perfect haven where, as Sir Oliver St John wrote in 1914, '300 sail may ride without annoying each other ... in 20–24 fathoms of water'. The anchorage, surrounded by farming and seafaring communities, and the number of small streams that flowed into it, could easily supply plenty of food and fresh water to a considerable number of ships.

The castle at Inver is one of a chain of castles running from that other haunt of the renowned pyrates the O'Malleys and Martins in Greatman's Bay, through Connemara and Mayo. They straddle the coast in strategic places, often within sight or signal proximity of one another. The castles were homes and fortresses and were in such positions as to be able to forewarn adjoining ones of any approaches by land or sea. Many, if not all, of these were used by the local clans such as the O'Malleys.

Inver Castle was in sight of another of Barret's castles, situated on the opposite side of the Broad Haven estuary, near Ballyglass, and also in signalling proximity to the castle on the cliffs at Doonaninon (Doonanierin, Dun Keegan, Dun Keeghan) to the north. It is reported that this castle also came into the ownership of Michael McCormuck as early as 1618 (Sir William Monson puts McCormuck in the castle as early as around 1614), as did Dooncarton soon after. This castle stood on the headland of the inner southern side of Broadhaven Bay.

A significant feature of Inver harbour, or just Inver, is its ancient Gaelic origins. The name remains in use right across the British Isles, and is also spelt as Inbhir or Inbhear. Its meaning refers to an area where rivers or streams meet: a river mouth, estuary and also a sea lough. For obvious reasons now, the area was also known as Dun Inbhir.

During the seventeenth century, this part of Mayo had already gained an unexpected and seemingly unlikely reputation for itself. A small number of actions by privateers off the Inniskea islands and around Erris are described in news media, state papers and in some publications. These do not match the inflated opinions reported by Sir William Monson after he was despatched there in around 1614 with a view to clearing out a place that had become 'the well-head of all pyrates'.

In an almost Shakespearean-like recollection, Monson recalls how he posed as the most famous English pirate, Captain Henry Mainwaring, when he dropped in on the McCormucks at Inver and hanged a pirate or two before he left. The story is extremely entertaining, but none of his victims were members of the McCormuck clan.

He later wrote that, 'Ireland was the great clearing house, rendezvous and playground of pirates from Ireland, Iceland, and the Baltic to the Straits of Gibraltar. In those out of the way places a pirate may trim his ships without affront from the country.'

When it was learned that Monson's ship was approaching the bay, McCormuck would seem to have fled the castle – done a runner, in today's parlance – leaving the greetings to be performed by his wife until he considered it safe to return. Monson remarked that: 'The gentleman of that place (Mr Cormac or McCormac) like a wily fox absented himself and left his wife and hackney daughters to entertain the new guests till he beheld the coast was clear.'

Interestingly, the very same approach seems to have been taken by McCormuck sixteen years later, when the diver Jacob Johnson arrived at Inver in search of Spanish Armada guns – i.e. leaving the greeting of the strangers to his wife, Ellen. Or he might just have been a very busy man?

Blessed with not a single harbour in north Erris, there is also a remarkable haven for mariners on the opposite side of the head, in Blacksod Bay, or 'Black Harbour' as it came to be known. This large expanse of water, if not offering a superior facility, at least offers equal protection for large ships from the elements and trading. It is a large harbour that cannot be seen from the sea and it too has a number of castles around it. It was an area described in such godforsaken terms as the 'black peninsula' where the people are 'wild and up to mischief'.

Once a very small village at the head of this estuary, the town of Belmullet is situated on a narrow isthmus which joins this most westerly peninsula with the rest of the County Mayo. Also known as the Mullet(s), this name was given to a species of sea fish as far back as Roman times. As Beal Muilleat it has the meaning the 'mouth of the fords'. The mullet species of fish flourishes on organic material such as rotting seaweed, leaves and even bog material in low-lying coasts and shallow estuaries. And God knows there is no shortage of bog in Mayo. The village is a fairly large town now, boasting a number of hotels. The reason for its significant growth is not welcomed by everyone.

Versions of history

These remote lands belonged to ancient Irish clans and were expropriated by the Tudors by law and by force – in many cases the same thing. As a consequence of constant warring between the English and the clans, and between the clans themselves, poor inhabitants were driven into the useless higher lands, which were suitable only for the most tenacious livestock. They became those cottagers who lived in bog huts and boolies and less kindly, but probably more accurately, described by mid-nineteenth-century travellers as tottering hovels.

The land had once been heavily forested and then cleared of the timber. Stone was moved to provide for planting and it is also a land that has no shortage of stone. Knowing little of money until it was demanded for rents and tithes, a system of bartering had survived among the population. These people were made unbelievably poor, but had at one time lived in harmony with nature from a land that was made rich and fertile in areas and teemed with fish. Thousands were condemned to famine and disease and the tearful train of emigration began.

It was known that, as Samuel Lewis put it in *Topographical History of Ireland* in 1837, 'Mayo, in the Roman provincial called Magee, was replenished both with pleasure and fertility, abundantly rich in cattle, deer, hawks and plenty of honey.' Regretfully, in its more modern history, right up to the end of the twentieth century, the north-west of the county remained a relatively poor and desolate part of Ireland, having suffered the ravages of emigration and the depopulation of its islands. Its inhabitants nevertheless remained very proud of their land and heritage. Since the recent exploration and exploitation of oil and gas which has come to this part of Ireland in recent times, Erris and Belmullet are no longer the unknown places they once were. Unfortunately, the 'progress' that came with it has fractionalised its communities and only time will tell how divisions and the impact on its future will mend.

The canvas that is history has continually been reworked in order to provide new understanding of our past. Some of it is enlightening and some of it has been truly regrettable. Particularly lamentable is the commentary on Ireland's Great Famine period by some contemporary journalists.

It is remarkable how, when a convenient scape-goat is discovered, one can salve the conscience. How quickly the vultures circle to feed. Referring to fishermen along the western coast, a journalist in the *Galway Vindicator*, in July 1849, was able to claim that: 'Whilst the whole world has been advancing in skill and acquiring fixed capital, they are little if anything, more skilful than long past generations, and families may be said to be their only inheritance – these are the effects of ignorance.'

The acquisition of capital always seems to have been used as a measure of success. As one of ignorance, it is new. Today, success is measured in the same way. Unless profit continually grows, a company is considered to be stagnated. Any profit actually represents growth. The ignorance to which the journalist referred is that of not being able to fish. This is completely ignoring the fact that man has fished since he came out of water, and the inhabitants of the west of Ireland had been good at it for centuries.

What he was specifically referring to in this issue was the deep-sea fishing off the west coast, for which the natives didn't have the more suitable larger craft. Why did they not build them? And why could a market distribution for larger catches not be developed, and prevent the starvation of the interior's inhabitants?

To be fair to the journalist, he did say the west coast fishermen were not entirely to blame and took a swipe at the 'Capitalists of Connaught' for having no interest in the industry.

But the journalist also seemed to have been unaware that a national scheme for such an industry had been proposed two centuries earlier.

Around the year 1629, a plan was mooted to create a national fishing fleet – a corporation. Appearing to be the basis for the form which the great British fishing fleet eventually took, the plan proposed to establish a fleet of fishing boats, 'busses', to be built for the fishing population around the British Isles and supplied to them under a national purchase scheme. Fishing with them could remain local to coasts, but a fleet would be established to pursue the different species of shoaling fish, pilchards, herrings, etc.

Considerable thought was also given to the white fish stocks and of maximising catch prices.

The voyages were planned to take them from Broadhaven northabout down the North Sea, into the English Channel and back around the south of Ireland. In *The Project of Fishing* it is written that: 'The busses must then return to winter at Broadhaven in Ireland, there to be trimmed and fitted for the next June, and the men to be employed in making nets &c.'

Considered again some thirty years later, the quality of the fishing and agriculture was expressed a little differently. Contained in the 1670 calendar of state papers for Ireland, but attributed to '1661 about', the landlord Shaen, Cormuck's successor, expressed his own ideas for fishing and agricultural opportunities in the area of Belmullet and Broadhaven: '... the commodiousness of the port, and the fishing upon that coast, it is a fit place to make a plantation of English and foreigners [Scottish?], both for manuring the ground and driving on the fishing, which may in time prove very advantageous to us'.

The value of the land, and its proximity to the rich fishing grounds off the west coast of Ireland, was well-known but, sadly, it lacked men with enough intellectual foresight and sufficient capital to develop it for its nearest communities. Instead, the seeds of sectarianism continued to be sown with the import of Protestant settlers. Sectarianism in a country is one thing, in Mayo it was plague.

English and Scottish fleets came to the west of Ireland in pursuit of the large stocks of fish there while the inadequate Irish vessels remained confined to inshore fishing.

Before then, those living in the west of Ireland had no need to venture deep-sea in order to catch enough fish to feed themselves. There was already an abundance of a wide variety of species inshore, on which they had successfully sustained themselves for centuries. This included vast numbers of the high-protein salmon that were caught in fish traps without ever going to sea. Without any assistance, they managed this on an almost industrial scale. These fish were not only eaten locally, but were exported for centuries until the landlords saw the value in the fish.

This happy time continued until a man could be sent to the colonies and never seen again, for stealing, or being suspected of stealing, one of the fish of his forefathers.

After landlords and bishops began to demand a bigger piece of the pie, through edicts such as the 'Right of the Sea All Round Erris' granted to the Protestant Bishop Stafford in the seventeenth century, the local people's share just kept diminishing, leaving only the remnants of catches that could barely sustain them. Living in the most remote parts of Ireland, these people were impoverished. They lacked the wherewithal to even build themselves decent accommodation, never mind large boats. When they attempted to improve their property, their rents were increased.

And as for the tithes and taxes, could these not have been invested in developing fishing? Could the capitalists of Connaught not have reinvested their tax money in boatbuilding, and hired local fishermen to crew the vessels, making profit and a living for everybody?

The suggestion of a corporation was by no means a new one. The Basques of France and Spain had also been fishing off the coast of Ireland since the beginning of the sixteenth century, and probably before. Their approach, though, was a more enlightened and cooperative one, sharing between the supporting merchants, captains and crew and reaching a very satisfactory measure of division. The ideas had been around for centuries but for some reason, in Ireland, there was a failure to step up to the plate.

This beautiful and self-replenishing food resource continues to be misunderstood and abused. In the case of Ireland, it is a resource that is now exploited by many others on a far greater scale than the Dutch in their busses ever did. Salmon are now farmed in cages for the masses, while our wild heritage remains in the possession of those who can afford it.

When the potato failed in these parts of Ireland, thousands starved and thousands more fled. It is sometimes mischievously suggested that it was the population's own fault – that they were ignorant and couldn't fish to save themselves. There were of course other factors involved, as those who starved or fled were certainly not the only poor people in the country at the time eating potatoes.

In desperate efforts to stave off starvation, there was a rash of piracy by small boats in the west of Ireland in 1847. Their quarry was not fortune but corn. Hopelessly ill-equipped for their forced new predatory occupation, they were soon rounded up by the lawmen and harshly dealt with.

The situation in Belmullet in 1847 was past being desperate and had descended into pure hopelessness. The inhabitants were dying in their hovels in the bogs and on the side of the road. Seasoned travellers to the area struggled with their emotions and a vocabulary ill-equipped to describe the scenes of famine, disease and the emaciated skeletons that were strewn across the bog, waiting for death.

Fortunately, there were those like William Bennett, who visited Belmullet during March 1847. He produced a significant report that would have been the envy of Dante and was later reproduced by the Society of Friends. These extracts from his report are truly upsetting:

Many of the cabins were holes in the bog covered with a layer of turf and not distinguishable as human habitations from the surrounding moor, until close down upon them. The bare sod was about the best material of which any of them were constructed. Doorways, not doors, were usually provided at both sides of the bettermost – back and front – to take advantage of the way of the wind ... Outside many were all but unapproachable, from the mud and filth surrounding them; the same inside, or worse if possible ... avoiding only such as were known to be badly infected with fever, which was sometimes sufficiently perceptible from without, by the almost intolerable stench. And now language utterly fails me in attempting to depict the state of the wretched inmates ... We entered a cabin. Stretched in one dark corner, scarcely visible, from the smoke and rags that covered them, were three children huddled together, lying there because they were too weak to rise, pale and ghastly, their little limbs, on removing a portion of the filthy covering, perfectly emaciated, eyes sunk, voice gone, and evidently in the last stage of actual starvation. Crouched over the turf embers was another form, wild and all but naked, scarcely human in appearance. It stirred not, nor noticed us. On some straw, soddened upon the ground, moaning piteously, was a shrivelled old woman, imploring us to give her something – baring her limbs partly, to show how the skin hung loose from the bones, as soon as she attracted our attention. Above her, on something like a ledge, was a young woman, with sunken cheeks – a mother I have no doubt – who scarcely raised her eyes in answer to our enquiries, but pressed her hand upon her forehead, with a look of unutterable anguish and despair.

Regarding the matter of the Great Famine in certain parts of Ireland, the stark reality of an uncomfortable truth remains. It proved an opportune blight, one which nailed the coffin shut for impoverished and unwanted tenants, those who were already on their knees. It presented an opportunity to get rid of them, or let them die.

'The Law of the Land' has, in times past, been taken to mean the privilege of the power to interpret it.

Shipwreck, wrecking and salvage around Erris and Broadhaven

Dotted with islands that show signs of being inhabited for thousands of years, such as the beautiful windswept and abandoned Inishkeas, the coast from Broadhaven Bay around to the entrance to Blacksod Bay at North Achill is a fiercely rugged landscape and one that has had its fair share of shipwrecks. Understandably, the geography of this part of Ireland was misrepresented on charts by early cartographers, even as recently as the late seventeenth century. By contrast, however, its harbours were well-known places of refuge for ships battered by the Atlantic weather.

Notwithstanding the knowledge that many mariners possessed about this area, there are at least 212 shipwrecks recorded between Broadhaven Bay and North Achill. The true figure probably amounts to many more. Despite having a number of safe bays and anchorages, much of this coastline is impossible to access either by land or sea. Completely exposed to the Atlantic Ocean, it lacked any navigational markers or lights until two lighthouses were commissioned on Eagle Island, to the west of Erris, in 1835. It might seem surprising, then, that there weren't many more maritime casualties.

Taken from Galway to Killybegs, there is probably a lower than average number of recorded shipwrecks per mile of coastline than elsewhere around the coast of Ireland. The isolated and sparsely populated shores of West Galway, Connemara, Achill and Erris, and their comparative geographical positions, were always considered to have had a lot less maritime traffic than, say, the east or south coasts of Ireland. Given this area's strong trade links with Scotland and elsewhere, it might be the case that coastwise traffic was probably no less prevalent there than anywhere else in Ireland, and maybe more so.

Notwithstanding its remoteness, the maritime commerce of these areas was probably even considerable at one time, when one considers the extensive trading practises of maritime families like the Burkes, O'Malleys, O'Flahertys and many others. They, and the foreign fishing fleets, as well as the wool and wine merchants of Galway, traded up and down the coast of Ireland to Scotland and to the western shores of Europe for centuries.

Another reason for only a modest record of significant shipwrecks lies in the fact that the course of deep-sea traffic between northern Europe and the Americas, and beyond, passes either to the south or north of Ireland. Exceptions to preferred routes were made during time of war and storms. If the vessels of the Spanish Armada had not wrecked in the remote areas of Ireland that they did, records of shipwrecks of any significance along this coast would have been sparse and the subject would have received very little attention.

Even long lost and unknown shipwrecks have a role to play in tourism today, and frequently figure now in the 'about' bumf relating to the 'Wild Atlantic Way' and its places of interest.

Marine casualty returns can only be reported if the incident is known about and communicated to others. Correspondence and the news media were the first order. Both suffered proportionally with remoteness and isolation, but especially so around Erris. There are many places in Ireland that can claim to have been remote and that the reporting of vessels in distress there went undocumented. In north-west Mayo, there were added reasons.

The area was the target of a continuous tirade of derogatory slurs, and the description of being 'a stronghold of freebooters' was the least of them. The area was one of the last places in Ireland to be subdued by English rule, and some local feelings still hold that they were never subjugated. Having experienced so much suffering after been cast into the 'Hell of Connaught', bitterness was branded into the souls of its inhabitants and is still palpable. It remains a wild, remote and beautiful land, and much to the chagrin of the likes of Royal Dutch Shell its people have retained a very independent spirit.

The more removed a place is from the centralised administration of law, the more stories regarding wreckers seem to prevail. Broadhaven and Erris are no different in this respect. There are a small number of stories regarding luring lights on cliff tops, looting and one of murder at Shank's Cave, where a sailor named Shank, or a crew member of a ship of that name, succumbed. Other than word of mouth and some exceptions regarding looting, no supporting documentation for these reports has been found.

There are records of a number of Ireland-based privateers who operated off, and probably out of, Erris – no different to many other places around Ireland. There are also records of a number of English and French privateers who operated out of the Inishkea Islands.

Much to my own surprise, during research for these stories I discovered that Ireland's geographical position in the Atlantic meant that at one time it was a veritable island of privateers, a staging post for their voyages that ranged over a huge expanse of seas and oceans.

At first glance, piracy would seem to have been less prevalent off Erris than in other places around Ireland. The act of piracy itself may have been, but, as we will discover, there were no shortage of pirates in Broadhaven, or around the rest of Ireland.

There seems to be no getting away from the existence, however, of an above average number of hard-hitting reports describing threats made by local people against shipwrecked survivors around Erris, and the exploitation of wreck and flotsam from shipwreck. Curiously, though, the activities of these local people were not at the expense of lives. Neither do they seem to have resulted in any violence or injury, at least on the survivors' side. And once more, here in one of the remotest places of Europe, local inhabitants with precious little to sustain them rushed to rescue and to care for the survivors of shipwreck.

Where a landlord might not have been seen to enforce his right to wrecks that occurred on his land, or in the sea off it, it could not be assumed that local folk, or anyone else, could just help themselves to it. In many cases, the local coastguard or revenue officials took the opportunity of seizing the wreck and laying claim to it under the law of 'Droits of the Admiralty', as in the case of Richards' reaffirmation of his entitlements to 'the wrecks of the sea, jetsam, flotsam, lagan, and derelict' on his lands at Erris, which was a consequence of officials challenging his right to wreck in 1843.

The following example of shipwreck, and of accusations levelled at wreckers, is presented in some detail. The reason is not a wish to dismiss out of hand all blame that might otherwise be intuitively attributed to some coastal folk during the incidence of shipwreck. It is alternatively presented as such to dispel the myths that quite often surround these events – these myths often leading to blame where it doesn't belong. Given the bigotry and the animosity that existed between the classes, landlord and tenant, and the former's superior access to the written word and the press, the case against the wrecker has too often been portrayed without balance – to put it kindly. And in the following example, mischievously and almost criminally so.

In 1863, newspapers, led by the *Sligo Chronicle*, reported that the American ship *Veturia*, captained by a man named Booth and carrying grain, was driven ashore and broke up on the rocks at Inver in Broadhaven on 2 November. The 470-ton barque had been on a voyage from New York when she ran into Broad Haven harbour, seeking refuge during a storm. Both anchors were let go but failed to prevent the ship from striking the rocks.

The initial reporting of the shipwrecking was typical, and as the crew and valuables were all saved, there was no cause for extended concern. However, the *Mayo Constitution* saw it differently and digressed with a vitriolic tirade of poisoned reporting. This version then began to appear in newspapers across the British Isles. Once again, one reporter copying another verbatim – each presenting his story as fact.

In light of a letter published over a month later, in the *Belfast Newsletter*, earlier bylines were proved to be scandalously libellous, and among some of the worst ever used to falsely describe the actions of wreckers. The *Mayo Constitution*'s attack first appeared around 10 November in an article which contained phrases, such as '… the peasantry behave with shocking barbarity … cruel monsters'.

What the article 'Wreckers on the Coast of Mayo' suggested had taken place was as follows: The *Victoria*, the incorrect name of the *Veturia* that was repeated incorrectly almost everywhere, dragged her anchors until she was blown onto the rocks at Inver. Local people had gathered on the shore and beckoned the captain to throw a rope. He did, and with that they began to haul a heavier one to the shore. The first rope was called a hand line. The journalist then reported that those on shore were looking for more rope and the captain, becoming wary, refused. The would-be rescuers then proceed into the surf, as far as they dared, and cut the rope and retrieved it before stealing it away.

The captain was reported to have then swam ashore with another line and set up a station on the shore, from which he rescued all twenty-two of the crew and their valuables before the ship broke up. The ensuing articles, one after another, reported that the ship had been wrecked 'among savages, and the cruel monsters' that were prepared to risk the lives of the whole crew on board the ship for a length of rope.

Having given the dog a bad name, it was then time to hang it. Trying and convicting the shore men, the *Mayo Constitution* also stated. '... We know of no felons we would feel much pleasure in having punished, as much disgraceful savagery has been unknown for many years on the wildest portions of our coast.'

The reputation and sensibilities of the more sane people of Ireland were by then at stake, and 'the peasantry who behaved with such shocking barbarity' had to be brought to justice. As if to confirm that the wrongdoings had been thoroughly investigated, the Archbishop Designate of Dublin, the Reverend Trench, lent voice to his solemn conviction of the men's guilt and to the accuracy of the reporting.

Having read hundreds of these shipwreck accounts, and even though it is more than 150 years later, this did not ring true.

Regarding what is more likely to have happened at Inver that day, the following account seems more fairly balanced and has the ring of truth to it. It is reproduced in full as it represents a conscience-stricken and just contradiction by a well-respected eyewitness in this case. More generally, it supports a warranted criticism of the slanted and mischievous comments that have been penned so often against coastal folk through the centuries.

The Wreck of the Barque *Veturia*, of Sunderland, in Broadhaven Bay.
Inver, Belmullet, Erris, 2 December 1863.
To the editor of the *Belfast Newsletter*.
Sir

I have just received through a friend a copy of your paper on the 16th ult., containing an extract from the *Daily Telegraph* on the above occurrence, and to which you add some remarks.

The story copied into your journal and commented on, would be, if true, I fully admit, a great disgrace to the country; but I have good grounds for believing, and am happy to be able to state that the facts are otherwise, inasmuch as the 'Irish Peasants' who succeeded in catching the 'hawser' pulled to shore to save the lives of fellow creatures, and cheerfully volunteered on the occasion, be it known, at no small risk. Instead of committing the inhuman and barbarous crimes, with which they stand charged-viz., 'when no more rope could be obtained by treacherous signs, rushing to the shore, cutting the hawser as far out as they could reach, making off with their booty, and heartlessly abandoning their fellow-men to fate' – the Irish peasants, as I am informed and believe, firmly held on the 'hawser' first caught by them (just as Irishmen know how) and manfully struggled on the rocks, amidst raging surf, until six out of eight hands on board were safely landed upon it. The two other men, as the tide receded, got ashore on spars, hanging from the vessel's side, and four of the crew previously left in one of the ship's boats. There were, in all, only twelve hands – accounted for and saved as above.

Another charge requires some notice, such as 'the wholesale robbery, by the said peasants, of such bags, boxes, etc., as were either cast or taken ashore,' which is not true, though I am sorry to say I cannot wholly excuse their conduct on this head; as after the men were safely landed, and such bags, boxes, etc. as were removable were drawn to shore, by-the-way, on the very same 'hawser', I believe as much of it and the hand line as could be got at was cut and carried off by some dishonest person or persons. I also believe that from the luggage & c., piled on the shore, one bag – the boatswain's property – was stolen. But with these exceptions, all other things taken to shore on that night were preserved, and safely carried to my house.

I could willingly conclude here, but as the *Telegraph* is anxious to know 'what landlords live about there;' and though I do not think it necessary to answer for others, for myself I will say, I am a member, but a very humble one, of the class, and particularly the proprietor of the shore on which the vessel struck; that my house is three quarters of a mile of where the accident occurred; and that I was on the spot in less than 2 hours after it took place. The writer further insists on finding out the perpetrators of the crime he describes – which would be rather a difficult job. However I will give him a few names from a list of the actors in the scene – viz., half dozen of the men who held, but did not cut, the rope on which the sailors landed, as follows:- Martin Cuffe, Inver, Belmullet; John Cuffe, Inver, Belmullet; Pat Lally, Inver, Belmullet; Pat Lally, Inver, Belmullet; John Donnelly, Graghet, Belmullet; Owen Ginty, Graghet, Belmullet; all who individually and collectively, with a least a half-a score of helpers, are anxious for the fullest and most searching enquiry into their acts, hoping thereby that something more agreeable than abuse may be their reward.

You note some unjust inferences, into which the *Telegraph* is drawn. It is plain that he travels out of his course to attack and offer insult to the Roman Catholic Church, in which religion there are just as respectable, high minded, and honourable men as there is in his creed, whatever that may be.

Further comment I consider unnecessary; but as the articles in your paper receive wide circulation, and doubtlessly arouse various feelings faraway and near to home, I will ask, as a an act of simple justice to the poor Irish peasants, for publication of this note, and will hope that such papers as copied the articles of accusation, will copy the reply. – I remain your faithful servant,

Isidore Peter Blake.

The Blake name is a significant one in the history of Connaught.

Mentioned above, John Donnelly was a neighbour of Mr Blake and a blacksmith and fisherman at Inver. At risk to his own life, he is also reported to have taken his currach and rowed to the stricken vessel and then took the rope to the men on the shore, whereby the entire crew were saved. The wrecking and the rescue was remembered long after, and John Mulldowney penned a song in remembrance:

Come all ye jolly seamen bold throughout old Erin's Isle
I hope you'll pay attention to these lines I now compile
Concerning the *Victoria*, her loss we do bewail
That was bound for Sligo town but alas it did not f(s)ail.
[The name of the ship continued to be misspelt as *Victoria*, when it should have been *Veturia*.]

I am unaware if Mr Blake's magnificent note appeared elsewhere. It wasn't long, however, before Mr Blake got wind of some criticism being levelled at him and charges reiterated against the people of the locality (Inver) by the *Mayo Constitution*. In response, he wrote to that paper directly and they published his letter on 16 December.

Mr Blake was also accused of not been present at the subsequent salvage court that was convened shortly after the incident and for not having attended the scene of the wreck until some hours after the event.

Mr Blake admitted he:

> ... was not present at the Salvage Court, where a reward was claimed on the distinct grounds of saving life and property – where a decree awarding James Caulfield of Inver £3, for distribution between himself and others, which determination in my humble judgement would never be arrived at by the upright gentlemen forming the court, if the atrocious crime charged by your correspondent in the letter published on the 10th ult. were in any way sustainable.

Mr Blake took the opportunity in this second fine note to reiterate that 'not one inch of the hawser was cut or injured, either before or while the crew were being landed'. What was cut was the end of the hand line that had been thrown ashore in order to pull in the heavier hawser and get it around a fixing.

Mr Blake finished off: 'Meantime, invite an enquiry, and await the result.' Put today, it would appear as 'Put up, or shut up!'

Not a stranger to pro-establishment, and often controversial conservative opinion, no reason was given for the vitriolic and untruthful position taken by the *Mayo Constitution* against the shore people at Inver. The incident regarding the hawser from the wreck to the shore, and the false accusation that it had been cut by the shore men, might have had less to do with their barbarity and more to do with any subsequent claim for a salvage reward.

In any event, the American owners of the *Veturia* thought that saving the lives of their captain and crew was only worth £3. The bad smell of the story and the false accusations just slinked off into obscurity.

It is no coincidence, and not just a matter of proximity, that the rescue and life-saving services that had already been established around Great Britain and Ireland by then, and which still exist to this day, are still comprised almost exclusively by those who live at and from the sea. They have in the past risked their lives repeatedly, and continue to do so, without favour or reward and they do it in that higher regard.

In his defence of the peasants involved, Peter Blake's rebuttal and straightening of the record has never been disputed. He does indeed appear to have been one of the few landlords that were an exception to the rule.

In the interest of balance, we might look at this earlier account recorded in the *Connaught Telegraph* of 27 October 1830, which was equally scathing of the treatment of shipwreck victims but might have had some justifiable cause. The 194-ton Austrian ship *Maria*, owned by the widow Rushton of Trieste and captained by Alexander Alexandrina, wrecked under the cliffs of Erris at Timber Cove, opposite Eagle Island. The ship was carrying a large cargo of fish and sundry goods. The wrecking was caused by poor visibility and piloting error.

Three crewmen were killed on the rocks and six were marooned there. A number of local people soon arrived, climbed down the cliffs and began to loot the wreck. Some harsh words and threats were traded between the surviving crew and the locals, but didn't become violent. Later the police arrived, and at least one local man was put in irons. Lord Bingham ordered their release and although there was a complaint made to the magistrate, no further action taken against the wreckers is recorded.

Much of the above was penned by J. P. Lyons, the parish priest of Kilmore, Erris, in a lengthy account. He expressed contempt for the 'denial of mercy and protection to wounded and shivering, shipwrecked and heartbroken strangers' by those who in his opinion were guilty of 'treachery and plunder'. He also considered the alacrity with which the wreck sale followed to be hurried and opportunistic.

Father Lyons' anger was directed at what he considered to be more a crime of neglect than violence against the shipwrecked mariners. No mention was made of mysterious lights or the lack of any warning ones. The captain and five other crew members reached Belmullet unharmed.

The Spanish Armada episode in Erris

A warning contained in the sailing instructions to captains of the Spanish Armada invasion fleet 1588, in the event of having to circumnavigate the British Isles, reads: 'And then take heed lest you fall upon the island of Ireland for fear of the harm that may happen unto you upon that coast.'

Regarding the fear of harm contained in the sailing instructions above given to captains of the failed Spanish Armada fleet in 1588, one has to wonder. Was it a warning to avoid wrecking on the wild and scarcely inhabited coastline of the west coast of Ireland at all costs? Or was it a warning as to what might befall survivors if they did happen to get on shore?

In the past, when we decided to visit a remote coastline, either to sail there or in search of shipwrecks, one of the first things we would do is refer to an Admiralty chart for that area. Making the visit much easier today, there are a considerable number of additional sources we can reference such as Google Earth and various types of seabed surveys, etc. In addition we will always consult with local people. The folklore and stories that have been handed down through generations are fast disappearing, and much of it cannot be found on charts.

The point being made is that local people, in the space of a few hours, can guide one to the whereabouts of safe moorings and inform you on how to avoid any uncharted and dangerous maritime anomalies. Maybe helped by a few nice pints, they can surprise with a canny knowledge of local shipwrecks and point convincingly to places named after such incidents. By your consultation, you have also paid them the courtesy of flagging your visit to their neck of the woods.

Centuries before, if a captain was about to set out on a voyage into unknown waters he would equip himself with the available charts relating to his voyage. His first port of call was to the cartographer. Sixteenth-century cartographers' faint knowledge of the North Atlantic was manifest in the charts they produced of the west coast of Ireland. Their accuracy varied from one to another, and for a while one just copied another. It is remarkable to look at these charts today and see just how the interpretation of the coastline varied during earlier centuries, with that shown on later charts not necessarily more correct.

Over the passage of time, navigational and geographical maps
have improved. At times, though, they also became victims of
interpretation. Some features have been interpreted more accurately
with time and research, while others have been deleted altogether,
some because they were no longer visible. The rush to placate
consensus and dismiss story, myths, folklore and even fact is a
regrettable frailty that can result when one is faced with the 'tut tut'
of peer overview.

The charting of the island Hy-Brasil by cartographers in the
fourteenth century and thereafter, and that it remained on Admiralty
charts until the late nineteenth century, is a fact. Considered mythical
by many, its record remains a fascinating enigma. First shown on
ancient maps as being a couple of hundred miles off the west coast
of Ireland, the same position is now plotted as being on the edge of
some famous offshore fishing grounds, the Porcupine Bank. Oil and
gas have recently been discovered here.

The reference for the origin of the recording, its accuracy or its
truth remains a mystery. The stories that grew up around its existence
seem extraordinary and doing more harm than good for a fascinating
possibility was the mention of 'gold'. Some believe it is a fanciful story,
but cartographers and sea captains believed it was there and had a
very distinct shape and that it was in a specific position.

Academic opinion is often confused on the subject. On the one
hand, surprise is sometimes expressed at the accuracy of very old
charts and, on the other, uncomfortable anomalies on the same charts
are described as mythical. There is much in Irish folklore that supports
the existence of such an island. Among this is the story of a race of
people, Tuatha de Danann, who lived there, and visited Ireland.

Mirages of islands have come and gone, and so too have real
islands, and they continue to do so to this very day. Whatever the
truth, the name of the island lives on and can be seen on many
houses throughout the west of Ireland.

Many recorded the western shores of Ireland, this most western
and remote area of Europe, as a coastline that was ragged with
inlets, but almost perpendicularly straight from north to south, as
we can see in Speed's sixteenth-century map and others.

The coastline is by no means straight, or anything like it, and here
lies an explanation behind the warning to the Spanish captains. Many
of the Spanish commanders knew that their charts were not accurate

representations of this remote coast, but used them as a general guide to navigate clear of its dangers. Those who did approach the coast, just like all the mariners before them, used known geological features such as mountains and large river estuaries to guide them.

To approach these parts of Ireland from northabout was probably a very new experience for many of the Spanish commanders. To help in this, they had consulted with local knowledge before the Armada set sail. Even so, some captains probably already had a detailed knowledge of the coast as they and their ancestors had been trading with the clans there for many years.

Travelling with King Philip's Armada were a number of pilots or steersmen who had emigrated from Ireland and England. The Spanish had not intended to navigate the west coast of Ireland, but they had made provision for such an event and hired a number of Irish pilots. The fleet also included a number of Irish sailors from impressed seamen to revered captains, with a few bishops thrown in.

The danger that lay in the Atlantic off the west coast of Ireland was that inexperienced captains could steer too close to the land. The navigating instructions broadly suggested that captains should keep well out west of Ireland, providing themselves with plenty of sea room. Considerable sea room was required in order for these ungainly square sail ships to successfully manoeuvre clear of the west coast of Ireland and into Biscay. They would have anticipated the predominant south-west winds, but did not anticipate any sustained northerly ones at that time of the year. These could drive them south and home to Spain. Neither would they have expected the ferocity and unseasonal nature of the storms that beset them.

After many of the ships were sunk and badly mauled in the English Channel the weather remained contrary, helping the English ships to impede their escape. The only clear means of escape left to the Spanish ships was to go northabout. All things being equal, being late summer/early autumn, they would have expected to fare better than they did. With no friendly shores between them and Spain, beset with damaged and overburdened ships, lack of supplies and fresh water, and running headlong into the storm of the century, the Devil seems to have snaked through the Spanish ships like a plague while Drake's sails filled with the wind that blew from God.

Most of the remainder of the fleet made it around Scotland and, given their terrible condition, with fewer losses than one might have expected. They continued to beat westward into the Atlantic, but with the onset of September, and winds developing in strength from the north-west, they began to veer southward towards Ireland. Not all managed to navigate sufficiently far from the coast of Donegal before a series of terrible storms began, lasting for three weeks. The winds veered north-west to south-west and even abated for a while, with a short intervening spell of easterly winds. The ferocity and persistence of the north-west winds was unseasonal and most destructive. The mixed collection of Mediterranean vessels was scattered before the wind, and only small numbers remained in sight of each other.

Some were blown out to sea, some were lost and others were cast dangerously close to the west coast of Ireland. One can imagine the stragglers being swept down the west coast of Donegal, the only course that allowed them to avoid sailing against the storm. Despite the warnings, the tired ships, full of weary captains and soldiers, began to fall on the Irish coast.

The sailors aboard the racked vessels, those who understood that the coast of Ireland would continue southward without any great geographical change, can only have been terrified when they realised they were trapped in Donegal Bay. With the shoreline of mountains on their port side, and unable to make sufficient way to the west, terror must surely have given way to despair when they eventually caught site of the 30-mile line of high cliffs directly ahead on their horizon. The dark border of the extended headland was trimmed with a boiling white ocean stretching from Erris to Sligo, and stood between the ships and Spain. The only possible refuge for a square sail was Sligo Bay or the large bight of Killala Bay. You might be cautious if you were not familiar with these places, but in desperation the low-lying land would have appeared tempting.

The scattered flotillas consisted of roughly two categories – ships that were helpless for one reason or another and were being blown before the wind, and those that could manoeuvre or steer. The latter would have been seeking a place in which to shelter, but couldn't alter their course sufficiently to escape the high stone barricade of the north coast of Mayo.

Three vessels were blown onto the strand at Streedagh, north County Sligo, with terrible consequences. More than 850 drowned (though some historians have estimated it as high as over 1,200), died on the shore, or were put to the sword by Richard Bingham and his agents.

An unknown ship was lost on a coast known as Tirawley, somewhere between Killala and Erris, where as many as 150 survivors were brutally slaughtered by a group that included Scottish mercenaries led by Melaghlen McCabb. The remainder were put to the sword or hanged.

Another unknown is believed to have been lost between the Stags of Broadhaven and Kid Island.

The ship *Santiago* is presumed to have weathered the approach into Broadhaven Bay, and probably steered through the mouth of Broad Haven harbour, only to end up on the rocks at Inver Point.

The large *Rata Encoronada* steered in under the Mullet, but failed to make it into Blacksod Bay and was blown onto Fahy Strand, in front of Fahy Castle.

Yet another, the *Santa Ana*, followed the same route between Achill and the Mullet, but managed to get into Blacksod Bay, where she anchored safely in Elly Bay.

The *Señora de Begoña* may have followed into Blacksod shortly after that, but is said to have sailed away again soon after.

Survivors from the *Rata* and *Santiago* made the difficult march around the Mullet to where the *Santa Ana* lay. It was probably clear enough to local inhabitants that they would almost certainly suffer at the hands of the likes of Bingham for helping the Spanish survivors. And although there is no mention of a march by the group of survivors from the *Santiago*, it is almost certain they were also helped to escape. It is quite feasible that, in both cases, some of the survivors may have travelled by sea to Belmullet and Elly Bay. The water is well sheltered in both cases.

Those that did reach the *Santa Ana*, and sailed from Elly Bay, Blacksod, to Killybegs in Donegal, had the second misfortune to wreck again off Killybegs. Once more they escaped and eventually boarded another Spanish ship anchored here. She was the *Girona*, on to which a motley lot of survivors from various ships boarded in their next attempt to escape the coast of Ireland. Their final voyage was back in the direction of Scotland, where they hoped to gain sanctuary and eventually return to Spain.

Yet another, a third shipwrecking, was a wreck too far for Lady Luck. The *Girona* was lost trying to reach Scotland and it is believed that there were at least 1,300 soldiers and sailors on board her, of which only nine survived. She was dashed to smithereens on the rocks under Dunluce Castle, Benbane Head, County Antrim, on 28 October.

The reasons advanced for such brutal slaughter of shipwrecked mariners on the coast of Ireland were few. The most obvious was that these were the same men who intended to occupy England, and would certainly have done some slaughtering of their own had they been successful. More strategic was the example that had to be shown to other Spaniards, the French and the Irish themselves. England would not tolerate sympathy shown for any threat to British rule in Ireland, armed or otherwise.

The legacy of Richard Bingham, the 'Flail of Connaught', and his terrible slaughter of the Spanish shipwrecked mariners has never been forgotten. The part some Irish natives played in assisting him and the authorities, and performing some terrible slaughter of their own, is another regrettable legacy. The fact that the Irish could not, or would not, seize the very real military opportunity that had presented a seemingly rare opportunity to throw off the shackles of English tyranny is another for the list.

A countering argument for some of the treatment meted out to the Spanish at the hands of the Irish lies in communication, or lack thereof. There were approximately twenty-five incidences of Armada shipwrecks in Ireland in 1588. Not all of these resulted in mariners or troops coming ashore, but many did. Irish citizens and their chieftains had to decide on the spot whether or not to help enemies of the Crown. A chieftain in Donegal couldn't lift the phone and ring his counterpart in Kerry and enquire as to how many he had ashore in order to assess the possible success of an armed rebellion.

This, in all probability, may not have been a real option at all as the Spaniards showed no interest whatsoever in remaining in Ireland. And it was no wonder, when both sides were exclaiming that the Spanish defeat, and the hurtling of its bedraggled survivors on to the rocky shores of Ireland, was the handiwork of the Almighty.

Supporting poorly conditioned Spanish troops in Ireland at this time would have been unrealistic. Giving the circumstances that prevailed, the result was probably inevitable. Some were helped, others were given up, and some were even killed. It was a mopping up operation of a bedraggled army that had just wanted to get home.

Sir George Carew would seem to have had his finger on the pulse of the feelings in Ireland at the time when he wrote the following to Walsingham in an almost mocking tone:

Before the defeat of the Spanish fleet, the English nations as well as the Irishery, stood agaze how the game would be played. They did not certify their masters as they were commanded by the Lord Deputy, until after the news had arrived, when they not only put to the sword, them that had arrived, but the gentlemen are now ready to attend. There is no rebellion in the whole realm, so much terror prevails.

The whole episode of the action, inaction and attitude of the Irish to the helpless Spaniards, to one another and to the English, was noted across Europe and any future military adventures in Ireland would forever be viewed with a jaundiced eye.

Diving in Broadhaven

Our small group, Leinster Divers, were by no means the first divers to travel to Erris and the Mullet Peninsula in search of shipwrecks. Men have travelled there in search of sunken mysteries since the year of the Armada, 1588, when so many ships were wrecked on the west coast of Ireland. It wouldn't surprise me to discover that they were fishing for wrecks there long before that.

It would appear that the Dutch diver Jacob Johnson, aka Jacob the diver, received a warrant from the Crown bestowing on him the right to salvage wrecks in England and Ireland in 1629, which at the time included those from the Spanish Armada. He was, however, not the first man to salvage the wrecks, as it is known that several were salvaged by local chieftains and others. Using free divers and basic tools, they recovered a number of anchors, furniture, chests and cannon by 'fishing the wrecks'. Some of the salvage was exported under licence or seized by the authorities, and some was spirited away.

Our group decamped from Ballycotton to Belmullet in 1986. I had been trawling through every bit of available material concerning the loss of Lord Cloncurry's ship, the *Aid*, at Wicklow in 1804 when I came across a report in the *Cork Mercantile Chronicle* concerning the sinking of the *Sovereign*. A Guineaman, she was lost in 1804 off Smith's Rocks, a nasty submerged reef around 2 miles to the west of Ballycotton Island, East Cork, and the nearby harbour village and lifeboat station of the same name.

Our families were young at the time and, with all our children, we spent a memorable summer together there. Subsequent visits were confined to just the lads. Our boat was a reasonably large Avon inflatable, powered by a Yamaha outboard – a sturdy workhorse that stood us in good stead. Again we used a magnetometer, which we hoped might detect some of the iron cannon that were carried on the ship.

If the reader is familiar with this part of the south coast of Ireland, he might be aware that the visibility in the water is very good. The result, of course, is that light penetrates further down through the water, promoting sea life – including wrack. Prolific growth of wrack can be found down to 15 metres off Ballycotton, which is great – but not when you are trying to tow a magnetometer fish over it. Invariably the fish ends up on the wrack, transmitting a confusing plethora of magnetic signals.

I think we threw it there soon afterwards and just relied on a swim search. Swimming or, more correctly, wrestling your way through a dense forest of wrack while trying to maintain a compass bearing, and remain in some kind of relative position with other divers while buried in wrack, is not the easiest thing to do. Frequently unsure of your relative position, one had to keep popping up above the forest of wrack in order to see where the nearest set of bubbles where.

The cargo carried in Guineamen (slave ships) was classic. 'Elephants' teeth' (Ivory tusks), lignum vitae, precious gems, etc. It represented the return leg of the typical triangular voyage of these ships. The voyage began in London a year earlier with a ship packed with general merchandise of trinkets and hardware, the first leg bound for the coast of Guinea.

Having exchanged wares in Africa, a cargo of slaves was loaded and transported across the Atlantic to the sugar plantations in the West Indies.

The *Sovereign* returned in convoy from the West Indies through fierce storms, which very few ships survived. The story of events leading up to, and including, the loss of the *Sovereign* is a typically dramatic and unfortunate one. Equally exciting was the story of the rescue that was performed by local men after she struck on the rocks off Ballycotton and sank.

The men rowed out from Ballycotton harbour and then turned between the two small islands just offshore in terrible weather. Heading westward into the storm, they eventually reached the wreck and saved those still clinging to the mast of the sunken ship. It was a remarkable feat against the elements. It was reported at the time that details of the incident were sent to the Royal Humane Society for the consideration of medals and awards to be made to the men. There is no record in the society of a commendation having been received.

The rescue and lifeboat service at the Ballycotton station has a long and very proud record of life saving, which includes the Fastnet tragedy in 1979. If we had been able to locate the wreck, we may have gained enough publicity and got the *Sovereign*'s case reopened. A belated award might have been added to their already cramped roll board of honour and bravery, which would have predated their earliest entry. That was the idea anyway.

We failed to find that wreck, diving before we left on the remains of the famous paddle steamer *Sirius* and discovering some bits and pieces from a nineteenth-century transport ship that had been carrying men and horses.

The search for an Armada wreck at Inver

Basing ourselves at Poul an Tomais, we made diving trips to the Broadhaven area for six years from 1986 to 1992. The area was chosen as a result of a tip-off. One of our group, the proprietor of the popular outdoor sports shop Great Outdoors, Leslie Laurence, had struck up a friendship with the colourful character Michael Max, a geologist-diver newly ensconced with the Geological Survey Office of Ireland. Max had been working in north-west Mayo when he had been told the story of some shipwrecks at Inver Point in Broadhaven. The information was apparently relayed to him by a local diver, who unfortunately suffered a fatal car accident soon after. Rather than let the information just disappear in the mists of time, Max passed it to us with the proviso that we must do something with it. We were delighted to comply.

Our first visit to Inver and Broadhaven did not yield any finds whatsoever. Inver Point is not a large area, but when a blank is drawn in a high-probability area, focus is infected and belief in the value of alternative sites can often overcome reason. We left Inver empty-handed and chastened, but we had gained an insight into that phenomenon of sideways rain in Mayo, and further experience of heavyweight wrestling with giant wrack seaweed.

The following year we set ourselves up in the McGrath's pub guesthouse and spread our business with another great pub just around the corner, McGuire's in Poll an Tomais. A pub is a great place from which dive operations can be carried out, but early morning starts tend to suffer.

We launched our sturdy Avon on the tidal slip at Inver the following morning and recommenced our search at Inver Point. After two days we had dived every nook and gully around the Point – at least we thought we had – and harvested a couple of tons of the stalky wrack in the process. Still there was no result. While the last diver was still down, sucking the bottom of his bottle dry, I popped in on a snorkel and swam a little closer inshore. Armed with an Aquascan underwater metal detector, I held it as far down and as near to the bottom as I could get it, and began to search between the rocks. Still no joy. The other divers had returned to the boat, and were all now anxious to pack up and start the long drive back to Dublin.

The head of the metal detector was still swinging well above the seabed, so I disconnected the head and let it swing loose on the wire, which allowed it drop another few feet. The extra few feet did the trick. The increasing frequency of the clicks in my earpiece was exhilarating, and soon blended into one continuous din just minutes afterward. It had detected the huge iron object that is every diver's dream find – a cannon. We motored back to the slip, filled a couple of bottles and returned to the site to discover two more. We had found the site of a very old shipwreck at Inver Point, but what ship was it?

Staying in pubs, an An Oige hostel, and rented cottages, we dived at Inver and the surrounding areas each summer until 1992 and made a number of finds at Inver Point. We had seen six different cannon, recovered some pewter bottle tops, Belarmine jars (broken and whole), a number of lead ingots, and a host of other small finds.

The cannon were heavily concreted and very difficult to identify, but the lead ingots – pigs or sows – had a considerable number of marks stamped into them. At least one of these marks, a Jerusalem cross, also appears on ingots that had been recovered from the *Santa Maria de la Rosa*, a wrecked Spanish Armada vessel in the Blasket Sound, County Kerry. We thus assumed that this was the wreck of another Spanish Armada vessel. This could only be the *Santiago*, which tradition had firmly put at Inver Point.

The marks on these pigs, and on others from wreck sites around the world, have undergone considerable study in the intervening years. It has since been discovered that the marks were used by merchants and traders to denote quality, value and ownership, much like trading certificates for diamonds and valuable objects today. Although appreciably different to any present-day marks, they were used over a prolonged period from the sixteenth century and possibly before – which didn't help with precise dating.

Further analysis of the ingots and the Bellarmine jar might also indicate that this wreck is that of the Dutch vessel *Zeepaard*, which was wrecked at Inver in 1665. If so, then where is the *Santiago*? Is it the wreck discovered in the mouth of Blind harbour? Complicating matters, there is also evidence of at least one later shipwreck at Inver Point. This wreck produced artefacts from the middle of the nineteenth century including bricks and iron knees. Might this be *Veturia*?

Flush with success and some pride, a considerable number of photographs were taken which, eventually, and with the help of another diver not part of the group, found their way into the hands of the authorities. It might seem naive and useless to proclaim now that it had always been our intention to interpret as much as possible from the finds and to submit them to the same authorities for conservation and display. When one considers what cannot be done with a half dozen ingots weighing a hundredweight each, it might not be that hard to believe.

Notwithstanding, we delayed and then came the fall. They beat us to it, and we received a polite but terse letter offering to receive the artefacts we had illegally removed from the wreck site. We gladly complied and received a nominal financial reward for the finds. It was a salutary lesson in several respects.

A little bruised after the unscheduled encounter with the long arm of the state, our activities took a holiday. I returned to dive there with my club in subsequent years. During one of these later visits, some local people pointed to Rin Roe Point and described how divers came there years ago and located cannon. We decide to pop in and have a look.

We soon came across some artefacts, chain and fixings, with the remains of a nineteenth-century shipwreck at Rin Roe Point, but failed to find any cannon. The divers that the local people might have been referring to were probably Sydney Wignal and his cohorts, who decided to venture up the west coast of Ireland in search of Armada treasure after his sojourn on the *Santa Maria* in the Blasket Sound.

I loved the remoteness and rugged geology of the place, but we had two regrettable incidents there which left a bad taste.

During one of these incidents, while divers were diving at Kid Island we were approached by a fishing boat which accused us of diving for, and taking, crayfish and lobsters. There were no crustaceans in the boat and the accusation was totally unfounded. With the exception of a very odd one for the table, I have yet to meet the sports diver who has an unhealthy and illegal interest in taking crustaceans from the seabed, but on that day the crew of the fishing boat were in no mood for talking.

These fishermen would have been better employed preventing their kinsmen divers in Belmullet, who had been raping the seabed of crayfish for years with scuba gear and monofilament nets and shipping container loads of them to France every summer until the area became devoid of the beautiful creatures. The fishermen from east of Portacloy threatened to drop chain on the divers below and to sink our inflatable! We experienced a similar occurrence in the same area and in almost identical fashion a year or two later – these were not pleasant encounters.

Neither incident was reported to the authorities. The scenic diving in this part of Ireland ranks among the best in Europe and beyond. Friends and I continue to have short breaks in the area. Despite its sideways rain, I still love the place and its people.

A review of significant shipwrecks, maritime-related events, and diving operations around Erris and Broadhaven

In order for us to obtain a wider understanding of the shipwrecks around Erris and Broadhaven, what may have already been discovered there and what might one might expect to find there in the future, the following chronological inventory of events might be useful.

It is a compilation of known shipwrecks, of discoveries that have already been made around Broadhaven by ourselves, those discovered by Sydney Wignal in 1969 (and referred to in his 1982 book *In Search of Spanish Treasure*), and with some reference to finds made by the Underwater Archaeological Unit of the department of Arts, Heritage & the Gaeltacht in 2013/14.

It also includes some record of early diving and significant maritime operations relative to this area.

By and large, the shipwrecks south of Erris Head, and in the Blacksod area, have been omitted, as are references to insignificant and smaller craft. To view a more complete list, one should visit irishwrecks.com.

Pre-1588

We must assume that there are few, if any, records available to support the occurrence of shipwreck or salvage attempts around Erris or Broadhaven before accounts erupted into the public domain after the arrival of the Spanish Armada vessels in 1588. As there are records indicating wreck and salvage elsewhere in Connaught and around the coast of Ireland during earlier times, the conclusion can only be reached that such events in north-west Mayo were not recorded or are well-hidden – or just lost.

1588

In September 1588, the Armada vessel *Santiago*, captained by Juan de Luana, known locally as *Long Maol*, was reported to have wrecked at Inver. The incident and the subsequent happenings are the subject of an interesting story now embedded in the folklore of the area (see below, 1588–1600s). Dismasted, the ship is said to have been towed into Inver (Donegal is also suggested) by a turf boat. It is also reported that this ship struck the rocks at Inver and that the sailors landed there.

Nearby Inver Castle was occupied at the time by the Munster man Barrett, who may have helped the sailors to reach another ship anchored in Blacksod Bay. Many of the Barretts were killed during a rebellion the following year, but Pierce Barret is believed to have been still there in 1607.

A second vessel was also said to have wrecked in Broad Haven (sometimes known as Toorglasse), which may have been the *San Nicolas Predaneli*.

And another at Kid Island, in the north of Broadhaven Bay.

A large Armada vessel, *Duquesa Santa Ana*, had entered Belmullet for shelter and anchored in Elly Bay. The survivors from the *Santiago* marched, or were brought by boats, to Belmullet and into Blacksod Bay to meet this ship. Quite extraordinarily, another Armada vessel, the larger *La Rata Encoronada*, had grounded at Fahy Strand further south, in the entrance to Blacksod Bay. The stranding occurred close to Fahy Castle, where the crew camped for a while.

It wasn't long before the Spaniards who had come ashore and camped at Fahy observed the *Santa Ana* come in under the Mullet and enter Blacksod Bay, where she anchored safely. The soldiers and crew of the *Rata* gathered up their stuff and set their stranded ship on fire. They marched around through Belmullet until they reached Tiraun and the anchored *Santa Ana*. Given the fact that there were no roads, and barely tracks, in parts of this difficult terrain, it should be safe to assume that the Spaniards were guided and helped by local people. It is also possible that some of them got to Elly Bay by boat.

The incidents of the Armada vessels wrecking at Inver and Fahy Strand are very strong in local tradition. Accounts of the *Santa Ana* taking on fellow shipwrecked sailors are equally persistent. Unfortunately, their reprieve proved to be short lived when the *Santa Ana* wrecked later in Donegal Bay. The survivors, who boarded another ship in Killybegs, weere wrecked a third time when their ship, the *Girona*, was lost on the north coast of Ireland.

1588–1600s

Official correspondence indicates that Spaniards from the Armada vessels were still being rounded up in Erris in 1589.

Folklore of this area tells us that treasure in the form of silver, and possibly gold, was recovered at Inver from one or more of these wrecks, or possibly later ones. As with all stories regarding treasure, not a word can be can be relied on.

The site of the wreck at Inver is still pointed to, and it is said that a great treasure of gold from this ship was entrusted to the keeping of a simpleton and buried by him 'in a moor between two strands just under the moon'. It is not clear what vessel or period the folklore refers to.

To this day, local people will still point to Inver Point as being the sight of an Armada wreck.

Another tantalising piece of folklore recalls that in Inver there lived a man called Brian Carabine, also known as Brian Rhua. Said to have been born in the early part of the seventeenth century, he became known for his prophecies. He is said to have foretold that a mastless ship would come in from the sea with gold. A short time later, one fitting that description was driven onto the coast. As handed down, this could not have been an Armada vessel, but it could have been another, one mentioned later by O'Malley the smuggler.

A local priest is reported to have told his congregation in 1678 that they should not heed the prophecies of Brian Rhua because he was mad! Dutch salvors arrived at Inver in 1630 but left empty-handed. A Dutch East Indiaman carrying silver later wrecked at Inver in 1665.

1600s

A wreck was discovered at the mouth of Blind harbour, on the north coast of Erris, in around 2013. Karl Brady of the Department of Arts, Heritage and the Gaeltecht recalled in 2014:

> All twelve cannon recorded are cast-iron muzzle-loaders and are of similar size, being around 2.20m in length, which indicates that they are likely to be small to medium sized guns, possibly ranging from minion to saker if English in origin, or 3 to 8 pounder if they are of the Dutch continental system. The initial assessment of the cannon has also indicated that they broadly date from the seventeenth century based on their calibre, size and the style of their buttons, cascabels, breeches and trunnions.

A Dutch wreck dating from the seventeenth century is being suggested.

1600

In a letter to Sir Robert Cecil, Sir Ralph Lane informs him that two frigates 'laden with friars and munitions from Spain' arrived at Broadhaven. The landing was at Inver and is thought to have been only some piece of a squadron from the main fleet. Probably more soul hunters than wreck-hunters, it is nevertheless interesting to note that Spain might have continued with such adventures so soon after their previous bloody nose, unless there is some confusion in the correspondence.

1601

Coastguard Captain Robert Cecil reported that two ships from Spain with treasure and munitions entered Inver the previous Christmas to harbour themselves and take in pilots. This may be the same incident as the previous one but, again, it is surprising to hear of Spaniards on the west coast of Ireland so soon after their regrettable experiences earlier.

1611

Warrants were issued to James Steward and Maximilian Vandeleur allowing them to recover certain pieces of brass ordnance 'cast away by shipwreck on the coast of Ireland in the year 1588'.

An export licence was later granted for 'ellevin piece of brasyne ordinance.'

1614

After Broadhaven was described as a wellhead of pirates and a nest of all the sea rovers by English planter Mathew de Renzy, Admiral William Monson sailed there in 1614 to root them out. Posing as the famous English pirate Henry Mainwaring, he gained the confidences of the Cormucks. The story is a charming but a lengthy one. Suffice to say, he presumed to have taught them a lesson of sorts and went on his way. A later account of events at Broadhaven, read: 'The pyrates ever after became strangers to the harbour of Broadhaven and in a little time wholly abandoned Ireland which was attributed to the execution of this man; for before that time, they were in those parts rather conniv'd at than punished.'

This view, although rather over optimistic, was true in certain respects. The pirates hadn't gone away at all, but as with all pirates they cannot operate without the connivance of the landsmen.

1626

On 18 March, Captain Campaines was reported as being in Broadhaven harbour, which he was in possession of, and to have taken two small ships of Galloway. He declared that he would keep the ships until he had his pardon in his custody.

The presence of this particular man in Broadhaven at this time is interesting if taken with the following. Whether it is Galloway in south-west Scotland or Galway, Ireland, that is referred to is uncertain.

Born in 1587, Claes G. Compaen became a successful merchant and privateer. Commissioned with a letter of marque from the Dutch government in 1621, he headed west. He eventually turned rogue and began a life of indiscriminate piracy, seizing and selling everything from or to anyone. He operated mainly in the Mediterranean, the Levant and the western Atlantic, where he had his pirate's nest at Salee in Morocco.

He also operated in the English Channel, the Irish Channel and along the west coast of Ireland, where he seemed to have operated with impunity and went unmolested by the authorities. He traded his cargos with merchants, officials, and VIPs around the coast of Ireland, and he ingratiated himself so well with the authorities that he had at one time been granted the official protection of the British Crown.

Compaen eventually went too far and found himself seeking a pardon from both the Dutch and English governments in order to make a return to Holland.

Having recruited men from all over, he was supposedly returning to Europe and dropping off some of his Irish crew to their native land in the west of Ireland when he found himself holed up in Broadhaven in 1626. Appearing to have put contriteness on the back-burner, he seized the ships from Galloway (probably Galway) mentioned in the calendar of state papers and remained at Broadhaven – presumably at the safe haven of Inver – Cormuck's country. Whether Jacob Johnson, the Dutch diver, was also at Inver in 1626 is probably unlikely. See 1630/1631.

Seemingly cruising the region, it was also reported in 1627 that Compaen and his flotilla had been in Killybegs and that 'the Dutch pirates possessed plenty of Spanish silver and ducats ... and glutted themselves on drinking and whoring'.

Despite generous offers of endowments by Compaen, and protracted efforts by the English Crown to cajole and coax him with a pardon, their efforts to bring him in at a previously agreed rendezvous at Long Island in west Cork in 1625, where he was much favoured by Sir William Hull, failed. Compaen did not receive the pardon and eventually returned to his lair in Morocco. Despite an earlier refusal of a pardon from his own country, he finally relented and returned to Holland, where he fell before William of Orange to beg for forgiveness, which was granted.

Having led a life of piracy – looting, blackmail, illegal trading with corrupt officials and possibly treason – he achieved the reputation of being the 'most notorious Dutch pirate'. Portrayed as a colourful character in his own fantastically successful autobiography, and many other publications concerning piracy and privateering, he nevertheless died a pauper in Holland, in 1660.

1630/31

Contained in the warrant issued and signed by the Lords of the Admiralty to Jacob Johnson (John Jacop Janson) on 8 June 8 1629 was the following:

Whereas we are informed by reason of shipwreck and other casualties there have been lost in the sea and divers roads harbours and creeks and places in the coast of England and also at Castlehaven and other parts on the coast of Ireland within the jurisdiction of the Admiralty of England divers pieces of ordnance as well as brass or iron much money and bullion anchors cables and commodities of good value for recovery whereof we do hereby constitute appoint and authorise you Jacob Johnson divers to employ your best art and industry in diving in all and every road port harbour or creek either on the coast of England or Ireland ...

Armed with the document, Jacob Johnson and William Broderick arrived at Inver with West Indian divers. Another Munster family, the Cormucks, had obtained the Barrett lands in around 1610. The foreign divers' attempt to secure the whereabouts of a Spanish wreck, or any other for that matter, would seem to have been a ham-fisted and naive attempt. The salvors were made unwelcome by Cormuck's wife, Ellen, and at first would not point to the site of any wreck. Ellen then supposedly relented for a £20 fee for each cannon recovered. Jacob recovered a brass cannon from a nearby wreck, but he and it were promptly returned to the castle by Cormuck's men, where the cannon was taken from him.

Realising they were getting nowhere, the salvors returned empty-handed, and a long-running legal battle ensued between Johnson, the Crown and Cormuck. This was not Jacob's first or last brush with the law, or disgruntled local inhabitants, over unsuccessful salvage attempts.

All attempts to salvage wrecks at Inver were abandoned by Jacob, but the disagreement was still being mentioned as late as 1649.

This event is recorded in *Where The Sun Sets* as having occurred in 1626. This seems unlikely as Jacob's warrant was not issued until three years later. In 1625/6, Jacob was busy with salvage work in the south of England. In 1629 and 1630 Jacob was involved in salvaging the *Leopard* and *Santa Ana Maria* in Castlehaven, Ireland.

1665

It was thirty-five years before there was mention of another significant shipwreck occurring around Erris. Official records of events are not insignificant, but they lack first-hand eyeballing accounts of the actual wrecking incident. This was an extremely remote place and there was no media to interview witnesses or report events. Local people could be fiercely loyal, even to their landlords, and the result is a story which again suggests that those who lived from the land and sea around Inver and Broadhaven did pretty much as they pleased, despite threats from officials of the Crown.

The first mention of a ship coming to shore, or possibly wrecking, is contained in a letter from Sir Oliver St George at Coloone to Ormond, dated 19 September 1665: 'In a late journey through the county of Mayo, the writer received information of the landing of a boat's crew in the island of Glanmoran [Glean Moran], not far from Broadhaven, when landed set themselves to dig around and kept the country people aloof by force.'

Morahan near Elly Bay? 'Moran' became a common name in the region of Erris. Morahans also lived at Blind harbour, on the north Erris coast. This was possibly the location of Glanmoran. Morans also had a significant piece of land that jutted into the south-west area of Broadhaven harbour. Is there a connection with the finds – cannon and lead ingots – made at Blind harbour by the underwater archaeological diving team from the department of Arts, Heritage and the Gaeltacht in 2014?

1665

The 25–28 December edition of the *Oxford Gazette* reports:

> There is lately another vessel run ashore in the county of Mayo, which is supposed to be a Dutch Man. The vessel is richly laden, and had 100 men aboard; Sixty of them are come ashore and have been several days, endeavouring to patch her up and get her off; but orders are sent hence to secure her.

In respect of any letters or reports dated before and after this one, the use of the words 'another vessel' is interesting. Does this mean that there was more than one Dutchman wrecked there around this time? Was there a ship ashore at Glanmoran, as reported by Sir Oliver St George in September? Or was it one of a number of ships contained in a report of wrecks on the coast of Ireland?

1665

The *Zeepaard*, a 400-ton jacht en route from Wieligin to Batavia, was lost near the Shetlands.

In December, the Lord Lieutenant of Ireland informed his peers in London that:

> A ship has lately run ashore in County Mayo. She is richly laden and supposed to be a Dutchman. She has 100 men on board and sixty of them have come on the shore and have been so several days endeavouring to patch her up and get her away. For it seems the place is so very thinly peopled that the country people durst not venture to secure her. But I hope that before you get this she is made safe enough by order from hence.

Given the short time span of a couple of months, it would seem that both statements refer to the same ship?

However, this might also be disputed. In view of the subsequent reports, which indicate that December's vessel is the same one referred to from here on, the September reference by Sir Oliver might then stand alone, casting doubt on the identity of this earlier wreck – the Dutchman *Zeepaard* which did not leave Wieligin until October.

1665/6

The 28 December 1655 to 1 January 1666 edition of the *Oxford Gazette* reports from Dublin:

> The ships mentioned in the last, to have run ashore in the county of Mayo, proves a ship of Middleborough of 500–800 tons; the *Sea Horse* (*Zeepaard*), bound for the East Indies, having in her arms and six chests of silver; she was much beaten at sea by storm, having spent her main mast and foremast, and lost her rudder on the rocks near Broad-Haven. The ship was beaten in pieces and sank, about 100 of her men escaped on planks, and by such fhifts [shifts] the rest, about seventy-four were all drowned. Some of the goods are cast up by the sea; four of the chests of silver recovered and we are not without hope of getting the rest of the money and

the guns belonging to the ship, and saving the rest of the lading that is not perishable by water.

The 'Dutch Wars' were in progress, and Britain was seizing Dutch vessels anywhere it could. The English Channel was effectively blockaded, which meant that Dutch vessels had to go northabout in order to travel to and from the Atlantic.

The following correspondence from George Larburton to Lord Joseph Williamson that was returned from Ireland on 25 August 1666 is telling, and confirms the fate of the vessel in question – but after it had left:

> One of the prize ships taken into Crookhaven has been sent to Sligo to recover anchors, cables, etc. left by the Dutch ship that was lost on the Mayo coast eight months ago [Dec 1665]. She has returned with them. I am sorry not to have more news; but this place in [is?] very quiet.

Does this mean there was no one around – or that those who were around did not say anything?

Despite all the official reporting and instructions concerning what should be done with the Dutch wreck at Broadhaven, nowhere does it mention any follow up to the initial reports of the Dutchmen that came ashore or the chests of silver mentioned in the *Oxford Gazette*.

It would appear that there was at least one wreck of a Dutch ship in Broadhaven in December 1665 and that it was badly damaged and that men and chests of silver came ashore. As there is no further mention of the ship or the sailors in the place that it first came ashore, we might assume that it was repaired and the men paid the local landlord for help, and the right of passage in silver, and then left. Leaving behind some anchors and cables. As the ship was also said to have been lost on the coast of Mayo, perhaps it was wrecked soon after, elsewhere.

1667

29 January. A letter from the Archbishop of Glasgow to Ormond:

Accredits Captain Binning of the King's horseguards. Who is about to visit Ireland; and also a merchant, who with his partners, has sustained heavy loss by the recent wreck, on the coast of Ireland, of a ship laden with French wines. Mention supplies voted to the Kings by the Convention of the Estates of Scotland.

1675

See 1969. Sydney Wignall's find and identification of Dutch pipe and cannon on wreck site at Rin Roe Point/Inver.

Is this wreck site that of 'Crann Casta' (Twisted mast) at Rinn Roe Point, recorded by irishwrecks.com and Sydney Wignal?

1691

In March 1691, a petition to the Crown was made by Thomas Neale Esq. He was looking for rights to wrecks and permission to fish up silver from wrecks that occurred before 13 February 1688 within 10 leagues of the Stags of Broadhaven.

1694

This was followed on 27 October 1694 with a petition from Lt Colonel Edward Pearce. In Pearce's case, he was willing to pay for the privilege to fish for wrecks in Mayo, Ireland, within 50 leagues of the Stags of Broadhaven.

There seems to have been no shortage of treasure hunters, which might suggest that there was some kind of valuable cargo still not recovered from Armada or Dutch wrecks in the area.

1696

Correspondence from Sligo in September 1696 outlines another victim at Erris:

A vessel with wine, brandy and salt, driven by the late storms
into the barony of Tereragh about 20 miles from Sligo, and also a
Deans [sic Danes's] ship of twelve guns driven in near the others,
and cast away near Broadhaven.

Lands and Inver Castle had passed on to Lord James Shaen at this
time. There is record of a family by the name 'Deane' residing at
Inver in 1765.

There are two ships mentioned in the above. The first of these is
not likely to have been anywhere near Erris, but the second is clearly
wrecked in the area of Broadhaven. The interesting word is 'in'. This,
I believe, should be interpreted as meaning the ship had been driven
into the broad reaches of Donegal Bay before being cast away near
Broadhaven.

Were there additional vessels in company?

1703

The 240-ton frigate *Chamberlain*, armed with sixteen guns and
captained by William Soyarce, was cast away near Blacksod on 10
December 1703, according to Collector Henry Arkwright of Galway.
Salvage of guns, indigo, cotton and logwood was performed by
Michael Cormack.

A foremastman, William Robinson, was lost on the frigate
Chamberlain when it was cast away on her homeward bound
voyage to England in April 1702. This report appears to be another
reference to a loss of the same vessel.

1706

State papers reveal a bid by the next owner of the lands around
Inver, Sir Arthur Shaen, to improve his holdings when he petitioned
the Duke of Ormond and the Queen to:

Erect lands within the barony of Innis [Erris?], County Mayo ...
into the manor of Shaen, and to grant a weekly market at the
town of Broadhaven ... and likewise ... at 'Black harbour'. The

petitioner has agreed with 130 Protestant families to settle there, which should prevent the recurrence of the occupation of Inniskea by French privateers as in the late wars with the government and the county and Her Majesty's forces had to besiege them to oblige them to surrender.

1710–1893

According to a report made in 1819, Captain O'Malley, a local smuggler, reported that a Spanish galleon, without a mast, from South America laden with gold was wrecked along the coast of Erris.

The following is a continuing account of shipwrecks that are believed to have occurred in the areas of Broadhaven Bay and north Erris between the eighteenth and nineteenth centuries. Extracted from a database, the list does not include what the author considered to be small local fishing vessels or other less significant vessels wrecked later.

1728 – The sailing vessel *Katherine of Londonderry*, skippered by Captain Hugh Davey, wrecked at Broadhaven.

1743 – The sailing vessel, *Good Intent* [*Adventure?*], skippered by Captain Jackson, wrecked at Broadhaven.

1770 – The sailing vessel *Rain*, was lost at Broadhaven on 23 April 1770.

1771 – The sailing vessel *Mary* was lost at Broadhaven.

1771 – The sailing vessel *Greyhound of Whitley* was lost at Broadhaven in 1771.

1797 – An armed smuggling vessel commanded by Captain Doyle of Rush landed at Erris.

1799 – The sailing vessel *William Bouch* of Workington wrecked at the Stags, Broadhaven.

1800 – The sailing vessel *Robert* was lost ashore at Broadhaven en route to Derry on 28 October 1800.

1805 – An unknown sailing vessel was lost at Shank's Cave in Broadhaven. Mate 'Shank' was murdered.

1807 – The sailing vessel *Favourite* was lost at Broadhaven on 17 March 1807.

1810 – An unknown sailing vessel was lost at Swallow Rock near Broadhaven.

1811 – The gallliot *Anna Hulk Klays Boys*, skippered by Captain Morris, was lost onshore on 28 November 1811 between Porturlin, Billings, and Broadhaven.

1819 – The sailing brig *Thetis* was lost at Broadhaven, skippered by Master Morrison, on 26 November 1819.

1822 – An unknown large sailing vessel was lost at Erris on 28 February 1822.

1822 – HMS *Arab*, armed with eighteen guns, was lost in Broadhaven on 18 December 1822. There were no survivors.

1830 – The sailing vessel *Maria* was lost in Timber Cove in Erris on 10 October 1830.

1841 – The sailing vessel *Ann* was lost on 6 October 1841 at Broadhaven.

1843 – The sailing vessel *Volant* was lost on 21 February 1843 at Doonkeeghan, Rin Roe Point.

1844 – An unknown sailing vessel was lost at Erris on 28 November 1844.

1847 – The sailing vessel *Emerald* was lost on 12 January 1847 at Broadhaven Bay.

1847 – The sailing vessel *Ranger* was lost on 12 July 1847 at Erris Head.

1847 – The sailing vessel *Albion* was lost on 12 November 1847 in Broadhaven Bay.

1847 – The sailing vessel *Three Brothers* was lost on 22 March 1847 in Broadhaven Bay.

1850 – The *City of Limerick* was lost on 20 November 1850, ashore at Broadhaven. It was towed off.

1853 – The emigrant sailing vessel *California* was lost on 5 October 1853 at Broadhaven Bay.

1863 – The American barque *Veturia*, skippered by Captain Booth, wrecked at Inver, Broadhaven on 2 November 1863.

1877 – The collier brig *Sinai* was lost on 1 January 1877 at Inver in Broadhaven.

1882 – The sailing collier *Magdala* was lost on 14 April 1882 at Broadhaven.

1890 – The sailing vessel *Annie*, of Greenock, was lost on 1 January 1890 at Inver in Broadhaven.

1893 – The sailing vessel *River Nithe* was lost on 1 January 1893 at Inver in Broadhaven.

1969

Sydney Wignall, in company with Colin Martin, departed their excavations of the Armada vessel *Santa Maria De la Rosa* in the Blasket Sound in search of other Armada wrecks on the west coast of Ireland in 1969 and located the remains of a wreck at Broadhaven. In Wignall's *In Search of Spanish Armada Treasure* it is said the site yielded:

> Large lead boat-shaped ingots, similar to our Armada lead ingots, lay in a stack in only 6 feet of water, cannon lay among rock gulleys ... glass bottles and clay pipes ... identified as Dutch in origin and dated about 1675. The site was pointed out by local people to Mr Wignall, and described as Crawn Casta (twisted masts), and was allegedly close to Rin Roe Point.

The finds, however, are almost entirely consistent with very similar finds made at Inver Point by the author and Leinster Divers in 1987. Describing the finds being made at Rin Roe Point may have been Mr Wignall's deliberate attempt to try and conceal the whereabouts of this site. As he said himself after salting confusion around another archaeological site, 'I was simply continuing the old English tradition of sowing confusion wherever we travel.'

Notwithstanding a potential ruse, however, finds from a later shipwreck were also made at Rin Roe Point by the author in 1996.

1996 – present

The author has made two visits to Rin Roe Point. Some local people had said that divers visited there many years ago and that there were cannon lying among the rocks. No cannon were found, but very old chain and some small ship's fittings, indicating a mid-nineteenth-century wreck, were located.

In 2010 local divers discovered cannon at Blind harbour.

In 2013/4 Karl Brady and the underwater team from the Department of Arts, Heritage and the Gaeltacht investigated the site of a seventeenth-century wreck in the entrance to Blind harbour on the northern coast of Erris. Early conclusions are that it is of Dutch origin. Further surveys are planned.

A conclusion in progress

Despite its long held reputation of being a wild, remote and scantily habited part of Ireland – and indeed maybe because of it – it was in fact a veritable hive of European travellers of one kind or another, particularly the Dutch in earlier years. There was more going on in this part of the west of Ireland than many of us have realised.

As Doctor de Courcy Ireland once recalled: 'There is ample record to show that large fishing fleets worked off Erris, and along the west of Ireland, from very early times.' Surprisingly, there is also significant evidence to show that Dutch privateers, pirates and merchant ships were not only seen off the south coast of Ireland but right along the west coast too. When weather was bad, they knew exactly the places to run for in one of the most remote regions of Europe.

A little less clear is the extent of their relationships with local people, the likes of Cormuck – yet another man who seems to have been very successful at playing both ends against the middle.

There is no doubt in my mind that one of the ships from the Spanish Armada of 1588 wrecked at Inver. As there is no record of prisoners being taken in this instance, or any execution of survivors, I believe they were helped to escape. The ship most likely carried cannon, and these were the same guns that Jacob Johnson sought, but failed, to recover in 1630. So, where did these go? Did Cormuck recover them? Did he sell them on? Or are they ones that are still there?

It would seem that there were many descriptions of the same ship, an Armada vessel, which suffered the same fate as other shipwrecks at the hands of multiple story tellers.

There is no disputing the fact that the Dutch ship *Zeepaard* was either wrecked or damaged at Inver. I say damaged as those aboard attempted to repair the ship. You don't try to patch up a ship that is wrecked. Some of the language used in the subsequent reports suggests to me that it, or another, left afterwards. Was there more than one Dutch ship? And what became of the 100 men who came ashore?

The fact that some chests of silver were recovered from this wreck, while others were not, seems to have prompted the interest of would-be salvors – those who applied for 'fishing' rights. The waters then became muddied with time.

Indicating a wreck, the guns located at Blind harbour would seem to be from a seventeenth-century vessel. This does not rule out the HMS *Arab*, which was wrecked somewhere in the vicinity in 1822, but a satisfactory conclusion is unlikely.

The mention in state papers and other records of yet another ship shipwreck, the 240-ton, sixteen-gun frigate *Chamberlain*, having been cast away at Blacksod in 1703, is tantalising. Some cargo, rigging, and her guns seem to have been removed from the vessel by Michael McCormack, who undertook the salvage. At the time of writing, nothing more has been learned about this incident.

In respect of the long-running saga of confusing accounts of shipwrecks at Broadhaven Bay and around Inver, the Deans (or Danish) ship carrying twelve guns, which was driven in near the others and cast away near Broadhaven in 1696 is the only remaining incidence which might provide a fit with the finds to date.

The author and a new team of divers will return to Broadhaven in 2015.

Bibliography

Publications, websites and songs

Albert, Fred, *A Cheer for Plimsoll* (1876).

Appleby, John C., *Women and English Piracy* (2013).

Ashworth, W. J., *Customs and Excise: Trade, Production, and Consumption in England 1640–1845* (2003).

Bald, *Map of County Mayo* (1830).

Barkham, M. M., *The Fishing Industry in the Spanish Basque Country* (2003).

Beesly, Patrick, *Room 40: Naval Intelligence 1914–1918* (1982).

Bennett, William, 'Visit of William Bennett of London', *Transaction of the Central Relief Committee of the Society of Friends during the Famine in Ireland in 1846–1847* (1852).

Bourke, Edward J., *Shipwrecks of the Irish Coast*, 4 vols. (1994).

Brady, Karl (ed.), *Shipwreck Inventory of Ireland* (2008).

Bolts, William, *Considerations of Indian Affairs* (1772).

Calendar of State Papers Relating to England and Ireland.

Carr, Peter, *The Big Wind* (1993).

Crothers, W. L., *American Built Packets and Freighters of the 1850s* (2013).

Falconer, William, *The Shipwreck* (1813).

Fallon, Niall, *The Armada in Ireland* (1978).

Geological Survey Office of Ireland & Marine Institute, *INFOMAR: Seabed Surveys of Ireland*

Gosse, Philip, *History of Piracy* (2012).

Hashegan, Ernst, *Westward: Log of a U boat Commander* (1931).

Isaac, Lynn, taffthehorns.com.

James, G. P. R., *Contraband and Corruption in World History* (2011).

Lavery, John, *Life of a Painter* (1940).

Lloyd's List

Lloyd's Register of Ships

Lockhart, G., *The Story of the Mary Russell* (2009).

Masters, David, *The Wonders of Salvage* (1924).

Masters, David, *When Ships Go Down* (1932).

McCarthy, Michael, *Ships' Fastenings* (2005).

McCoole, Sinead, *Hazel: A Life of Lady Lavery* (1996).

McGlue, Thomas, 'Recollections of the W. M. Barkley', *Guinness Time* (1950).

Monson, W., *Sir William Monson's Naval Tracts* (1703).

Morphy, John, *Recollections of a Visit to Great Britain and Ireland in the Summer of 1862* (1863).

Noone, Father Sean, *Where the Sun Sets* (1991).

O'Danachair, Caomhin, 'Armada Losses on the Irish Coast', *Irish Sword* (1956).

Otway, Caesar, *Sketches in Erris and Tyrawly* (1841).

Ritsema, Alex, *Pirates and Privateers from the Low Countries* (2008).

Roddie, Alan, 'Jacob The Diver', *Mariner's Mirror* (1976).

Stokes, Roy and Liam Dowling, www.irishwrecks.com.

Stokes, Roy, *U-boat Alley* (2004).

Symes, R. S., W. A. Trail and A. McHenry, *Geological Survey of Ireland* (1881).

Tennyson, Alfred, *The Kraken* (1830).

Teresa, Bridget and Richard Larn, *Shipwreck Index of Ireland* (2002).

Traditional song (collected by John Short), 'Heave Away My Johnnies' (1914).

Trewald, Martin, *The Art of Living Underwater* (1734).

Wanner, Michael, *Imperial Asiatic Company in Trieste: The Last Attempt of the Habsburg Monarchy to Penetrate the East India Trade 1781–1785* (2008).

Wignall, Sydney, *In Search of Spanish Treasure* (1982).

Williams, Glynn, *Prize of All the Oceans* (1999).

Archives, museums and additional sources

Antwerp City Archives.

Austrian State Archives.

British Newspaper Archives.

Dalhousie University, Nova Scotia (Personal papers of James Dinwiddie).

Department of Arts, Heritage and the Gaeltacht, Underwater Archaeological Unit.

Fishermen at Dun Laoghaire and at Wicklow, courtesy of Martin Roe.

Gloucester Record Office (Personal papers of Charles Spalding).

Hyperbaric Medicine at Dublin.

Irish Newspapers Archives.

Lincolnshire Archives.

Liverpool Central Library.

Merseyside Maritime Museum.

National Archives at Dublin.

National Archives at Kew, London.

National Library of Ireland.

Royal Library, Brussels.

State Archives, Bruges.

U-boat Archives, Cuxhaven.

United Kingdom Hydrographic Office.

Washington State Archives. (Microfilm records of First World War U-boat logs.)

While collecting material for this book, I have spoken with many divers and storytellers around Ireland, some of whose names I have been remiss in recording. They might recognise their contribution within these stories, which provided a lead and unlocked sources to further material that enhanced the story. I took great enjoyment in collecting such tales, and I thank them all most sincerely.